Stuttering

STUTTERING

A Short History of a Curious Disorder

Marcel E. Wingate

BERGIN & GARVEY
Westport, Connecticut • London

Library of Congress Cataloging-in-Publication Data

Wingate, Marcel E. (Marcel Edward), 1923–
    Stuttering : a short history of a curious disorder / Marcel E.
Wingate.
        p.   cm.
    Includes bibliographical references and index.
    ISBN 0–89789–530–4 (alk. paper)
    1. Stuttering—History.   I. Title.
RC424.W549   1997
616.85′54—DC21   97–10408

British Library Cataloguing in Publication Data is available.

Library of Congress Catalog Card Number: 97–10408
ISBN: 0–89789–530–4

First published in 1997

Bergin & Garvey, 88 Post Road West, Westport, CT 06881
An imprint of Greenwood Publishing Group, Inc.

Printed in the United States of America

♾™

The paper used in this book complies with the
Permanent Paper Standard issued by the National
Information Standards Organization (Z39.48–1984).

10 9 8 7 6 5 4 3 2 1

Copyright Acknowledgments

The author and publisher gratefully acknowledge permission for
use of the following material:

Excerpts from W. Johnson, *Because I Stutter*, New York: Appleton
& Lange, 1930. Used by permission of Appleton & Lange.

To Seattle — in the good years.

Faithfulness to the truth of history involves far more than a research, however patient and scrupulous, into special facts. Such facts may be detailed with the most minute exactness, and yet the narrative, taken as a whole, may be unmeaning or untrue. The narrator must seek to imbue himself with the life and spirit of the time. He must study events in their bearings near and remote; in the character, habits, and manners of those who took part in them. He must himself be, as it were, a sharer or a spectator of the action he describes.

Francis Parkman, *Autobiography* (1868)

Contents

Figures and Tables

FIGURES

TABLES

Preface

In preparing this book I have had in mind the conviction that anyone interested in this disorder, particularly persons who might be contemplating a professional involvement with it, should have the enlightened perspective on the disorder that only a familiarity with its history can provide.

An adequate perspective can be provided without apprising the reader of the full body of content that the topic might permit. This is particularly true of a topic like stuttering, where so much, in fact excessive, material exists. The fundamental substance of a history of stuttering lies not simply in a recording of events and dates, but in recognizing the significance of relevant contemporaneous intellectual and cultural contexts, and especially the influence of certain individuals. In undertaking this broad objective I have endeavored to be succinctly comprehensive, to condense reasonably and yet remain faithful to the important major dimensions of the subject over time.

I sincerely hope that the book will be interesting as well as informative; that the reader will be able to acquire a substantive understanding and valuable perspective without being burdened, or perhaps confused, by an excess of detail or reference. This objective expresses a motivation based in a long-term personal recollection of having been required to read, in my undergraduate curriculum, the excellent *History of Psychology* by E. G. Boring. The scholarship and breadth of knowledge represented in that source was indeed impressive, yet the extent and depth of detail seemed, to us, to be burdensome.

Over the years I have maintained a more-than-casual interest in various dimensions of history, and I have been particularly appreciative of historical accounts that make the effort to interrelate various events and circumstances, to consider the focal topics in respect to influences that contributed to shaping them. In this respect I should like to mention having been particularly struck by the fairly recent BBC television series, and book, titled *Connections*, authored by James Burke. The format and theme of that production, and publication, have stood in my mental background as an idealized structural reference throughout the conception and organizaton of the material contained in this special history.

I hope this book will approach the level of interest, for others, that the Burke series has had for me. Understandably, there are not as many "connections" in the history of stuttering as were revealed in Burke's broad historical series; they are especially scant in the remote centuries. However, the evidence of clear "connections" for stuttering in even those early times is itself significant. Their number slowly increases as the long periods of time go by, and as the nineteenth century passes they not only appear more frequently but are also more notable, both in breadth and specificity. This trend quickens as the twentieth century unfolds, the "connections" therein having more determining influence on the slow groping toward an understanding of this curious disorder.

The book is intended primarily for students of stuttering. However, anyone with some professional, or personal, interest in the diosrder should benefit from acquaintance with its content. The book should provide, for any reader, not only the core of a general orientation to the topic of stuttering but a condensation of its major trends and issues. I believe that an appreciative readership will include many lay persons who are simply curious about the disorder; stuttering seems to be of perennial interest to the public, as reflected in the recurring articles and stories about it that appear in various lay periodicals. At the same time it should have unique value to persons, in specialties other than speech and hearing science, who should be able to make use of its susbstance professionally. In particular, however, I hope that it will be read widely among students preparing for a career in speech pathology, as well as practitioners in the field, especially by persons who have a special professional interest in stuttering.

In respect to its potential didactic use I believe it can serve not only as a text that presents realistic content, but also as a source from which specific topical areas, in various dimensions, can be expanded further via the References and Further Reading.

I should like to acknowledge, in reference to preparation of this book, a long-term influence that I have not had an appropriate opportunity to make known formally in previous writings. The acknowledgment is pertinent in a general sense to the matter of scientific attitude, but in part it relates specifically to certain material that will appear in the final chapters of the book. While a graduate student in Psychology at the University of Washington I included in my curriculum a course in Comparative Psychology taught by Dr. Roger B. Loucks. I much appreciated the course at the time, but only gradually over later years did I become aware of the extent to which it had contributed to my education as a psychologist. A more specific recollection of Dr. Loucks centers on the one instance in which I showed him some data representing the "adaptation effect" in stuttering. His immediate, succinct remark registered indelibly in my mind because it cut abruptly to the truth that I even then realized, but of which I was not then confident. He said, in his incisive, direct manner, "Those don't look like learning curves!" Dr. Loucks was a scholar of keen intellect and extensive knowledge, straightforward and clear in his thinking and expression. He remains, for me, a model of the behavioral scientist; I remember him well.

I should also like to thank two colleagues, Dr. Curtis E. Hamre and Dr. Anthony Seikel, for their review and helpful comments on the manuscript, which resulted in a number of improvements over the original version. I should note, as well, the valuable contribution of several students in Speech and Hearing Sciences at Washington State University who, anonymously, gave encouraging reviews of an earlier version of the manuscript.

CHAPTER 1

Introduction

Over the centuries, "stuttering" has referred to the same kind of observable events and thereby to the same disorder — as a recounting of its history will reveal. This point is critical to clear thinking about stuttering, especially in view of the persistent efforts made over the past fifty odd years by certain vocal sources to deny the distinctiveness — and from that, the reality — of stuttering.

The word "stutter" is a uniquely appropriate name for this disorder, as reflected in its etymology, its onomatopoeic structure, and its use in metaphor.[1] However, the term "stammer" has also been used. In fact, "stammer" is still used regularly in Great Britain and some of the Commonwealth countries. British use of "stammer" is itself rather curious and the origin of this usage is unclear. The Modern English word "stutter" derives from the Middle English (c. 1150-1475) "stutten," in which the phonetic similarity is obvious. Francis Bacon (1561-1626; see Chapter 3) used "stutter," and the word "stutter" is found in numerous English sources of the fourteenth to nineteenth centuries. Clearly, the early British settlers brought the usage of "stutter" to America (see Chapter 3) where it established precedence over some use of "stammer," and has continued to be used as the appropriate term for the disorder.

In regard to British use of the term "stammer" it is pertinent to note here the commentary on this word in the *Penny Cyclopedia* (Volume 22, p. 429) published as part of the thirty volume *Library of Useful Knowledge* (London, 1833 to 1858): "In the looseness of language . . . all kinds of difficult and defective utterance are misnamed 'stammer'."

Over many years notable and respected authorities who dealt with speech disorders, especially stuttering, have made firm statements regarding the im-

proper use of "stammer."   James Hunt, the outstanding nineteenth century
English authority on stuttering, remarked that in his country the two words
("stutter" and "stammer") had, improperly, been used synonymously. He attempted to put the matter right by setting forth the "distinctive character of
each affection," as follows:

Stammering (per se) is characterized by an inability or difficulty of properly enunciating
some or many of the elementary speech-sounds, accompanied or not, as the case may be,
by a slow, hesitating, more or less indistinct delivery, but *unattended with frequent
repetitions* of the initial sounds, and consequent convulsive efforts to surmount the difficulty. *Stuttering*, on the other hand, is a vicious utterance, manifested by *frequent
repetitions* of initial or other elementary sounds, and always more or less *attended with
muscular contortions*. (Hunt 1861: p. 12)

A few pages later he added:

The main feature of stuttering consists in the difficulty in conjoining and fluently enunciating syllables, words, and sentences. (p. 17)

Hunt's quotation identifies stammering as an articulatory defect, a distinction
also made by Klencke (1844), Schmalz (1846), and other nineteenth-century
writers. In the latter part of the nineteenth century and very early in the twentieth century certain writers attempted to apply "stammer" in reference to the
tonic form of the disorder and "stutter" for the clonic form.[2] This distinction
was never very widely accepted. In fact, it too was pointedly criticized and fell
into disuse in the second decade of the present century.

It seems entirely possible that modern day British use of "stammer" originated as an instance of euphemism, for which the motivational source remains
obscure. However, in a seemingly relevant vein, it has often been said that,
among individuals in higher levels of British society, "a slight stammer" is
sometimes affected as a kind of quaint personal idiosyncrasy. A recent allu-
sion to this allegation appears in an article (Remnick 1995) that reviews current
books about Kim Philby, the notorious spy, whose success was due in con-
siderble measure to his having perfected upper-class characteristics, including
"a disability of English privilege: a slight stammer."[3] However, whatever the
source of the preference for "stammer" in the United Kingdom, it is clear that
for many years this term has referred to the same disorder known as "stutter" in
other English-speaking countries.

A SHORT HISTORY

The impetus for this book has a history of its own; it reflects a long-held
conviction that anyone seriously interested in this unique disorder of speech
should be familiar with at least a synopsis of its lengthy history.

My concern that interested persons, particularly practitioners in the field, should have at minimum a passable acquaintance with the history of the disorder was galvanized some years ago in my reaction to an article in which stuttering was claimed to be a product of modern times, engendered through an emphasis on communication that purportedly characterizes the modern world. Although not particularly knowledgeable then about the history of stuttering, I did know enough to seriously question whether anyone could say that there ever has been a time when communication involving the spoken word was not important. For instance, to quickly span many centuries of recorded history, one can call attention to the runner at Marathon, Paul Revere's ride, the message to Garcia, and so on.[4] Moreover, as will be documented in Chapter 2, there is compelling evidence that not simply verbal communication, but the ability to speak well, has been valued since very ancient times. So, with a sense of irritation, I dismissed the article out-of-hand and therefore I cannot cite the reference; but I do recall that the author was known in the field of stuttering, a matter that sharpened my reaction.

Many examples in the literature of stuttering reveal an ignorance of its history similar to the one just noted. Substantial documentation would be tangential to the objective of this book, yet a more contemporary instance bears mention. Perkins, Kent and Curlee (1991), for example, evidently believe that "perceptual" (objective) definitions of stuttering are "rooted in the work of [Wendell] Johnson and his colleagues" (circa 1935). To the contrary, as will become clear in subsequent chapters, such definitions of stuttering far predate the twentieth century.[5]

However, examples like the foregoing were not the sole basis for my growing concern that persons in the field should have some familiarity with the history of stuttering. George Santayana remarked that, "Those who cannot remember the past are condemned to repeat it."[6] Although certain matters from the past may well deserve repetition, these must be separated cleanly from others that are best discarded. In the total picture, they who know nothing of the past are in an indefensibly vulnerable position.

At the very least, one should not only be clearly aware that his subject matter *has* a history; one should also have some appreciation of its extent. Beyond this, and ever more important, being knowledgeable in a subject requires familiarity with matters in the past that are pertinent to its present and its future.

TO BE BRIEF . . .

In view of the plethora of the literature on stuttering,[7] it is quite possible to write a very lengthy history of the disorder. However, there are at least three good reasons to write only a short one. First, although people generally seem able to enjoy the occasional historical anecdote, they also seem to become easily bored by history, especially if reading it alone. Second, even a moderately lengthy history of stuttering would surely be boring, because so much of the same content appears again and again. A common fault of works on the history of stuttering is that their major substance is essentially a catalogue of names, with attendant viewpoints, many of which are, at best, variations on a theme. Third, most of what is relevant to understanding stuttering and its present circumstances, can be conveyed without overburdening the reader with an account of the many persons who have written on the subject and what each of them thought. Much duplication and redundancy would have to be endured without acquiring any better appreciation for the history of the disorder than from a less elaborate account.

At the same time, a better understanding of the disorder should follow from an awareness of significant dimensions of its history. I believe that a properly instructional history should elucidate the major themes involving the disorder, presented in the context of a broad general history of human development, within which appropriate references highlight particular significant events and outstanding or representative individuals. A major theme in this book is the abiding interest in speech and in speaking well, a theme within which stuttering assumes its uniqueness and significance.

My intent, then, will be to cover the range of substantive content that is most pertinent to an understanding of stuttering from the breadth of a long-term perspective. Serious students, as well as those using this work as a textbook, can expand this knowledge by consulting the Bibliography.

Liberal use of notes in many chapters has allowed me to include important relevant material without impeding the flow of the main narrative. Similarly, the Glossary includes information that, although of special significance to certain topics in the text, would encumber the narrative.

NOTES

1. For elaboration see Wingate 1976, p. 40-41; 1988, p.9.
2. See Glossary for use of "clonic" and "tonic" relative to stuttering.
3. In this article, a review of recent books on Kim Philby, "the spy of the century," Remnick details how Philby so carefully prepared, over most of his life, the personna with which he could achieve his profound deception. Remnick writes: "He had an unerring education in the trappings of class, camouflaging himself with memberships in the right clubs and with the proper eccentricities. Even his disability was '*a disability of English privilege: a slight stammer.* ' " (Italics added.)

It is germane to note here the occurrence of stuttering in the genealogy of British royalty; which suggests a possible source of the affectation of a "slight stammer" among the British upper class.

The surmise regarding preference for "stammering" as euphemism seems supported by a recent survey conducted by the (British) Association for Stammerers in which there was an almost ten-to-one (317 to 37) preference for "stammer" over "stutter." (See *Speaking Out*, Vol. 15, No. 4, Winter, 1994. London: The Association for Stammerers.)

4. Marathon is a plain about twenty-five miles from Athens where in 490 BC the doubly outnumbered Athenians and Plataeans defeated the Persian army of King Darius. The Athenian general, Miltiades, fearing that the people of Athens, unaware of the victory at Marathon, might capitulate to the Persian fleet, sent his swiftest runner, Pheidippides, to carry the news. Arriving at Athens completely exhausted he fell dead after gasping, "Rejoice, we conquer!"

In the night of April 18, 1775, Paul Revere (and others) bore to the Minutemen the message reporting British troop movements out of Boston. The episode was immortalized in Longfellow's poem "Paul Revere's Ride."

Garcia y Inigues was a Cuban army general in the revolt of 1895-1898 that preceded the Spanish-American War. Lt. A. S. Rowan carried a message to Garcia asking what aid the United States should send. The event inspired Elbert Hubbard's 1899 essay "A Message to Garcia."

5. Moreover, as will be reviewed later, especially in Chapter 7, "objective" is hardly an appropriate term to associate with Johnson's writings. Further, in particular regard to the matter of defining stuttering, "Johnson and colleagues," including those who have perpetuated his teachings, have pursued an active policy of blurring the identification of stuttering.

6. *The Life of Reason, Vol. I: Reason in Common Sense.* New York: Charles Scribner's Sons, 1954, p. 82.

7. Throughout history, more has been written about stuttering than about any other disorder of speech. Relevant documentation is presented in Chapters 4 and 6.

PART I

LONG AGO AND FAR AWAY

CHAPTER 2

Eoanthropus to Anno Domini

In the beginning was the word. . . . And even from the limited information now available to us, it seems most likely that not long after "the beginning," the word was stuttered, by someone.

Reference to "the word" implies speech as we know it today, the form and level of oral language expression that presumably has been much the same over the centuries of recorded history. Of course, we do not know what oral communication was like in those long, long epochs of prehistory during which mankind was developing its modern form.[1] However, we are constrained to assume that for thousands of years oral communication was rudimentary relative to speech as we know it today. Similarly, we also do not know when "true" speech (that is, speech as known today, presumably unchanged over recorded history) was first uttered on the face of the earth. We have only inferences drawn from anthropological study of human remains, and most of these remains are relatively modern in anthropological terms.

It is especially worth noting, then, that early written records contain no description of what speech was like. Evidently, even by this time the human ability to speak was taken for granted; the matter of speech *per se* did not command any special notice or interest. The extant statements on speech recorded in ancient history (see later) make reference only to its quality: good (valued, admired) speaking, in contrast to poor speech — *and* speech defect.

NOTES REGARDING EARLIEST SPEECH

Before considering the interesting and notable ancient records of speech defects it seems appropriate to consider, at least briefly, the probable nature of speech itself in those eons that predate formal record. Inferences that can justifiably be drawn regarding the origins and development of speech contribute substantially to understanding the nature of this capacity. The serious student of speech disorders should make the effort to learn much more than will be presented here.[2]

Estimates of the age of the human race vary, and so too do estimates of how long humans have used a form of oral communication that could defensibly be called speech. Even if one accepts the most conservative estimate of the latter span of time and further qualifies it with a probable error of several thousand years, it is clear that humans have been able to communicate orally for a very long time.

Inferences about the speech of prehistorical humans are, understandably, addressed to the matter of a *capability* for speech, and in an abstract and generalized sense. The speech capability of early man has been deduced from anthropometric analysis of human and humanoid remains. It is based on physical evidence from ancient skulls, such as the size of the brain case; the probable configuration of the vocal tract and its important structures; the size and shape of the resonating chambers; and the inferred size, relationships and mobility of the articulators. However, although such evidence strongly supports the deduction of a capacity for speech, it cannot yield a very clear picture of the nature or character of this very early human oral communication.

At the same time, linguists knowledgeable about the anthropological record seem clearly to agree that from the time Homo sapiens had emerged in the anthropoid evolution, this unique animal species possessed a form of oral communication describable as rudimentary speech. There also seems to be clear agreement that this special human function did not emerge full-blown, appearing *de novo* in its present day, essentially historical record form. There is good reason to posit, from indirect evidence, that speech itself has an evolutionary history, one that parallels and reflects the development of the human central nervous system and its refinements in capacities. Deductions from relevant data suggest that in its early forms speech was crude, simple in structure, and poorly articulated. In essence it was, reasonably conceived, not too far removed from the cry communications of animal forms predating it in the evolutionary sequence. It is eminently reasonable to propose that speech evolved concurrently with man's evolving brain; that it proceeded from a very simple form of oral communication that was elaborated with other, primarily manual, gestures; and that very gradually this system came to focus mainly on the oral gestures, which became more complex in their underlying systems and more refined in execution.[3]

Speech—oral language—is undeniably a function of the human nervous system, and there is considerable evidence that it is a species-specific capacity.

We have come to think of it as either integral to or closely imbricated with man's intelligence, and there is considerable evidence to support this position. For instance, among tests of intelligence, or parts thereof, measures of vocabulary have the highest correlation with overall assessment of intelligence. Also, from a somewhat altered perspective, inability to speak is the hallmark of the lowest level of intelligence.

Speech is commonly considered to be a function of the highest, and phylogenetically the newest, levels of the central nervous system: the cerebral cortex. However, we still know little about the "where and how" of this marvellous capacity of the central nervous system. Even so there is growing evidence that "lower," at least *older*, levels of the brain — those we share with even our pre-hominid ancestors—participate importantly in speech processes. I am referring here to certain vital mid-brain structures, in particular the limbic system and thalamic nuclei, but also the cerebellum (see Wingate 1988, Chapter 9).

I believe it is critically important that students of stuttering recognize thoroughly the linkages between human speech and the oral communication forms of non-human species; that they be well aware of the discernible commonalities and continuities among, as well as the evident differences between, these modes. Both of these facets of comparison can tell us much of great value in moving toward an essential understanding of the nature of oral language, and then of stuttering.

As noted in Chapter 1, attention to stuttering has reflected the broader interest in speech itself, a connection that will be evident throughout most of this book. However, as content in some later chapters will reveal, this connection became essentially eclipsed in the twentieth century and, interestingly, soon after speech pathology began to develop as a profession. The fundamental reference to speech was abandoned in favor of attractions that were to be found in psychology.

In very recent times there is evidence of a renewed interest in speech as the fundamental reference, a revival that can be expected to benefit the study of stuttering. There are signs of a renewed awareness that stuttering is a disorder of speech, and a realization that anyone who wishes to understand stuttering must first understand the nature of speech — "speech" used here in its fundamental, comprehensive sense, as *oral language expression*. Unfortunately, for the most part twentieth century attention to stuttering has largely ignored such fundamental inquiry. This serious omission and the sources underlying it come into focus in later chapters, especially in Part III.

DEFECTS IN EARLIEST SPEECH?

One might well posit that in those ages when speech had much simpler form and substance, there may have been no disorders of speech. In other words, one might suppose that speech disorders, as breakdowns in function, may have made an appearance only after speech became more complex and intricate, and therefore more subject to defect. This supposition would be consistent with the fact that the audible communication systems of non-human animal forms do not evidence anomalies in any way analogous to disorders in human oral communication. However, although human speech has always shared certain very basic features with the oral communication of other animal species, the features that most mark it as unique, phonemes and syllable structures, are the dimensions most involved in defect.

On logical grounds alone there is every reason to suspect that defects of speech have been an aspect of the human condition ever since there has been a human condition. This inference is supported by the historical record, in which statements noting speech defect appear almost as early as do comments lauding qualities of normal speech (see below). The prominence of references to stuttering in these records is especially pertinent.

There is some basis for making a reasonably sophisticated guess about the approximate time that stuttering appeared in the evolutionary progression of Homo sapiens. It is frequently observed that in contemporary humans stuttering is usually first manifest when the affected child has reached the level of using word combinations. From this observation, and accepting the axiom that "ontogeny recapitulates phylogeny," one might assume that stuttering first appeared in the history of our species soon after man had become capable of what today is called "connected utterance."

The foregoing statements are, of course, highly speculative. But one need not reach   into our lengthy prehistory to be impressed that stuttering has been a human affliction for a very long time. Recorded history is impressively lengthy and, as noted above, within this historical record one will find convincing evidence for the antiquity of the speech disorder called stuttering. Although the pertinent records are scant, they are clearly sufficient to document that a variety of speech disorders, including stuttering, were recognized ages — in fact, millenia — ago. The documentation is presented later in this chapter.

EARLY WRITTEN RECORDS

There is clear evidence in the very earliest written records that attention was paid to the quality of an individual's speech, and that speaking well was laudable and admired. In the twentieth century BC, the king of Heracleopolis, in a treatise on kingship addressed to his son, Merikare, exhorted him, "Be skillful in speech, that you may be strong." References to speech quality occur in the oldest chapters of the Old Testament, which scholars estimate to have been written in the tenth century BC. In the Song of Solomon 4:3, one finds, "Thy speech is comely." Proverbs 17:7 states, "Excellent speech becometh not a fool." In Ecclesiasticus 4:23-24 appears the exhortation, "Praise no man before thou hearest him speak; for this is the trial of men." [4] Further, recognition of speech defects is well reflected in Moses' famous demurral in Exodus 4:10

(written circa 1000-1400 BC) in which he offers the excuse that he is "of slow speech, and of a slow tongue." And it is of particular significance that evident reference to stuttering occurs three times in the book of Isaiah (28:11; 32:4; 33:19), which is estimated to have been written in the eighth century BC.

Interest in speech and in speaking well evidently was developed to an even higher level in another part of the ancient world — India. Savithri (1987, 1988) has reviewed a considerable amount of such information garnered from Sanskrit texts written between 2000 BC and 1633 AD. These extensive sources contain many works addressed to analyses of speech, to criteria of good speech, and to recommendations for speaking properly (see also Allen 1953; Catford 1977). Moreover, they also include writings concerned with the identification of speech disorders, including stuttering, with suggestions for their management. According to Savithri, the Sanskrit sources reveal that speech disorders were attributed to several different causes, with the implication of neurological involvement being most frequent. (It is not clear from Savrithi's review how early any of the cited causes were suggested.)

Catford (1977) notes that, in more recent historical times (500-300 BC), the classical grammarians of Greece and Rome made remarkably sophisticated attempts at phonetic analyses. Such endeavors clearly reflected an interest in speech. So did the development of oratory which, beginning with Corax in the 460s BC, became a hallmark of the democratic form of government first nurtured in that same era. Clearly the ancient Greeks, at least from the fifth century BC, had an active interest in good speech. Speaking in public was a major vehicle for the expression of their experiment with democracy. Citizens could participate in the formulation of public policy at general assemblies. They also presented their grievances or defended themselves in public courts. The principles and art of public speaking — known as oratory, or "the Rhetoric" — is one of the significant Greek contributions to Western culture. The first major figure in the history of rhetoric was Pericles (461-432 BC), whose name is synonymous with the Golden Age of classical Greece. Many more great orators were to follow, the most outstanding of whom was Demosthenes, a figure of particular interest in the history of stuttering, about whom much more will be said presently.

A DISTINCTIVE SPEECH DEFECT

A notably specific reference to stuttering appears in ancient Egyptian hieroglyphic records. This ancient reference is reproduced as Figure 2.1. The pairs of abstracted characters (left to right) have a general meaning and also a phonetic value. The little human figure at the far right is a *non*phonetic type of symbol, called a "generic determinative"; it determines the specific meaning of the entire glyph by indicating how the abstracted characters are to be interpreted. The phonetic transcription of the abstracted symbols of Figure 2.1 yields the word "ketket" which, when used with certain other determinative

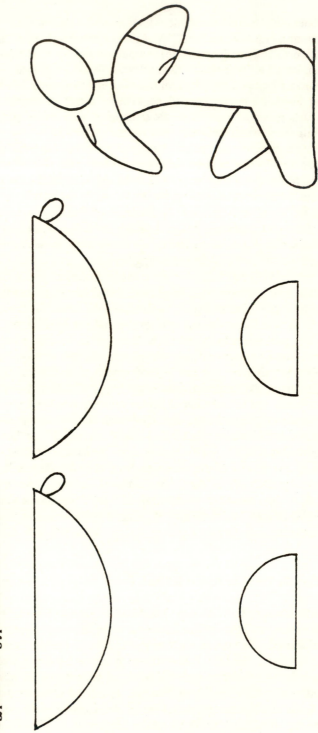

Figure 2.1
Egyptian Hieroglyph Translated as "to stutter"

symbols, carries the meaning of "to beat," "to shake," "to walk with short quick steps," or "to quake." The generic determinative of this glyph indicates that the meaning of the abstract symbols applies to actions of the mouth, so this particular set of symbols has the meaning "to stutter." [5]

As noted by one Egyptologist who was consulted regarding the phonetic value of the glyph, "it is clearly structured like a word for stuttering." That is, it is onomatopoeic — as are most words for stuttering in the languages of present day as well as older cultures (see Chapter 3; also Van Riper 1971: p. 5; Wingate 1976: p. 40).

It is appropriate to mention here a report made some years ago of another ancient hieroglyph that was interpreted as referring to stuttering (Paconcelli-Calzia 1941). In that instance too a pair of abstract symbols, rendered phonetically as "nitit," was followed by the same determinative symbol as in Figure 2.1, indicating that those symbols also referred to the mouth. However, in the interpretation of that glyph the author committed the kind of error found much too frequently in the literature of stuttering — making an unwarranted interpretation. Paconcelli-Calzia claimed, largely in respect to the determinative symbol, that the hieroglyph "expresses very definitely that it deals with an individual who, because of deep fear-depression, does not have 'his heart in his hands.' " Actually, there is nothing about the hieroglyph itself that in any way supports such a surmise, nor does the context in which the glyph occurred.[6] Significantly, "nitit" has the general meaning "to hesitate." Thus the hieroglyph that was given the fanciful interpretation by Paconcelli-Calzia evidently means simply "to hesitate in speaking."

The existence of these two different references to departures from literal fluency indicates that the ancient Egyptians too made the distinction between normal and abnormal types of fluency irregularity.

Particular kinds of speech defect were recognized by the Greeks at least as early as the era of Pericles. Herodotus (c. 484-424 BC) specifically mentioned a case of stuttering and the treatment recommended for it. Hippocrates (c. 450-357 BC), "the father of medicine," also described cases of stuttering and his medically based treatment for it. However, the most informative account of early Greek knowledge of speech defects is supplied by Aristotle (c. 384-322 BC).

Aristotle is one of the two greatest intellectual figures produced by classical Greece, the other being his teacher, Plato. Aristotle's achievements were outstanding in every branch of knowledge extant in his time,[7] although his major contributions were in biology and history. Aristotle has been identified, with good reason, as "the original scientist." He favored exploratory method and was systematic in his observations and analyses. Many of his descriptions were remarkable for their detail and accuracy, and his materials were organized intelligently and significantly. His sciences were based on a multiple system of classification rather than on a simple scheme of mutually exclusive and independently existent categories. In fact, in his *History of Animals* he seemed to be moving toward an ordering of genera and species. We can assume, then, that he approached the study of speech disorders with the same attitude or orientation.

In his Problemata[8] (Chapter 11, p. 30) Aristotle described several kinds of speech defects. One of these, *ischnophonos*, has been translated as the ancient Greek word for stuttering. Aristotle described this particular defect as "due to the inability to join one syllable to another sufficiently quickly." This description seems to indicate clearly the fracture of an utterance at the syllable level, and well reflects the essence of stuttering; namely, the inability to move forward in the speech sequence — the "block." In the same work he states that the disorder "is due to the movement of the tongue; for they [stutterers] find a difficulty in changing the position of the tongue when they have to utter a second sound." This characterization is augmented by other statements by Aristotle about *ischnophonos* in which "hindrance," "impediment," and "force" are key words. In the same chapter he writes:

Why is it that those who (*ischnophonos*) in their speech cannot speak in a low voice? Is it because they are hindered from using their voice by some impediment? Since, then, there is not equal force exerted and similar movements set up when there is some impediment to the movement than when there is none, a violent effort is required. Now the voice is a movement, and those who use more force speak louder; and so since they have to force the hindrance out of the way those who (*ischnophonos*) in their speech must necessarily speak louder. (p. 35)

Another statement contains an observation commonly reported about and by stutterers in modern times; namely, that they stutter more when "nervous."[9] This second statement also illustrates an explanation of cause couched in the terms of the ancients' concept of the "cardinal humours" (See Chap. 3, specifically Figure 3.1). In this instance the explanation is cast in terms of the opposing elements of cold and heat, thought to be aspects of certain humours, as follows:

Why do those who (*ischnophonos*) in their speech become worse when they are nervous but better under the influence of drunkeness? Is it because their condition is a state resembling apoplexy of some interior part of the body which they cannot move and which by its coldness hinders their speech? Wine, then, being naturally hot, tends to get rid of the coldness, but nervousness creates coldness; for it is a form of fear, and fear is a chilling condition. (p. 36)

Note here the reference to fear. Clearly, there is a lengthy history to the practice of invoking fear as the source or at least the major determinant of stuttering.

Evidently the concern for speech excellence in classical Greece centered around performance in public, and was therefore addressed largely to statesmen and civic leaders. Typically, these individuals came from the upper classes and had the means to pay for the services of a tutor.

As noted earlier, Demosthenes is a figure of particular interest in the history of stuttering, largely because he is the first person identified by name as having stuttered. In a more general context he also seems to have become something of a folk hero of the Horatio Alger type in that, through dedication and persistence, he succeeded brilliantly in overcoming personal limitations and adversity.

A contemporary of Plato and Aristotle, Demosthenes is recognized as the greatest of the ancient Greek orators. He was born into a wealthy family, and at age seven was left a large inheritance at his father's death. However, his guardians were unscrupulous, and little of his fortune was left when he came of age. Demosthenes was described as physically delicate, which prevented him from receiving the customary Greek education via the "gymnasium." This limitation, coupled with his intense motivation to sue his guardians, led him to prepare as an orator and to study legal rhetoric. Plutarch, in his *Parallel Lives,* related that Demosthenes had an articulation defect as well as stuttering, and that he overcame these limitations by exercising his voice, speaking with pebbles in his mouth, practicing before a large mirror, and reciting verses when running or climbing a hill. It is of considerable interest that these exercises were reportedly prescribed by a Greek actor, Satyrus, whose assistance he sought and obtained.[10]

Demosthenes is said to have built himself an underground study in which to work on these techniques, where he would stay for two or three months at a time, shaving one side of his head so that he would not be tempted to appear in public. Despite these strenuous preparations his first efforts before the public Assembly were disastrous, and the audience laughed at him. However, he persisted in making speeches, and learned much about speaking method and strategy. This led to his becoming a "logographer," a writer skilled in preparing speeches for wealthy clients. It was not until he was thirty years old that he made his first major speech before the Assembly, "On the Navy Boards." Its objective was to persuade the Athenians to increase their naval strength to dissuade the Persians from initiating hostilities. The speech was an outstanding success and marked the beginning of his long career as a prominent civic leader in the service of Athens. His continued achievements in that service were secured through his skilled use of oral language.

Perhaps Satyrus should be installed by speech clinicians as something of a patron saint, in view of his evidently having been, as noted centuries later by Chervin (1867), the first person to treat stuttering through "lessons of diction." A further note by Chervin should also be given due consideration; namely that, in his own time, the extent of success in working with stutterers had been in proportion to "the nearness of approach to the simple and natural means which antiquity has transmitted to us."

At the very least, the story of Demosthenes contains much of instructional value for the treatment of stuttering in any era.

NOTES

1. Nonetheless, some very shrewd deductions can be made about the probable speech of early homo sapiens, and certain precursors (see, for example, Lieberman, 1988: Swadesh, 1971)

2. One's time is well spent reading sources such as Gans (1981), Lieberman (1988), Stam (1976), Wells (1987).

3. Note that the account presents speech as essentially gestures-made-audible. In this respect see sources such as Armstrong, D. F. et al (1995), Kelso, et al (1986).

4. Predating by some twelve-and-a-half centuries Ben Jonson's challenge, "Language most shows a man. Speak, that I may see thee." *Explorata, "Oratio Imago Animi."*

5. Budge, E. A. W. (1978) *An Egyptian Hieroglyphic Dictionary.* New York: Dover. (Republication; originally published by John Murray, London, 1920.)

6. I am indebted to Dr. Emily Teeter, Assistant Curator of the Oriental Institute, University of Chicago, for the authority of this criticism. Personal communication.

7. The study of nature, philosophy, psychology, ethics, politics, grammar, rhetoric, aesthetics, epistomology, logic, metaphysics.

8. Translation by E. Forrester. Oxford University Press, 1947.

9. Another current-day observation, less frequently made, is the tendency to stutter less when slightly inebriated. See second Aristotle observation above.

10. See later (Chapters 4 and 5 especially) in regard to the efforts, and achievements, made by persons concerned with and knowledgeable about good speaking.

CHAPTER 3

Anno Domini to 1700

Covering a span of seventeen centuries within a relatively short chapter may seem to require substantial condensation, but with the topic of stuttering, there is very little to condense. For instance, the article by Klingbeil (1939), which provides the most comprehensive list of historical sources that make reference to stuttering, contains only eleven entries over these first seventeen centuries of the Christian era.

As with Chapter 2, the primary concern of this chapter will be to note the recorded recognitions of stuttering. Relatively little space will be devoted to suppositions offered about the presumed source of the disorder and recommendations for its treatment, because ideas about stuttering were quite superficial and based on false premises about human nature. In most respects these concepts were simply modest variations on ancient medical lore passed down from preceding authorities.[1]

Nonetheless, it is important to the history of stuttering to acknowledge and appreciate the prevailing beliefs of this era for what they were. To gain an understanding of the context in which disorders of speech were then considered, the reader should have at least a general knowledge of the relevant intellectual climate during the bulk of this long epoch.

THE SHADOW OF ANCIENT MEDICINE

Over most of the centuries from the onset of the Christian era to beyond the Middle Ages, what little attention was paid to disorders of speech came principally from the "physicians" of those times.[2] To adequately appreciate how these learned men attempted to understand the many mysteries confronting them, two major themes should be kept clearly in mind.

First, "medicine" during most of this era was essentially a branch of philosophy—natural philosophy—and it lacked even the qualities of the early scientific attitude to be found in its classical origins. The practice of medicine during this long time was largely limited to knowledge passed down, generation to generation, from the writings of ancient authorities, with few alterations. Although minor revisions or minimal new contributions to knowledge were made occasionally, "progress" in medicine consisted predominantly of discussion and argument centering around those hallowed age-old writings, rather than from experiment and investigation.

Second, two ancient assumptions regarding human nature pervaded these deliberations and continually stultified meaningful progress. One was the doctrine of "humours"; the other centered in the concept of "soul." The latter preoccupation was closely linked to, and strongly supported by, the cultural ambience of most of this era, when almost every aspect of life centered around religion. Further complications, based in the notion of *spirit* in the body, were posed by accepted beliefs about specialized "spirits" as significant features in human body functions. An additional confounding influence was the persisting conviction that astrological events played an important role. A clear vestige of the latter belief is found to this day in the word "influenza." Present for centuries in the lexicon of medicine, it is an Italian word whose original meaning represented the assumption that the medical symptoms of this malady were caused by astral *influences*.

The historical figures in medicine, the "physicians" practicing and expounding over these many centuries, were not unaware of the important internal body structures and organs—including the brain and nerves — but the level of their anatomic knowledge was actually very limited. Much more serious, however, was their abysmal ignorance of physiology. Their most crucial limitation was that they had, and continued to perpetuate, only conjectural notions of the functioning of those body structures they recognized.

The ideas about physiological function in these times amounted to little more than a simple elaboration of Plato's writings on life processes, combined with the doctrine of body "humours." Plato had held that life processes were the reflection of three levels of "soul," or *pneuma*, that arose through the action of vital organs.[3] In this scheme, air, inspired into the lungs, was transformed into one kind of pneuma. Another form of pneuma was to be found in the veins. Venous blood, which supposedly moved with a tidal motion, carried this "natural spirit," which was elaborated from the alimentary tract. When this blood entered the heart it became transformed into a higher form of pneuma, the "vital spirit." In turn, this enriched form of pneuma was then passed to the *rete mirabile* in the base of the brain, where it was again transformed, this time into the highest form of pneuma, the "animal spirit." This most refined pneuma, the essence of life, was then diffused throughout the body via the nerves, which were thought to be hollow.

The notion of pneuma, or soul, was intermixed with ancient Greek ideas regarding the substance of the body, ideas dating from at least the time of Pythagoras (sixth century BC). The essence of these ideas was that the body, long known to be of the earth's substance, was describable in terms of the four dimensions thought to be the essential constituents of the world: earth, air, water, and fire. This belief underlay the doctrine of bodily humours, a doctrine that established a sweeping and long-lasting hold on "natural philosophy" relating to human health and body function.

The foundations of this conception can be traced to the earliest precepts of Greek philosophic reflections. As indicated earlier, medical explanation was only part of a general belief about human nature, accepted in essential form and substance from ancient notions about man's connection to the cosmos. The doctrine of humours is attributed to Hippocrates (fourth century BC) who reputedly based the concept on the belief proposed by Pythagoras that everything in the world consists of four basic elements; earth, air, fire, and water. These four basic elements are then expressed within each person as four "cardinal humours"—black bile, blood, yellow bile, and phlegm. This basic relationship is illustrated in the central portion of Figure 3.1. Note that each basic element is characterized by two qualities (for instance, fire: hot and dry) and that these qualities apply as well to the respective humours, although the humours had other qualities as well. Note further that the four qualities of the basic elements constitute pairs of opposites.

Not only was the doctrine of humours based on a ubiquitous reality (the obvious body fluids); application of the doctrine was all-encompassing. It was, all at the same time, a physiology, a psychology, and a pathology. According to the doctrine of humours, the ordinary healthy individual is characterized by a proper balance among the four cardinal humours, with "proper balance" meaning the particular humoural proportioning unique to, and correct for, any given individual. So, there could be as many different "proper balances" as there were individuals. Just as the proper balance of humours constituted health in any particular individual, so disease reflected an excess or insufficiency of one or another of the humours. Thus, both health and disease were highly individualized conditions. For instance, there was in those times no norm for body temperature; it was thought that people differed in personal temperature as a reflection of their humoural balance, their individuality. This belief was so pronounced that even for some time after the development of the thermometer the word "temperature" remained synonymous with "temperament," which meant the unique individual balance of the four cardinal humours.

In this system the physician's objective was to discover the unique "natural" balance of humours in each person and then, in case of illness, to determine which humours needed adjustment to restore the natural balance. Treatments to alter the presumed disturbance in balance called primarily for manipulation of the four "qualities" (heat, cold, dryness, moisture), the intended remedy being to induce qualities opposite to those believed to be at fault. The treatments could be directed to parts of the body as well as to the body as a whole. A few

Figure 3.1
Illustration of the Humours Concept

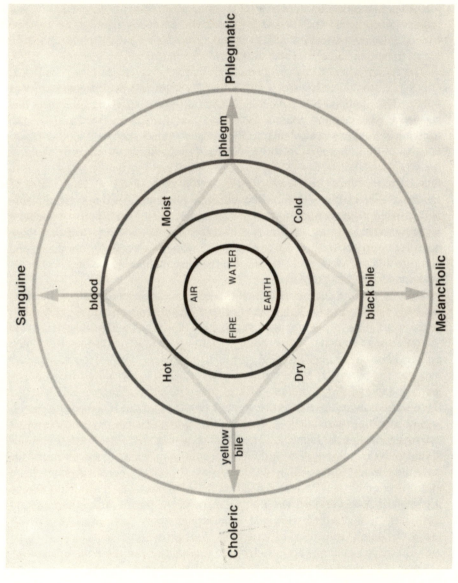

of the many such treatments were application of poultices; gargles; eating pungent substances; massage with various herbs; inducing sweating; vigorous exercise; change in diet; purgatives; inducing vomiting; and phlebotomy (bloodletting).

The extension of the humours doctrine to encompass psychological attributes is represented in the outer border of Figure 3.1. The four humours were linked conceptually to highly idealized types of personality known as "temperaments," which were conceived as being generally characterized by the qualities unique to each humour. Although people were typically classed as being one of the four types, it was accepted that individuals could manifest varying degrees of the four temperaments. As indicated above, all kinds of human functions and dysfunctions, including speech and speech disorders, were for centuries ac-counted for in terms of the humours doctrine. The notion was especially impor-tant in explaning speech disorders during the Middle Ages — and for some time thereafter (O'Neill 1980).

The pivotal, though unwitting, figure who served as the ultimate reference source in this age-long stalemate in physiological-biological-medical thinking was Galen, a Greek physician of the second century AD (c. 130-200). Galen's writings were most influential in the Western world—in contrast to the East. His teachings reached Europe originally as Latin translations but later, and with greater influence, through translations into Hebrew and Arabic that the Moors brought with them when they occupied the Iberian peninsula. His writ-ings constituted almost the sole basis for medical practice for fifteen hundred years — that is, until the Renaissance overtook the areas of natural philosophy. The Renaissance, which began in the 1300s, was initially expressed in art, ar-chitecture and literature; the rebirth of science, however, took considerably longer. Facing an extended struggle with the double reactionary burdens of religion and "Galenism," the renaissance of a scientific spirit therefore re-quired several more centuries.

Although Galen's works were the font of this encumbering morass, its persis-tence can be attributed to sources other than Galen himself. Galen's medical compilations were extensive and evidently thorough and well done for his era. He collected and organized the medical lore of earlier authorities, but his sub-stantial writings also contained many of his own treatises on anatomy and physiology, works that resulted from his own observations and investigations. Galen himself emphasized the value of experience, and he counseled against relying solely on written works. Ironically, this aspect of his legacy was ig-nored. However, this caveat may well have been overshadowed, or even nulli-fied, by his assertion that no man could be considered a true physician who was not also a philosopher.[4]

Galen's works in anatomy and physiology could be duly respected along cer-tain dimensions. In addition to undertaking careful analytic observation of healthy and ill individuals, he was for a time a physician to gladiators, in which capacity he had the rare opportunity of learning from what he saw in their wounds. At the same time, his writings contained many serious faults, not the least of which was that many aspects of this knowledge were based on analogy from other animals, not from examination of humans. A dramatic example of such error involves his description and discussion of the *rete mirabile* ("marvellous network") which was said to exist at the base of the human brain. There, it was claimed, man's vital spirit was transformed into the active agency of "animal spirits." This network (of *blood vessels*) which Galen (and later, others) had found at the base of an ox brain (present also in other ungulates) does not occur in man. However, this error persisted in medical lore until well into the sixteenth century!

These errors persisted for so long largely because of two suppressive influences. One was the church-based prohibition against dissection of the human body. The other was the monopolistic policy of the physicians, the "Doctors of Physick." These men were highly secretive about their learning; their knowledge was passed down to the initiated only in texts that were written in Latin, Greek, Arabic, or Hebrew.

Both of these negative influences were gradually mitigated through the spirit inherent in the Renaissance — and aided, as well, by many of its real achievements, particularly the development of printing. The taboo against dissection of the human body was gradually circumvented in one way or another. In the fourteenth century dissection gradually came to be used more openly in teaching human anatomy. The prestige, credibility, influence, and monopoly of the "physicians-after-Galen" steadily weakened.   Initially, their credibility and prestige were severely damaged by their complete inability to deal with the bubonic plague, which first appeared in Europe in the fourteenth century. Subsequently, their stature was increasingly diminished by findings emanating from the revitalized spirit of inquiry and experiment, Renaissance expressions in science that eventually became manifest in the sixteenth century.

Two significant early figures in this movement bear mention. One is Paracelsus (1493-1541),[5] a vigorous Swiss physician and son of a physician, whose iconoclastic, practical, yet visionary realism mark him as leading the way to modern medicine. The second, whose mark on history is more visible, is Andreas Vesalius (1514-1564). His 663-page printed folio of anatomical charts, *De Humanis Corporis Fabrica,* was based on his own dissections of human specimens. Known to thousands of students of anatomy over the centuries as simply the *Fabrica,* it is said to have been for anatomy what the work of Copernicus was for astronomy. It is of particular note relative to the history of scientific progress that both Vesalius' folio and Copernicus' "De Revolutionibus," which placed the sun rather than the earth at the center of the universe as then known, appeared in the same year, 1543.[6]

SPEECH, SOUL AND HUMOURS

Speech was a function that could not be analogized from another animal form, unlike many other bodily and behavioral activities. It was universally accepted that speech was distinctively human, although with variations in respect to what this meant. Speech could be observed in only its most superficial aspects, and then most briefly. Certainly its source within the human could not be inspected. Speech was acknowledged as a given, and widely accepted as an expression of the "soul."

As noted above, the concept of soul was a Platonic notion devised to account for human mental function. Plato conceived of the soul as separate from the body, a notion that appealed to religious, particularly early Christian, thinking. Aristotle, in contrast, viewed the soul as an epiphenomenon of the physical organism. Either version could be dealt with similarly by medieval medicine, and evidently there was little, if any, concern with the distinction. There was, however, concern about the location of the soul and its mode of operation. As might be expected with a concept so vague and impalpable as "soul," and in view of the general level of medical knowledge of the time, there was disagreement about where the soul was located and how it achieved results. Some authorities contended that the brain was the likely locus; many others argued that it was more likely to reside in the heart. The level of rationale offered in support of either locus matched the credibility of the claims themselves.

The doctrine of humours was a more comprehensive influence in Medieval medical accounts than was the concept of soul. A "humour," originally the Latin *umor* meaning fluid or moisture, was evidently a more credible concept than "soul" inasmuch as it was obvious that the body contained fluids of several kinds.

As indicated above, all kinds of human functions and dysfunctions, including speech and speech disorders, were for centuries accounted for in terms of the humours doctrine. At the same time, it was recognized that various influences, internal and external, could affect speech. Awareness of such influences was, for persons of this era, based in considerable measure on the effect of head wounds. However, other, more mundane observations also made some contribution. For instance, it is of particular interest that, in spite of very primitive ideas about speech production, some authorities of the time made a distinction between speech and voice, on the grounds that voicing could occur in the absence of meaningful verbal utterance; and, to the contrary, that verbal communication could be effected through whispering, in which instance the voice was absent. However, such observations and inferences evidently did not excite additional observation or reflection, and such realizations were not developed further. Invariably, the standard account of how the marvel of speech happened was cast in the medium of the humours doctrine.

STUTTERING IN THESE CENTURIES

The history of stuttering in the early years of the era covered in this chapter is marked through a personage who was undoubtedly the most powerful and influential individual of his time, Roman Emperor Tiberius Claudius Caesar Augustus Germanicus — in common reference, Claudius.

Claudius, step-grandson of Caesar Augustus, was the fourth emperor of Rome, reigning from AD 41 to 54. He is recognized as having been, on balance, a capable and good emperor who generally maintained enlightened policies and ruled effectively in spite of certain personal limitations. He stuttered, a characteristic that may have been one feature of a lifelong physical condition that had signs of neurological involvement; the nature of this condition remains unclear.[7] There is no record of efforts to treat his stuttering.

In the following century, the physician Galen described stuttering and, viewing it within the framework of the humours doctrine, spoke of it as due to excessive moisture, or in some cases dryness of the tongue, for which he recommended treatment by heating (including cauterizing) the tongue or wrapping it in cloth soaked with lettuce juice.

As noted earlier, the medical lore of classical Greece was assimilated and preserved by Arabian scholars, through whom it was eventually transmitted to Europe. O'Neill (1983: p. 108) relates that, in fact, the humours doctrine seems to have been organized into a definite system by Arabian scholars and, moreover, that they used it to explain disorders of speech.

Two key figures in this compilation and transmission of classical medical lore were al-Razi, who lived in the latter half of the ninth century (c. 865-925), and Avicenna[8] who lived almost a century later (980-1037). In al-Razi's writings the Arabic word "fa'fa'a" is identified as the counterpart of the Greek "ischnophonos." Such sources are among those that provide clear indication of the reference of the Greek term. Rockey and Johnstone (1979) note that medieval Arabs evidently were particularly impressed with the prevalence of the "fa" sound in stuttered speech. The Arabic word noted above also is clearly onomatopoeic, as is "tamtam," another term reported by Rockey and Johnstone.[9]

Actually, Avicenna has been accorded much more attention in sources dealing with the history of medicine than has al-Razi, probably because of the considerable extent of the former's writings (see, for example, Boorstin 1983; O'Neill 1980). Avicenna's *Canon*[10] is a vast medical encyclopedia consisting of five lengthy books, and it is matched by another work of equivalent magnitude dealing with other aspects of science.[11] Avicenna endeavored to bring together the medical writings of Hippocrates and Galen with the biological works of Aristotle, and in so doing he elaborated the system, described above, that dominated European medical thought from the late twelfth century to the seventeenth century. Although Aristotle was the major authority for Avicenna, the influence and status of Galen remained salient. The title "Galen of Islam" was the highest honor Muslim physicians could pay al-Razi or Avicenna, or any other great Arabian physician (see Boorstin 1983).

Avicenna noted particularly the iterative aspect of stuttering and commented on the patient's evident inability to emit words unless syllables were repeated several times. Both al-Razi and Avicenna directed treatment primarily to the tongue (see O'Neill 1983).

The final three authorities to be considered in this chapter, whose lives span the four hundred years from 1300 to 1700, essentially repeated what had been said long before them.

De Chauliac (c. 1300-1380), surgeon and physician to three popes at Avignon, authored a physician's manual that for three centuries was considered indispensible to the practice of medicine. He ascribed stuttering to either excessive moisture or dryness of the tongue or brain. Inasmuch as these attributions of cause were couched in the humours doctrine, the appropriate treatments were therefore obvious: application of various treatments or techinques that would presumably adjust the body's humours, as represented in Figure 3.1.

Mercurialis (1530-1606), a distinguished Greek and Latin scholar and physician, professor at Padua, Bologna, and Pisa, wrote a number of medical treatises including one on the ailments of children. In the first chapter in the latter work, titled "On Injuries to Speech in General" (see O'Neill 1980), he identified *ischnophonos* as hesitation of the tongue, and reported that persons so afflicted were compelled to repeat the first syllable of words. He was evidently well acquainted with a wide range of medical lore from famous predecessors and attempted to embellish such accounts by interweaving his own observations as well as folklore and legends. However, overall the fundamental theme was heavily infused with the humours concept.

Francis Lord Bacon (1560-1626) is most renowned as an essayist, philosopher and statesman. He was a keen observer and wrote admirable, influential essays on many subjects. Although educated in law and a very competent attorney, he was particularly interested in science, especially scientific method. He stressed the value of inductive reasoning and set out a description of the "rules of evidence" scientific inquiry should accept.

Although he was, thereby, a leader in the rebirth of science, certain agelong beliefs appear in some of his writings. One of his works, titled *Sylva Sylvarum,* first published in 1627, is a compilaton of observations on many subjects.[12] One entry is of special interest in the present context. Entitled "Of Stutting" (p. 85, No. 386), it captures the distinctive flavor of the humours concept in specific reference to stuttering:

Divers, we see, doe stut. The Cause, may bee, (in most,) the Refrigeration of the Tongue; Whereby it is lesse apt to move, And therefore wee see, that Naturalls doe generally Stut: And wee see that in those that Stut, if they drinke Wine moderately, they Stut, less, because it heateth: And so we see, that they that Stut, doe Stut more in the first offer to speake, than in Continuance; Because the Tongue is, by Motion, somewhat heated. In some also, it may be, (though rarely,) the Drinesse of the Tongue; which likewise maketh it lesse apt to move, as well as Cold; For it is an Affect that it cometh to some wise and Great Men; As it did unto Moses, who was *Linguae Praepiditae*; And many stutters we finde are very Cholericke men; Choler Enducing a Driness in the tongue.

Note that his statements relative to heat and cold are similar to ones made by Aristotle (see Chapter 2). Of more substantive significance, note the observation bearing on the matter of stutter locus: "in the first offer to speake," that is, initial position. Another comment is pertinent to stuttering in the mentally retarded: in Bacon's time "a Naturall" was a euphemism for someone who was mentally deficient.

PROLOGUE TO A NEW ERA

The pervasive influence of Galen would begin to dissipate as the seventeenth century passed, following particularly upon the momentous achievements that led to understanding how blood circulates in the body. First, through the work of William Harvey, in 1628, regarding the function of the heart and the roles of the arteries and veins. Then, in 1661, through Marcello Malpighi's discovery of the capillaries, which completed the basic understanding of blood circulation.

The broad realm of science received very substantial support and encouragement in 1662 when a group of learned English men of science, under the patronage of Charles II, established the Royal Society, an academy for the advancement of science. In 1665 the society began publication of *Philosophical Transactions*, which contained reports and exchanges of letters from men of science all over Europe. It was the first scientific journal. Note the word "Philosophical" in the title, reflecting the status of science at the time, still incorporated within philosophy. At the same time, the title of the journal and the transactions themselves, were printed in English, not Latin.

The pivotal event marking what is widely considered to be the beginning of modern science was the publication, in 1687, of Isaac Newton's *Philosophiae Naturalis Principia Mathematica*,[13] usually referred to as the *Principia Mathematica*, or simply the *Principia*. This benchmark in the progress of scientific method would gradually have a profound impact on other areas of scientific inquiry, although its relevance to the topic of stuttering would remain tangential. In fact, the level and quality of scientific orientation and inquiry that this great work encouraged in other fields has yet to overtake endeavors in the field of stuttering.

NOTES

1. It is instructive to note that some of the beliefs held during this period continued to find advocacy in the nineteenth century—and beyond. At the same time, in contrast, certain pithy observations occasionally surfaced during this era, as well in earlier times.

2. As later discussion will reveal, speech itself was perplexing to these men. For an excellent, relatively brief, review of the history of medicine, see Boorstin's *The Discoverers*, Part X, and certain other chapters in Book Three of that source.

3. It deserves mention that Aristotle, in contrast, saw life as a single process of the whole living organism, not as something that occurred when "spirits" or "pneuma" were added to bodily organs. Aristotle's view of the unity of life processes was an incentive to Harvey's work on the circulation of the blood.

4. It should be noted that Galen also wrote extensively on drama, grammar, philosophy and rhetoric.

5. A nickname by which he is known historically. He was born Theophrastus Philippus Aureolus Bombastus von Hohenheim.

6. Translated title of Vesalius' folio: *On the Structure of the Human Body*. Of Copernicus' work: *On the Movement of the Heavenly Bodies*.

7. See Scramuzza, Chapter II.

8. Al Razi's full name was Abu Bakr Zakariyya al-Razi. Avicenna is the Latinized name of Abu Ali al-Husain ibn-Abdallah ibn-Sina.

9. See also Van Riper (1971) who lists a variant of this word, and also "rattat."

10. "Canon" is the Latin title for this work. Its original title is the *al-Qanun fi al-Tibb*.

11. His known works also include close to one hundred treatises on art, astronomy, geometry, philology, philosophy and theology.

12. For example: "Of compound fruits and flowers."; "Of certain cements and quarries."; "Of the medium of sounds."; "Of caterpillars."

13. *Mathematical Principles of Natural Philosophy*. Note the title. The work was written in Latin; translation into English was published in 1729.

PART II

THE SIGNIFICANT INTERIM

CHAPTER 4

1700–1900

> Those who cannot remember the past are condemned to repeat it.
> George Santayana

By 1700, the spirit and effects of the Renaissance had spread to all the countries of Europe, and many of its achievements had become part of European life. Major developments in the new mold of science had occurred in the seventeenth century; in fact, the modern period in science came into being during that century, in which the Age of Enlightenment began. Also, the major theme of the Renaissance — humanism, the renewed interest in man and his life on earth — had found expression in many directions, several of which can be seen to have influenced an interest in stuttering. Not the least of these influences was the belief in the importance of the individual, but certain other important developments also prominently affected interest in and attention to the disorder as time passed.

Attention to stuttering was relatively limited in the eighteenth century, as reflected in the comprehensive survey by Klingbeil (1939), which contains only eleven entries from the 1700s. In contrast, interest in the disorder expanded remarkably in the 1800s, which is well represented in the 104 references in Klingbeil's review. Interest in stuttering in these two centuries, particularly the nineteenth, was influenced by three major intellectual and social forces, themselves interrelated in varying degrees: continued developments in science, especially as they influenced medicine; a broadly based interest in speech performance as an art, a skill, and a suasive medium; and a concern for education. The latter two influences, being intimately interrelated, will be considered together.

BACKGROUND: MEDICINE / PHYSIOLOGY

In the two centuries considered in this chapter, particularly the nineteenth, the study of medicine was more rapidly becoming truly scientific, although it was still considered a branch of philosophy until well into the nineteenth century. The anatomy and physiology of the human body were more widely studied and investigated, and much better understood. Yet, although many medical advances were made during the Age of Enlightenment, progress was, in general, remarkably slow. In particular, physiology, which would become the basis of modern medicine, did not become established as an independent sphere of scientific inquiry until the third decade of the nineteenth century.

The age-old treatments such as purging and phlebotomy persisted;[1] in fact, one form of the latter treatment, use of leeches, was in vogue as late as 1833. The superficiality yet pedantry of medical practice was satirized in the literary works of Johnathon Swift, in England, and in the plays of Jean Moliére in France. Moreover, the practice of medicine and access to medical treatment were limited largely to the upper classes. Most of the great names in medicine came from wealthy families and were identified with elitist groups, royalty, scientific societies, or the military.

Public health was seriously neglected all over Europe, which was becoming heavily industrialized. The Industrial Revolution brought overcrowded cities in which living conditions were incredibly loathsome and unhealthy. For many of the sick, hospitalization was considered simply a prelude to death. Recovery from surgery was rare, and was more a tribute to the patient's constitution and good fortune than to medical treatment. The importance of sanitation was not realized until well into the nineteenth century. Florence Nightingale's startling success in decreasing the death rate in Crimean War hospitals in 1855 from 42 percent to 2 percent in five months was due largely to her insistence on improved sanitation.

Although Antonie van Leeuwenhoek had reported seeing bacteria under the microscope in 1674, the role of such organisms in disease and infection was not realized for another two hundred years. It remained for Louis Pasteur to demonstrate, in 1861, the role of bacteria in putrefaction and disease. This achievement finally forced abandonment of the agelong belief in spontaneous generation. A few year thereafter, in 1867, Joseph Lister developed the first antisepsis, initially for use in surgery. However, major advances in bacteriology did not come until the decade of 1880-1890.

Surgery, in particular, was handicapped, and complicated, not only by sepsis but by lack of anesthetics. Not until 1846 did the medical world begin to realize that anesthesia, using ether, was a practical proposition.[2] In subsequent years some use was also made of chloroform, but ether was more widely employed as a general anesthesia and remained the principal anesthetic technology well into the twentieth century.

Understandably, in view of the technology available at the time, progress in understanding the nervous system was slow. A major achievement of the sec-

ond decade of the nineteenth century was the research of Charles Bell in Scot-
land (in 1811), and Francois Magendie in France (in 1822); working independently, they established the distinction between sensory and motor nerves.
However, physiology did not emerge as a scientific discipline until 1833. In
particular, investigation of brain functions, the mind, and the mind-brain relation was only beginning to be approached scientifically. The level of sophistication in such matters during this time is clearly reflected in the widespread
attraction of phrenology.

Phrenology was a conjectural explanatory scheme that related inferences
about individual mental "faculties" to features on the external configuration of
the skull. Interestingly, this notion emerged and blossomed in the same era as
the significant contributions in neurology made by Bell and Magendie. Although not generally accepted by scientists, phrenology seemed plausible to
many and continued to hold great attraction for many years. In fact, the idea
still haunts conceptions of brain function, through its influence on
"localization" views of cerebral organization. This general orientation received
encouragement some thirty years later from the reports of Marc Dax and then
Paul Broca, which seemed to identify "the language area" in the brain. A particularly notable figure of this period was Hughlings Jackson, whose work not
only yielded insight into cerebral function but had special relevance for speech
and language. Jackson conceived the important contrast between "automatic"
and "propositional" speech. The latter concept would eventually have considerable significance for understanding the nature of stuttering, although its value
in this regard is still to be adequately appreciated (see Chapter 9).

The middle of the nineteenth century saw the beginnings of physiological
research that was directly pertinent to speech processes, such as the study of
respiratory movements, the structure of the larynx, and the vibratory action of
the vocal folds. Major discoveries were made about the nature of sound, and
the sounds of speech in particular. Significant advances also were made relative to the receptive aspect of speech: namely, progress in study of the anatomy
and pathology of the hearing mechanism, notably the work of Alphonse Corti
and, of course, Hermann von Helmholtz. Important contributions in the study
of speech and hearing accrued during the remainder of the nineteenth century,
although it was not until the last decade of the century that one could speak of a
discipline of experimental phonetics.

Scientific study of various matters pertinent to speaking was to increase toward the end of the nineteenth century, yet certain aspects of even the peripheral speech process, especially the relationship between respiration and phonation, were generally not well understood in those times. Actually, the nature of
phonation was not fully understood until around the middle of the twentieth
century, when the myeoelastic-aerodynamic theory of phonation was accepted
over the neurochronaxic explanation (see, for instance, van den Berg 1957;
Rubin 1960).

At the same time, even well before the nineteenth century, it was obvious that
breathing and voicing (respiration and phonation) are closely related and di-

rectly involved in the act of speaking. This essentially lay knowledge constituted the core substance for practitioners dealing with varied interests in
speaking and singing and, particularly relative to our interest, in disorders of
speech. The relevance of these matters to the topic of stuttering will be discussed later in the chapter.

BACKGROUND: GOOD SPEECH / EDUCATION

   The other major influence on the study and treatment of stuttering was the
development of a broadly based societal interest in speech form and style. This
area of interest led quite naturally into study of the processes of speech production by certain individuals who were professionally concerned with ways of
improving speech expression.
   The latter part of the eighteenth century saw the emergence of a unique phenomenon that, in the following century, was to have considerable significance
for all speech defects,   including stuttering: the elocution movement. The
central focus of this movement, which began in England, was a sincere concern
for proper use of the language, especially as spoken. It was believed not only
that a higher standard of spoken English was needed, but also that improvement in oral verbal expression might "refresh ways of thinking."
   Several precursory circumstances influenced the development of the elocution
movement. For centuries Latin had been the language of the church, of natural
philosophy, and of medicine, and so also of science as it gradually developed
into an autonomous area of inquiry. In all of these areas the use of Latin was
exclusionary. The various professions were open only to those few who had
the resources to receive instruction and preparation in Latin. The masses of
communicants attending religious services did not know Latin; it was understood only by the few who officiated in the rites. There was, therefore, little
knowledgeable interest in what was said from the pulpit, or how it was said.
However, after the Reformation (beginning in 1517), and in England after the
separation of the Anglican Church from Catholicism (1534-1558,[3] church
services for other than Catholic denominations gradually came to be conducted
in the national language. This change held great import for the matter of interest in speaking. Additionally, the advent and spread of the printing press had
made books increasingly accessible to more people, in the language of their
own country. People were becoming literate and increasingly better educated
and, thereby, more active participants in their society.[4]
   At the same time, typical use of the native language evidently left much to be
desired, a condition that provoked much concern in a culture such as that
found in England. The first book written in English devoted exclusively to the
subject of speech performance was Robinson's *Art of Delivery*, published in
1617.[5] By 1750 many developments within the increasingly democratic society
in England had contributed to a critical attitude toward public speaking and
speakers. This attitude, which expanded into the elocution movement, is re-

vealed in the following statement by Thomas Sheridan, one of the earliest writers to stress the need for better speech. Lecture I of his *Lectures on Elocution* (1762) begins with this complaint: "That a general inability to read [aloud], or speak, with propriety and grace in public, runs through the natives of the British dominions, is acknowledged; it shews itself in our senates and churches, on the bench and at the bar." Later in the same work he describes good speaking as follows:

A just delivery consists in a distinct articulation of words, pronounced in proper tones, suitably varied to the sense, and the emotions of the mind; with due observation of accent; of emphasis, in its several gradations; of rests and pauses of the voice, in proper place and well measured degrees of time; and the whole accompanied with expressive looks and significant gesture.

Eventually, various systems of elocution appeared, some of which produced excesses in certain of their "principles," particularly the use of codified gestures and facial expressions. Nonetheless, this development of such systems reflects the great appeal and popularity of the elocution movement.

In America too the increased attention accorded public speaking produced a parallel interest in how to construct and present a speech. The works of the English writers on principles of speaking, especially the elocutionists of the latter half of the century, were circulated in America and emulated. Even early in the century elocution had come to occupy a prominent place in higher education. John Quincy Adams, who would become the sixth president of the United States, held the first chair of rhetoric at Harvard, in 1810. In the same year his book *Lectures on Rhetoric and Oratory* was published. By 1830 elocution was becoming separated from rhetoric. Both Yale and Harvard instituted separate instruction in elocution,[6] and in the latter half of the nineteenth century elocution was a required subject in many colleges throughout the United States.

The concern with ability to speak well was also clearly evident in educational practices in the primary and secondary schools throughout the nineteenth century. The major dimension of classroom instruction in the primary grades was reading, which meant essentially *oral* reading, with clear attention to articulation, enunciation, and pronunciation. Also, other kinds of speaking experiences were either included as curriculum, particularly at upper grade levels, or actively encouraged as extracurricular in the form of such activities as declamations, recitations, debating, formal conversation, and discussion.

In America the close connection between the elocution movement and a concern for education was reflected in the lyceum movement, started in 1826 at Millbury, Massachusetts, by Josiah Holbrook.[7] Originally, lyceums were local associations that gave people the opportunity to hear debates and lectures on topics of current interest — an early form of organized adult education. From the time of their inception their major interests were the establishment and improvement of public schools, classes for adults, and the development of libraries and museums. In 1831 the local lyceums united to form the American Lyceum, and by 1840 the organization was a professionalized institution that brought in lecturers from the outside. The lyceum popularized the lecturer as a form of entertainment combined with instruction, and often the entertainment value outweighed the instructional. The lyceum system flourished and spread across the land, keeping pace with westward expansion.

A parallel, and eventually superceding, movement arose after the Civil War at Fair Point on Lake Chautauqua in New York State. Essentially a summer teachers' institute in its early years, the program at Chautauqua gradually broadened to include general education, popular entertainment, directed home reading, and correspondence study. As with the lyceums, the Chautauqua movement extended its programs throughout the country via various regional "circuits." Known in the vernacular as "Chautauquas," the various educational and cultural programs were widely dispersed to a population eager to receive them. In fact, the Chautauqua movement remained vigorous through the early decades of the twentieth century.[8] However, in the early 1930s it collapsed under the massive societal changes that followed the development of radio, moving pictures, and the automobile.

In a time now distant from the days of the lyceums and Chautauquas[9] it is difficult to imagine the nineteenth century attraction of oratory. In its cultural as well as educational aspects, oratory in those times has properly been called "the literature of the masses." But the present-day reader must also recognize that, in addition, oratory had a substantial aesthetic appeal in those times. Catton (1963) presents the picture clearly when contrasting the speeches given by Abraham Lincoln and Edward Everett at the dedication of the Civil War cemetery at Gettysburg in 1863. Everett, America's most famous orator, was actually the featured speaker at the event, chosen because of the performance he could be expected to deliver. Oratory, Catton reminds us, had great popular appeal in those days, and the speaker's skills were greatly admired:

People greatly enjoyed listening to speeches — long speeches, done up in flowery language, with all sorts of classical allusions and quotations, going on and on and on until the listeners grew numb in their seats. . . .

Today's average American would probably pay good money to avoid having to sit through a speech of that kind, but in the 1860's it was top-flight entertainment. (p. 136)

The aura of this interest in speech is reflected in the existence of popular magazines like *The Voice*, a review of which is presented in the section addressed specifically to stuttering, later in this chapter.

The concern for education, in particular, found expression and support in legislation to limit child labor. Such legislation was established in England by 1833. In America, Massachusetts led the way in 1836. Other states were following by 1860, although a federal statute was not passed until 1911. With the gradually increasing limitations on child labor came requirements for school attendance. With more children in the schools, the numbers of children having various handicaps became more evident, which led to the development and growth of special education programs. This influence was to grow as the early twentieth century unfolded.

THE BROADER BACKGROUND

One cannot consider developments in the nineteenth century without making particular note of three marvellous intellectual achievements in that century, achievements that would thenceforth influence all human endeavors in some way and, in particular, shape the intellectual climate of the next century.[10]

The first achievement, founded in an increasing understanding of the earth's geological record, was the discovery of time— time, stretching back into a far distant past, immeasurably further than had ever previously been imagined. The second, which emerged from study of the fossil record, with its evidence of extinct species and of ancient hominid forms, was the realization that humans are just one species of animal, not a special creation. The third achievement, which emanated from the first two, was the concept of evolution.

The influence of these achievements on the topic of stuttering would be indirect and rather remote, but nonetheless eventually potent. The effect would come largely from changes in ways of viewing human nature, primarily as expressed through several disciplines whose foundations were established or gathering momentum in the latter part of the nineteenth century. The broadest of these influences would arise from the emergence of psychology as a separate discipline having a respectable research base. Another would derive from developments in psychiatry, notably the appearance of dynamic psychology. A third would emanate from cultural anthropology. These three disciplines share a common theme, namely, a focus on the individual and a bias toward invoking environmental factors as the major source of human behavior. The nature of their influence on stuttering will be considered in subsequent chapters, principally Chapters 5 and 6.

STUTTERING IN THE EIGHTEENTH AND NINETEENTH CENTURIES

Writings on stuttering were notably sparse in the eighteenth century, and consequently there is, for the 1700s, relatively little to condense. Nonetheless, the pertinent material is well worth noting.

It is of some interest that publications at the beginning and end of this century contain references of a psychological nature. A treatise published in 1700 by Johann K. Amman (1667-1724), a Swiss physician who was one of the earliest writers on the instruction of the deaf, proved to be a bellwether. Amman also worked with stuttering, which he called "hesitantia."[11] Although his treatment was directed primarily to control of the tongue, he considered stuttering to be a "bad habit." This may be the first written record that alludes to stuttering in terms of habit. The early years of the seventeenth century also saw the advent of the "associationist" school of psychology, initiated in David Hartley's *Observations on Man*, first published in 1749. Hartley's concepts, with their reference to a physiological basis for behavior, set the framework for much of modern psychology. They also influenced certain subsequent views of stuttering: eventually, notions that it is "acquired." Hartley himself made specific mention of stuttering, commenting that "as a rule stuttering seems to arise from fear." The reader should recall that fear has been invoked in explanation of stuttering since at least the time of Aristotle.

Other kinds of "psychological" accounts were offered. For instance, toward the end of the eighteenth century Moses Mendlessohn (1783) proposed that the main source of stuttering was the collision of ideas; and Alexander Crichton (1798) also attributed it to "conflicting thoughts." At the very end of this century Erasmus Darwin[12] explained (1800) that stuttering is due to emotions, which disrupt the movements of the speech organs. Of course, emotions are still frequently cited as the cause of, or a major contributor to, stuttering. It is especially worth noting, however, that writers in the eighteenth and nineteenth centuries who mentioned emotions included reference to positive kinds of emotion as well as the negative. This finding is in marked contrast to the clear preference found among twentieth-century authors to invoke — in fact emphasize — only negative emotions (see Chapter 5).

Other records from the 1700s yield references to stuttering that are more mundane, yet nonetheless notable if only to attest that stuttering was well recognized in those times. A review of periodicals published in several of the American colonies between 1720 and 1765 revealed frequent notices soliciting help in locating runaway slaves and bonded servants (Read 1938). These notices typically listed distinctive attributes of the persons sought, often including mention of various speech characteristics and speech defects, including stuttering.

Cotton Mather is undoubtedly the most famous stutterer of Colonial America. He was the scion of a prominent family, many of whom were clergy, including his father and eventually Cotton himself. Initially his stutter frustrated his aspiration to prepare for the ministry, and he and his father prayed long for his "deliverance." He began the study of medicine instead, and in 1724 wrote a lengthy medical treatise titled *The Angel of Bethesda*. This treatise contained what was most likely the first account of stuttering written in this country: a chapter titled "Ephphatha, or Some Advice to Stammerers." One should note that in this chapter Mather mentioned that stutterers are often "too choleric" in disposition, a remark that reveals the persistence of the old "humours" doctrine. Of additional interest is the term "ephphatha," a Biblical word meaning "be opened" (see Glossary). Mather eventually overcame his stutter, at least sufficiently to enter the ministry. For a fuller account of his efforts and success, see Bormann (1969).

On the other side of the Atlantic, stuttering was a distinctive aspect of the speech of Camille Desmoulins, an early leader in the French Revolution (see Morton 1950).

As noted earlier, the number of writings on stuttering increased markedly in the nineteenth century. Throughout most of that century writings on stuttering were authored predominantly by practitioners on the European continent and in England. Further, a majority of these individuals were either physicians or persons having medically related preparation. Americans who had an interest in stuttering were much inclined to accept the continental sources as authoritative.

The medically based interest in stuttering was pursued actively on the European continent and to some extent in England, but less so in the United States. These differences in orientation to the problem took on more definitive form as the nineteenth century passed, becoming more clear-cut toward the end of that century and persisting into the twentieth. On the continent, conception and treatment of the disorder remained more within the medical framework, a pattern that would extend into the twentieth century (see Chapters 5 and 6). In Great Britain and the United States the orientation was decidedly more along the lines of what might be called a functional theme. The British and American orientation came about largely as a result of the nonmedical influences mentioned earlier in this chapter, particularly the elocution movement and its derivative interest in speech processes.

The much increased knowledge of human anatomy and physiology that had accrued by the nineteenth century suggested and supported explanations of stuttering that focused on the body structures whose functions are obviously integral to speech performance, namely, those structures involved in the processes of articulation, phonation,[13] and respiration. Often stuttering came to be explained as a disturbance in one or the other of these areas of function — and, of course, as some incoordination among the three areas.

In view of the relatively early date at which incoordination among these three processes was offerred in explanation of stuttering, and of the fact that such accounts have been restated intermittently for over a hundred years, it is rather startling to find that "discoordination" among these processes was offerred as a presumably original hypothesis late in the twentieth century (Perkins et al. 1976; and again, 1986).

Especially in the early and middle 1800s one finds a considerable inclination to explain stuttering in terms of faulty anatomical structures. The tongue figured prominently in such accounts, with attention directed to its status (e.g., size, debility), its anatomical connections, and its control. However, this predominant focus on the tongue did not, of itself, reflect any actual sophistication in anatomy or physiology. For centuries the tongue has been identified as the essential organ of spoken language; consider, for instance, the frequency with which "tongue" occurs as a synonym for "language."[14] Thereby, the tongue has quickly become the primary suspect in cases of speech dysfunction. As noted in earlier chapters, the tongue was often cited as the source of stuttering, from antiquity through the Middle Ages — and into fairly recent times.

Some practitioners of the early nineteenth century believed that certain other structures seemingly related to the speech process, such as the tonsils, the uvula, and the hyoid bone, were somehow involved in the evident problem of control. However, the tongue remained the prime suspect in cases of stuttering in this era too. Of course, the resulting prescription for treatment was addressed to the presumed cause. Recommendations included various tongue positioning and tongue control exercises, and the aid of various oral devices. However, the most dramatic prescription, and certainly the most infamous, was surgery.

As one might expect, the tongue was the primary target of surgical intervention. Evidently, lingual surgery was first performed by a German named Johann Dieffenbach in 1840. It should be noted that Dieffenbach was a capable and highly respected physician and surgeon, knowledgeable for his time. He had had an interest in speech problems and had done good work with cleft palate. He had come to accept the view, rather widely held in those days, that the immediate cause of stuttering was spasms of the glottis. He had himself encountered several stutterer patients who also manifested a varying irregularity in oculomotor control. These and evidently other observations led him to suspect anomalies of motor control involving lingual and facial muscles as well as musculature in the larynx. His rationale for the lingual operations was that cutting into the base of the tongue would improve coordinative neural control of the tongue and the vocal folds, thereby quickly eliminating stuttering.

Dieffenbach performed three kinds of operations, all on the tongue. In the present context it is sufficient to make only brief reference to one of these three procedures. Dieffenbach's "favorite" operation was to excise a wedge-shaped section transversely across the dorsum of the tongue and nearly through it, the wound being then, of course, sutured. Keep in mind that effective anesthesia was not yet a part of surgical procedure, and that antisepsis too was still unknown! One can hardly imagine the suffering to which these patients were subjected.[15]

The interested reader will find descriptions in Burdin (1940) of a range of the many surgeries undertaken to "cure" stuttering. Incredibly, hundreds of patients underwent these operations, which were soon being performed in other countries of Europe, in England, and even in the United States. The surgical procedures varied somewhat among surgeons; however, following the lead established by Dieffenbach, almost all of the operations were performed on musculature of the tongue.

Fortunately, the major crest of this lingual surgery episode passed in about a year, but not until many patients had died either as a direct result of the operation or from ensuing complications. Many surgeons claimed successes for these operations — among those patients who survived[16] — but other surgeons acknowledged that the problem often reappeared even before the wound had fully healed.

The whole surgical episode provides a classic illustration of the folly that attends presumption coupled with ignorance, or belief not tempered by circumspection. It is a sort of folly that recurs in the field of stuttering, although in other instances not with such outrageous procedures or with such irremediable physical consequences. The unwisely trusting patients and their families, no less than the practitioners, seem to have participated in this lingual surgery fiasco through an expectation of quick results. Unfortunately, the search for a quick resolution continues to lure persons involved with stuttering.

Many physicians, especially in England and the United States, protested this evident fad of surgical intervention. Prominent among those who objected to "this butchery" was Edward Warren, an American surgeon whose early warnings of the futility of such methods had gone unheeded. Warren, a stutterer himself, lamented the general disinterest of the medical profession in stuttering. At the same time he insisted that stuttering could only be managed through didactic procedures, and that success could be expected only if such methods were "resolutely persevered in for one or two years." In this regard, it is notable that he spoke highly of the kind of instruction available from persons well trained in the principles of elocution.[17]

Both before and after this episode of lingual surgery, other methods were implemented to correct presumed limitations of the tongue or its control. For instance, the belief that stuttering was due to a weak tongue led to the prescription of mechanical devices or special techniques designed to give the tongue support. The most frequently mentioned device of this type, evidently the first one described (in 1817), was designed by Marc Itard, a French physician of considerable stature.[18] Described by later writers as a "fork," Itard's device more resembles a gibbous moon. A drawing of this little device, which was to be worn underneath the blade of the tongue, is pictured in Wingate (1976: p. 282). Devices very similar to Itard's *refoule langue* were described by other practitioners in later years, and oral devices of various designs have continued to appear well into the twentieth century (see later).

In the same era that devices were first reported (1820s),[19] there appeared a famous "system" or treatment technique that was intended to achieve an effect comparable to that of the tongue forks (that is, holding up the tongue). The objective of this technique, called the Leigh, the Yates, or the American method,[20] was to train the patient to keep the tongue in a "floating position." To this end various exercises were prescribed, as well as the use of tongue support during sleep (see Schoolfield 1938: pp. 106-107). The system was widely employed in this country and was reported to yield "striking successes." The method was bought by a Belgian named M. Malebouche who elaborated it and then sold it to several European governments. After several years of enthusiastic acceptance in this country and abroad, the system seems to have fallen into disrepute. Apparently the successes were not enduring, at least in many cases, although adequate records of success and failure were not kept.[21]

The contrasting belief that the fault in stuttering lay in an overly energized tongue led to recommendations for use of devices contrived to restrain its movement. Numerous oral devices having this objective were subsequently developed throughout the nineteenth century — and the twentieth. Some of these devices were very simple, such as Canon Charles Kingsley's recommendation of holding small pieces of cork between upper and lower teeth. Others were very complicated and cumbersome. Some are aptly described as mechanical contrivances, complete with moving parts. The interested reader will find a good sample of oral devices pictured in Katz (1977).

Some of the nineteenth century were not designed simply to influence tongue position or movement, but were addressed to a major dimension of the speech process. For instance, three devices developed by Robert Bates (patented in 1851) were intended to assist the patient to maintain "an uninterrupted current of sonorous breath" (that is, voicing).

Oral devices and their reported effects have been widely ridiculed and casually dismissed as "trickery," especially by sources that gained prominence after the development of the American Speech and Hearing Association (ASHA) in the 1920s. However, there is reason to suspect that these efforts should not be so readily denigrated. In regard to the Bates devices, for instance, an independent report (Meigs 1852) attested to their successful use by several persons.[22] Two years later the Committee on Science and the Arts of the Franklin Institute of the State of Pennsylvania, having appraised the efficacy of these instruments, awarded Bates the Scott Legacy Premium for his "ingenious and useful inventions" (Hamilton 1854).

Devices for the treatment of stuttering continue to have great appeal. Many oral devices similar to those just noted have been developed, and have received patents, well into the twentieth century, and at least as late as 1959! Moreover, technological advances in the late twentieth century have led to the creation of a new breed of devices employing modern electronic gadgetry that follow new treatment themes of a nature quite different from their predecessors (see Chapter 9 under "Modern Devices").

As noted earlier, practitioners in the nineteenth century had a partially sophisticated appreciation of the peripheral speech process that provided some embellishment of the essentially lay knowledge regarding the functions of respiration and voice. Beyond the anatomic preoccupation that focused principally on the tongue, a great deal of attention was directed to the functions of breathing and voicing. Many who wrote about stuttering in the nineteenth century emphasized disturbance in respiratory function, which led to recommendations for breathing exercises and systems of breath control. Others considered that control of the voice was faulty. In fact, in the latter half of the century many were persuaded that a major part of the problem lay in vocal control, leading them to recommend methods and techniques to "keep the glottis open," whereby the patient could avoid precipitating "spasms of the glottis" (that is, spasms of the vocal folds).

Because stuttering clearly reflects interruption and perturbation in making sound, the nature of stutter events indicated loss of normal control of such functions. This inference, enhanced by noting the exaggerated movements of certain more pronounced stutter events characteristic of some stutterers, had led to use of the descriptive term "spasm," a word consistent with the reference to stuttering as a "nervous affection." This inference was expressed fairly often, usually without further reference to central nervous system dysfunction. However, several writers (A. Guillaume, Charles Bell, James Yearsley) drew a parallel to chorea. Yearsley, in noting that stuttering resembles chorea, added the astute qualification that in stuttering the choreiform movements "occur only during attempts to speak."

Alexander Melville Bell was the only writer of this era to emphasize that speech is an *overlaid* function, which means that all the structures participating in the production of speech have first-order functions that are considerably more vital to the organism.[23] He made the further significant observation that the structure, or structures, that were supposedly "deranged" (as the presumed cause of stuttering) were able to function quite adequately in their ordinary basic duties. A potentially critical inference afforded by the observations of both Yearsley and A. M. Bell, although not expressed by either of them, is that stuttering must therefore be some function of oral language expression. This particular inference would not be expressed formally until well into the twentieth century.[24]

The view of stuttering as a "nervous affection" at least implicated the central nervous system, and certainly had a broader scope than those that focused attention on only those structures directly participating in actual speech acts. This broader orientation seems to have caused some practitioners to look carefully at other acts concurrent with stuttering, such as blinking the eyes, dilating the nostrils, or similar events. A preoccupation with such occurrences led to their being considered other "symptoms" of stuttering. This view led, in turn, to the proposal that there were many kinds of stuttering.[25] At the same time claims of this sort implicitly recognized that what might superficially appear as different kinds of stuttering actually comprised variant expressions of one disorder, in which the clonic and tonic "spasms," the speech features, were the central, common, criterial features.

The inclination to consider nonspeech features as actual symptoms of stuttering, which to some suggests different "types" of stuttering, has recurred as a misleading preoccupation well into the twentieth century. The attempt to identify different types of stuttering has ignored the consistently present compelling evidence that *all* cases of stuttering evidence the characteristic anomalies of speech — the clonic and tonic features. They are the universally occurring, *sine qua non* markers of stuttering. In contrast, nonspeech events are not characteristic of stuttering. Nonspeech acts that may be present during a stutter event do not typify stutters. Moreover, they are certainly not universal among stutterers.[26]

In spite of the recurring diversion to features other than the speech characteristics, most sources in the nineteenth century, and well into the twentieth, found stuttering to be appropriately described in terms of the simple classification proposed by Serre d'Alais in 1821, namely, that the true symptoms of stuttering are either *clonic* or *tonic* perturbations of speech — that is, that stutter events are characterized by either iterative (clonic) or perseverated (tonic) actions or postures (or both) that involve elements of words. These designations were widely used as the essential descriptors of stuttering for well over a century, due undoubtedly to their succinct yet distinctively encapsulating reference.

Because of the clarity and directness of their reference, the terms "clonic" and "tonic" might well still be used routinely in description of stuttering had their use not been discouraged when the term "spasm" was intentionally ex-punged from an influential literature source, the *Journal of Speech and Hearing Disorders*, between 1943 and 1948 by its editor during that period, Wendell Johnson. The circumstances underlying this action are considered in Chapter 7.

Notations relative to an analytic description of the actual speech aspects of stuttering appeared only sporadically during the era under consideration in this chapter. However, it is of considerable interest that as early as 1717 David Bazin remarked that stutterers have difficulty with one or another "letter," and in 1798 Alex Chrichton emphasized that stuttering involves sounds, not words. Further, he offered the inference that in a stutter event there is evident "a sudden immediate uncertainty about how a sound should be produced."

A number of writers in the nineteenth century listed particular sounds on which stuttering was most likely to occur.[27] As one might expect in light of what is known today, the sounds differed considerably from one list to another. Several authors reported stuttering to be related to special "types" of sound, according to how types of sounds would have been known in those times, for example, "gutturals." However, there was a growing tendency to speak of sound difficulty in terms of the consonant-vowel distinction, in which consonants were said to present the greater difficulty. This notation of consonants being more difficult than vowels is another report that has continued to be made well into the twentieth century. Even in what are, at this writing, the final years of the twentieth century, this particular contrast between consonants and vowels vis-a-vis stuttering remains widely accepted as a truism, in spite of key considerations that indicate otherwise.

Although, as the nineteenth century progressed, more attention was beginning to be paid to certain speech variables in stuttering, only rarely did a speech description proceed beyond the level of noting sounds or types of sounds. Nonetheless, the few such observations made were pithy ones. In 1803 Erasmus Darwin made the astute observation that the break marking a stutter event is usually between an initial consonant and the following vowel. James Hunt, in 1861, gave a more elaborate analysis along these lines and was the first to make the point that the essential problem seems to lie in making the transition between sounds, principally between consonant and vowel. Failure in connecting consonants to vowels also was mentioned by several other prominent practitioners of the era. Hermann Klencke (1862; see later discussion) made this observation, as did Adolph Kussmaul in 1877; somewhat later Kussmaul (1881), described the source of stuttering as an "irritability of the coordinating center that controls the formation of syllables." This unique description clearly implies defect in the integrity of the syllable. Some mention should be made here of Kussmaul's eminence as a physiologist. He was widely recognized for his outstanding work in the study of pulse and respiration. In the same era (1880) Alexander Graham Bell wrote that the failure to connect consonants to vowels is the hallmark of stuttering.

The content of the preceding paragraph should call to mind Aristotle's descriptions regarding "joining syllables sufficiently quickly" and "when they have to utter a second sound." Both of these descriptions clearly imply transition. Unfortunately, incisive observations such as these, and those noted immediately above, have been consistently ignored, overridden in the perennial rush to offer some broad conjecture on the cause of the disorder.

It is appropriate to make particular mention here of the well-known Bell family: father, Alexander Bell; son, Alexander Melville Bell; and grandson, Alexander Graham Bell. The latter, of course, is known worldwide as the inventor of the telephone. His father, less widely known, will be remembered in some disciplines for his development of "Visible Speech," a system for making a graphic recording of speech through the use of symbols based essentially on oral positions. All three men merit attention here because they were prominent figures in the field of elocution.[28] They wrote extensively about speech and problems of speech, and (notably Alexander Melville) particularly about stuttering. Their writings span much of the nineteenth century and well represent the contributions made by the field of elocution to the management of speech disorders. All three men emphasized that speech correction is the province of the educator, not of the physician or surgeon.

This claim that speech correction should properly be undertaken by educators was not simply an issue of prerogative. There was much empirical justification for the contention. Even in the many medically based approaches to dealing with stuttering, the treatment was essentially functional or didactic in nature— for instance, special exercises addressed to developing proper managment of respiration; the use of rules for acquiring control of the voice; or, combinations of such procedures. In most instances the treatment was broadly based, proceeding from a basic requirement that the individual be generally in good health. Specific treatment procedures were then addressed to what was understood at the time about the speech process as a whole. Here writings from the study and pursuit of elocution made major contributions.

One technique employed in the treatment of stuttering deserves special attention here: the use of rhythm. It deserves special note for several reasons: it was the contribution of an elocutionist (John Thelwall); it was initiated early in the nineteenth century; it was used extensively in the nineteenth century, and into the twentieth; it lost favor and in fact was openly denigrated during the second quarter of the twentieth century by persons influential in the field of stuttering, largely because it was a measure employed by the "commercial schools"; and it then resurfaced and received considerable, although passing, attention in the 1960s. However, the most important reasons for taking note of rhythm are that its unquestionable and dramatic beneficial effect and its value are still not understood.

John Thelwall was one of the intellectual liberals of his day, a friend and companion of men like Samuel Taylor Coleridge and William Wordsworth. Considered by some a radical, he was a champion of free thought and an eloquent early spokesman for democratic ideals. His extensive writings received only limited attention, but he was acclaimed for his skill with the spoken word. Immersed in the use of his language, he was especially attentive to its "rhythmus." He called attention to the prominent expression of rhythmus in poetry and also to its less evident but ever-present role and substance in ordinary speech (Thelwall 1810; 1812a, 1812b).[29] His emphasis that rhythmus was central to good speaking led to its recommendation for use in speech correction. Rhythm's remarkably beneficial effect on stuttering quickly became evident, and it was incorporated into many systems of treating stuttering.

Evidently rhythm came to be used by many practitioners in a manner that had lost sight of Thelwall's intent. In fact, Thelwall himself, as well as the substance of his contribution, was practically forgotten. Marc Colombat has often been cited as the person responsible for introducing rhythm, possibly because he devised an instrument called the muthonome[30] to assist the patient to follow a rhythm. However, Colombat also did not use rhythm simplistically, as twentieth-century references to him have routinely suggested. He was among those who directed his patients' attention to "the rhythm of the sentence," in the form intended by Thelwall.

Many sources, particularly later in the twentieth century, have dismissed rhythm as a "trick" or explained it as "distraction" and referred to those who have used it therapeutically as charlatans. However, the effect of rhythm, and its employ, cannot be dismissed so lightly or so simplistically.

A LATE NINETEENTH-CENTURY SAMPLE

As the preceding discussion suggests, the leading nineteenth-century authorities on stuttering were European. They were primarily continental, especially German, and most often physicians. Nevertheless (except for the surgery episode), their treatment consisted largely of methods stemming from, or at least highly consistent with, principles in elocution—and they incorporated the use of rhythm.

A brief synopsis of the management program employed by Hermann Klencke (1862) should be exemplary. Klencke was a highly respected German physician, recognized as probably having had the most experience on the continent in dealing with stuttering. His system was carried forward by A. Gutzmann, who had studied under Klencke, and then by H. Gutzmann, his son. This succession extended Klencke's methods through the latter half of the nineteenth century and into the early twentieth.

Klencke identified his method as "a medico-pedagogic system of speech gymnastics." He took only five or six patients at a time; the average length of stay at his institute was twenty to twenty-five weeks. He reported that a few had spent only twelve weeks, but their stuttering was relatively mild. He reported having dismissed 148 cases from his institute over a period of thirty-six years (1843 to 1879). Klencke warned of charlatans in the treatment of stuttering, stating that many persons who knew nothing about stuttering, including some physicians and surgeons, were willing to treat it and offered to do so.

Klencke's system placed initial emphasis on breathing exercises, then a combination of breathing and voicing ("vowel exercises") working on individualized vowels. He described these as "a system of gymnastics of the respiratory and laryngeal muscles." He used charts and diagrams that illustrated the combined exercises of respiratory and laryngeal gymnastics. By carefully following these charts,

The attention of the stutterer is firmly fixed upon his breathing function and his tone formation. He becomes able to inhale and exhale according to his volition—long or short, with vocal sounds or toneless breath, with a continuous air current or with interruptions, pauses and new attacks. It is indeed remarkable what a change in nervous action is wrought by these gymnastics of the respiratory and laryngeal muscles. This change is plainly shown in the patient's ability to regulate his respiration and in the liberation of his will power, which hitherto has been subordinate to his malady. He gains control of his voice which grows fuller-toned and more powerful. In order to specially exercise the voice muscles and make them still more pliable and subservient to the will, the patient should practice the vowels in octaves. (p. 72)[31]

Such exercises were also assisted by diagrams and directions.

The two foregoing parts of the system provided the principles and the experience that governed the treatment in the third part of his "cure." These earlier exercises "have drilled only the auxiliary organs of speech; now begins speech itself, with physical and mental activity, or cooperation." The stutterer was then given speech rules that he must not break and must observe with "the utmost rigor." "Henceforth the patient must not stutter." The procedure was as follows. Every morning the patient must repeat the respiratory and laryngeal exercises he had learned, at first alone and then with the other patients. Then:

He is allowed to speak only according to a prescribed measure, which he must himself meter visibly with his finger, either by striking a part of his body or some convenient object. Every patient practices measured talking an hour daily with me, during which I stand with the measure stick before him. He is not permitted to speak in mechanically-read or thoughtlessly-recited phrases, but must instantly give well-considered answers to questions. Usually the stutterer finds great difficulty at first in talking according to measure. He is strongly inclined to rush through hurriedly. If left to himself he is sure to quicken the beat, which is slow in the beginning, and he, without wishing to do so and without knowing it, goes faster and faster until stopped by stuttering. Slow measure also consumes his breath. He soon gets tired of it because he is not accustomed to slow talking. (p. 74)

Description of stuttering treatment in this era should also at least note briefly the work of the Englishman James Hunt, Ph.D., who is certainly one of the most notable figures in any nineteenth-century history of stuttering. His book, *Stammering and Stuttering*, first published in 1861, went through seven editions and was eventually reprinted in the United States in 1967. Hunt's method, employing exercises and techniques similar to those of Klencke, is best described succinctly in a statement attributed to Canon Kingsley,[32] namely: "naturally, and without dodge or trick, to teach the patient to speak consciously, as other men speak unconsciously." In this regard it becomes appropriate to note a statement by Aine Chervin, a French specialist of the same period as Hunt. Chervin (1867) made the point that Satyrus, who helped Demosthenes, should be recognized as the first person known to have treated stuttering through "lessons of diction." Chervin added that, in his own time, success with stuttering had been in proportion to "the nearness of approach to the simple and natural means which antiquity has transmitted to us."

A REVIEW BY A CONTEMPORARY

A notable contribution to the history of stuttering is contained in a small book that was quite unique for its time. Bearing the title *Speech and Its Defects* (Potter 1882), it was written as a special-project essay by a young physician who lamented the fact that standard medical textbooks either ignored the subject of defective speech or relegated it to the care of, in his words, "specialists"—by which he evidently meant persons with questionable professional background. He expressed concern that, because of the apparent indifference of the medical profession, treatment of these defects would be abandoned to

semi-professional empirics, who as self-styled "professors," conduct various "institutes," each claiming to be the possessor of a peculiar method, productive of better results than the system of any other institute. (p. 10)

This description reflects a situation that developed during the nineteenth century, concurrent with the expanding attention to stuttering, that would continue well into the twentieth century.

Despite its title, *Speech and Its Defects* addressed proportionately little discussion to speech processes or to deviant speech in general. The bulk of the book was addressed to stuttering, a disproportion occasioned by the fact that the author himself stuttered.

Potter commented on the "confusion in nomenclature" used for speech defects in general, but particularly in regard to stuttering. He complained that some authors in both America and England used the terms "stuttering" and "stammering" interchangeably, and he repeated the distinctions pointed out by Hunt, Klencke, and others (see Chapter 1), with which he concurred. He identified the defect as "difficult, interrupted speech" that is characterized by "clonic and tonoid spasms of articulation, and spasmodic hesitation." It is of interest that in his introductory discussion he used several technical terms to describe several kinds of speech defect, employing the term "dyslalia" for stuttering. Thereafter he used these two terms interchangeably.

A principal value of the essay lies in its compilation of the views of many "authorities," especially of the nineteenth century,[33] regarding the nature of stuttering and its appropriate treatment. From these sources the author distilled summaries of the presumed causes of the disorder and the various approaches to its treatment. He assessed the findings in both areas quite objectively and elaborated on treatment efforts that evidently were productive.

The professional credentials of some of the authorities Potter reviewed are not clear, and among these a few might seem to be questionable. However, it is significant that the majority of the authorities cited were physicians, and several more were physiologists. Potter's complaint about the medical profession's indifference to speech defects may seem contradicted by this finding. But although many individual physicians were concerned about stuttering, there was in fact no focalized or systematized interest that would underlie organization and integration of pertinent information. Establishing such a foundation was an evident Potter objective,[34] but in this aspiration he was far ahead of his time.

On the presumed cause of stuttering, the material in Potter's book is consistent with the reports from sources reviewed earlier in this chapter. The most prevalent notions among the old authorities linked stuttering to some organic structure, particularly the tongue. Significantly, these views persisted into the early decades of the nineteenth century. Then a shift to emphasis on some aspect of the nervous system began in the 1830s.[35] Typically, such presumed cause was spoken of as "derangement of nerve-function," as seemingly manifested in the evident faulty operation of one or another of the structures known to participate in the production of speech. Some of these accounts implicated the structures that are clearly involved in articulation; a few cited the breathing apparatus; and a dozen authorities emphasized lack of coordination among all systems participating in speech production. However, the majority of explanations focused on innervation of the larynx, a view epitomized in the frequent reference to "spasms of the glottis."[36]

Potter commented on the occasional statements regarding "forms and varieties" of stuttering by noting that "in all forms and varieties of the disorder the essential condition present is *spasm* of a greater or lesser degree" (p. 76).

In summarizing the treatment efforts recorded, Potter educed four "axioms." Three of them received only brief attention. The first was that the ineffectiveness of surgery had been clearly established. Second, no direct benefit, for stuttering at least, could be expected from "either medicine or electricity, alone or together." Third, mechanical appliances and routinized actions or postures were likely to afford only temporary benefit.

It seems pertinent to digress briefly here to elaborate a bit on the matter of "electricity." Electrical stimulation was used during most of the nineteenth century in the treatment (and diagnosis) of a variety of human ailments, especially those involving the nervous system. However, one finds only passing notations of the practice in sources addressed to the history of medicine, such as Castiglioni (1941), Haagensen and Lloyd (1943), and Mettler (1947). Brief, and nonspecific, mention of the use of electricity in the treatment of stuttering appeared sporadically in some sources in the latter half of the nineteenth century.[37] The rationale for its use with stuttering evidently was based on results obtained in "medical electricity" treatment of conditions like chorea minor and "various forms of local spasm." However, the rationale, objective and details of procedure in respect to its use with stutterers are obscure.[38] Potter noted that both "galvanic and faradic currents" were applied while the patient was seated on an insulated stool, but he made no mention of how the application was made nor with what objective.

The fourth axiom derived from Potter's review of treatment efforts is summarized well in his own words:

That the only rational and efficacious method of treatment is disciplinary exercise of the respiratory, vocal and articulating organs; conducted unremittingly and patiently, until a correct habit of speech is established, and aided by the use of the utmost degree of willpower of which the patient is capable. (p. 87)

The treatment procedures Potter himself set forth were consistent with this axiom. In fact, the outlined descriptive summary of his recommendations suggests that they were much like those of Klencke; they included a rhythm component, as did the procedures of a number of the authorities he reviewed.

THE VOICE: ALMOST A SPEECH CORRECTION JOURNAL

As a capstone to this chapter's review of the history of stuttering, it seems fitting to present a brief account of *The Voice* (1879-1892), a little-known publication that, although it reflected quite well the tenor of its times in regard to speech and speech disorders, was nonetheless considerably ahead of its time.

Volume 1, Number 1 was printed in Albany, N.Y. in January 1879. The editor and publisher, a Mr. Edgar S. Werner, stated that he planned to encompass a wide range of topics having to do with good speech, including contributions from authorities on voice, the mind, and the nervous system. At the same time, a principal objective was to provide a vehicle to aid the speech defective, "the thousands who are measurably deprived of one of the noblest faculties given to man." He would endeavor to present the systems of treatment utilized by various individuals from different countries to help "remedy defective utterance."

Although the purview of interest was good speech, with a major focus being a concern for the speech handicapped, he openly acknowledged in the initial issue that "stuttering and stammering[39] will be made a specialty." The reason for the emphasis on stuttering should be guessed readily — Mr. Werner was a stutterer. He reported having begun to stutter in early boyhood and having received treatment for several years with different persons in both the United States and Europe. The story of his stuttering was serialized in the magazine within the next few years, and he reported there the experiences he had had with various treatments in this country and abroad. However, he gave little description of whatever improvement in fluency he attained or of changes in his speech or manner of speaking. He himself treated stutterers privately, using elocutionary methods.[40]

The magazine remained in print for about twenty-two years — until just after the turn of the century — although it underwent several changes during that time. In the early years, articles included many contributions on speech problems, predominantly stuttering. However, the proportion of contributions on defective speech became progressively smaller, giving way to a heavier representation of articles dealing with public speaking, elocution, voice culture, and some impressively scientific articles on the vocal mechanism and the nervous system.

Throughout most of its life the title of the magazine remained unchanged; however, various subtitles reflected changes in orientation and content over the years. The original subtitle, "A Monthly Devoted to Voice Culture," was used for about three years. In March 1881 (Vol. 3, No. 3) the subtitle was changed to "An International Review of the Speaking and Singing Voice." There was now a great deal of material on elocution, care and culture of the voice, singing, and the physiological rationale for speaking. There was also quite a bit of emphasis on breathing: explanations of the act of breathing as well as techniques of breathing, and rationale for its control. Articles were contributed by physicians, elocutionists, teachers, actors, and many operators of schools of speaking, singing and voice culture. Many of the contributors were evidently well known in their day — including one who was to become much more widely known later, namely, Alexander Graham Bell. Each issue also included letters from readers, testimonials of various kinds, critical reviews of articles, and comments relevant to one topic or another, largely made by persons having some professional interest in speech.

Still, consistent with Werner's initial statement, stuttering was the special focus. The lead article in the first issue was the first installment of Hermann Klencke's book *Die Heilung des Stotterns*, translated by Werner himself, which was continued in serial form over a number of issues. Books by other contemporary experts on stuttering were also serialized in subsequent volumes of the magazine. However, Werner featured Klencke's work because he considered Klencke to be "the Columbus among the curers of stuttering," saying that there was no system for over a quarter of a century that did not include the principles of Klencke's method. Evidently Werner could speak with some authority on this matter, in view of his reported personal experiences with various treatments.   At the same time he received, and published, some criticism of Klencke's method by authors who offered their own ideas.

Among the testimonials that appeared from time to time one finds the type of report that would be discovered again almost a century later, in a study of recovered stutterers (see Wingate 1964). The following, which appeared in Volume 1, Number 6 of *The Voice* was a contribution from a J. W. Essig, D.D.S., of Owosso, Michigan, who described how he had cured his own stuttering by keeping his teeth closed while speaking. He said that he read aloud slowly, carefully, and distinctly while moving his lips but keeping his teeth abutted. He practiced speaking in this manner in two-hour sessions three days per week. He added that he had tried the system even though he was unimpressed upon first hearing about it. However, after working with it for a while he felt "as though something had loosened the speaking apparatus," and eventually his stuttering phased out.

In addition to the frequent contributions on stuttering (independent ones as well as the serialized) that appeared during this period, many articles bearing other content are represented by the following titles: "The False Vocal Cords"; "Gymnastics of the Voice"; "Elocution of the Delsarte Method"; "Aesthetic Physical Culture";   "The Audiphone";   "The Action of the Thyro-Cricoid Muscle"; "Articulation in Singing"; "Speech Reading"; "Articulation of the Deaf"; and "Visible Speech" (a series of articles by Alexander Melville Bell himself, in 1884).

For a period of time in the early to middle 1880s considerable space was occupied by discussions of the Delsarte method of speaking. This method, developed by a Frenchman, was touted as "the science of expressive man," in which "expression is the exterior in motion that is moved from the interior." This method placed great emphasis on the use of postures and gestures that, so claimed, should be part of effective speech-giving. This emphasis went so far as to codify the types of postures, gestures and facial expressions presumed pertinent to the varying content of the spoken message. Evidently the method received widespread attention in this country; it had numerous protagonists and severe critics. Delsarte himself never visited the United States; his major disciple in this country was a man by the name of Moses True Brown, who was on the faculty of Tufts College in Boston.

Although *The Voice* now devoted proportionately less space to content dealing with speech defects, an interest in speech problems remained the central theme during this period. In the November 1883 issue (Vol. 5, No. 11, p. 169) the editor made reference to *The Voice* as "the only journal in the world making the cure of vocal defects a specialty." He continued to publish contributions from experts on stuttering of the day. These articles were usually quite lengthy and were published in installments that appeared intermittently. The editor personally translated works from H. Klencke, E. Gunther, A. Gutzmann, and E.

Coen. Other contributors in the area of stuttering were W. Hammond, S. O. L. Potter, E. B. Shuldham, and A. Chervin.[41]

The only other kind of speech defect that received much attention was articulation problems associated with deafness. In the August 1884 issue (Vol. 6, No. 8, pp. 130-133) three pages were devoted to the program of a Convention of Articulation Teachers. This material reported that about 200 persons attended the opening meeting of this group. The convention was held June 25 to 28 at the Institute for the Improved Instruction of Deaf Mutes, located at "Lexington Avenue between 67th and 68th Streets, New York." Undoubtedly this "institute" is the facility now known as the Lexington School for the Deaf.

In subsequent years progressively less space was devoted to speech defects. In issues of the mid-1880s one finds increasing numbers of articles on various aspects of singing and vocal music. In June 1885 the magazine was moved from Albany to New York City and the sub-title (Vol. 7, No. 6) was changed again, this time to "Devoted to the Human Voice in All Its Phases." Evidently this time the shift in emphasis resulted in some measure from dissatisfaction expressed by subscribers. In the March 1886 issue (Vol. 8, No. 3) Werner remarked in one of the articles of his serialized autobiography that he had received mail complaining about so many articles on stuttering.

The following articles are representative of contributions to *The Voice* during the mid-1880s: "Breathing in Song and Speech, with Illustrations"; "Reading Aloud in the Schools"; "The Art of Oratory" (in installments); "The Study of Language"; "Speaking and Singing Contrasted"; "Physiology of the Larynx" (in installments); "The Face and Its Expressions"; "The Origin of Human Speech"; "Helmholtz on Singing"; "Vowel Theories", by Alexander Graham Bell.

In the December 1889 issue (Vol. 10, No. 12) the editor announced that, since he had not protected the title *The Voice* by copyright, a newspaper devoted to political issues had taken the same name.[42] Consequently, the title was changed in January 1889 (Vol. 11, No. 1) to *Werner's Voice Magazine*. At the same time the subtitle was changed to "A Journal of Expression—Vocal and Physical." The content then shifted more toward voice culture in regard to formal speaking and singing.

After 1901 the magazine entirely lost its unique identity. In that year it merged with a journal titled *Philharmonic*. This title appeared until March 1903, after which it was published as *Muse* for a span of about three months. Then it merged again, with a publication identified as *Rostrum*. Within a few years it disappeared in another merger, this time with a magazine called *Home Education*.

As mentioned above, *The Voice*, as a publication focusing largely on disorders of speech, was ahead of its time — in fact, about fifty years ahead of its time! It would require the eventual establishment of a professional-level specialty to provide the receptive audience and consistent support necessary for such an endeavor, a development that did not occur until well into the third decade of the twentieth century.

ADDENDA AND REFLECTIONS

For several reasons it seems appropriate to include here a brief summary of some material that could not be fitted easily into the historical narrative but that nonetheless merits special attention and commentary.

First, certain collateral observations about stuttering were made repeatedly by nineteenth-century practitioners. Many observed that stuttering occurred much more frequently in males than in females.[43] Many also reported that stutterers experienced no difficulty while singing. Several writers noted that their patients had less difficulty reading poetry than prose. Several also recorded clear evidence of a familial predilection for stuttering, suggesting a hereditary dimension. Fear was mentioned often; occasional references were made to imitation, to "external pressures," and even to "mental expectancy." Intermittency of the disorder was especially remarked by several writers; also, observation of a decrease with age, and instances of "complete relief through self-treatment in adult life."

Second, approaches to management having demonstrable merit were developed during this period, essentially from a pragmatic, mainly ad hoc, effort. The following list identifies nineteenth-century stuttering management practices in terms of how directly they addressed the speech process.

A. Speech Specific

    1. Slow reading aloud
    2. Rhythm
    3. Easy onset
    4. Continuous flowing manner of speaking
    5. Systematic voice training
    6. Disciplinary exercise of the organs of voice
    7. Drill in techniques of speech
    8. Didactic method
    9. Regular progressive language lessons
    10. Careful enunciation
    11. Practice in speaking
    12. Drill in the proper processes of speech
    13. Avoidance of musculature effort in speaking

B. Other

    1. Exercise of will-power
    2. Education of the will
       (These first two items emphasized that personal involvement in working at controlling one's speech was necessary.)
    3. Cheerful society (having friendly people about)
    4. Kind treatment
    5. Good physical regimen (good food, exercise, rest, etc.)
    6. Relaxation

It is important to recognize that no practitioner used any of the "other" practices exclusively. In contrast, treatment efforts always focused on, or made exclusive use of, measures directed at modifying the manner of speaking.

Students of stuttering have never reflected very long on why certain procedures (such as the Leigh-Yates method) or the mechanical devices of this era
"worked," at least for some indefinite period. The failure, and therefore also
the success, of these measures has typically been imputed to influences within
the patient's mind, via some grossly conceived notion such as distraction, suggestion, belief, or faith. No serious search was made, then or later, for some
possible principle(s) linked more closely to speech processes that might be
found to recur in these various effects.

It is germane to point out that all of the mechanical devices effected change
in manner of speaking, whether or not their employment was so intended.
Similarly, the Leigh-Yates-American method undoubtedly had such effect.
One should be able to readily appreciate that the (at least short-term) result of
surgery also had the same effect. As an approximation to the likely effect of
such surgery, consider how one speaks during an interval after having inadvertently bitten one's tongue. If one seeks a common dimension in all the influences noted above, at least two major features can be discerned: reduction in
speech rate, and an emphasis on the voiced basis of the speech signal. In fact,
the latter was the stated objective of some of the devices, namely, to induce "a
current of sonorous breath."

It is beyond the scope of this book to expand the above list, particularly the
first section, to the point of identifying the range of specific techniques actually
employed. For one thing, one can not readily distinguish between treatment
principles, treatment methods, and treatment techniques. In fact, many approaches may be all three in one; or simply technique; or only technique
thought to be something more. For instance, of the items listed as "speech
specific" above, the use of rhythm might be employed in one or the other of
these three levels, depending largely upon one's understanding of what seems to
be involved in the effect produced.

With this qualification in mind, it is of considerable interest that all of the
approaches to stuttering listed above, and the specific techniques contained
within them, have a direct equivalent or an essential counterpart in the treatment efforts of the twentieth century. In this vein it should be of particular
interest to note a few representative items that are to be found in both centuries. One such item, which appears in the list above, is "easy onset," which is
undoubtedly the all-time favorite technique. A related item, though frequently
used separately, is "prolongation," which consists of intentionally lengthening
a word or (most often) initial syllable. A third is the nineteenth-century (Arnott
1862) recommendation to say /e/ before a difficult sound (word). Twentieth-
century "experts" in the profession have criticized and denigrated this particular technique as another "trick," without any consideration of how it might
have been of value. At the same time, the technique is essentially duplicated in
the suggestion, made in very recent times, that a stutterer produce a slight

voicing in the identical circumstance (Lee et al. 1973). A fourth item of special interest is the routine utilized in the early nineteenth century by Good (1827) and by McCormac (1828) of having the patient begin treatment by saying only letters, then simple words, then words in sequence. This same technique has been offered late in the twentieth century, at which time it was presented as a newly devised procedure in a therapy program supposedly derived from, and expressing the principles of, the "operant learning" paradigm (Ryan and Van Kirk 1971; D. M. Mowrer 1975, 1980; Costello Ingham 1993).

Nineteenth- and twentieth-century correspondences will be considered again at the end of Chapter 9.

NOTES

1. Phlebotomy was probably the major cause of George Washington's death, on December 14, 1799. He was bled three times in less than twenty-four hours (for what retrospective diagnosis suggests was a strep throat). See Paster (1993) for an interesting review of the lore, beliefs, and practices of phlebotomy in early modern England.

2. William Morton, an American dentist, is usually credited with demonstrating the value of ether as a general anesthetic. Crawford Long, a U.S. surgeon, had used ether in his practice in 1842 but did not make his findings public until 1849. Humphry Davy had suggested the use of nitrous oxide as early as 1800, but its value was not demonstrated until 1844 by Horace Wells, an American dentist.

3. Henry VIII's Act of Supremacy (1534) made the king the head of the church in England; an independent Church of England was established in 1558 under Elizabeth I.

4. Latin continued to be the universal language of science until well into the seventeenth century, such that matters of a scientific nature were available only to the specially educated. As noted in Chapter 2, the works of Copernicus, Galileo, Vesalius, and Newton, for example, were all published originally in Latin.

5. Noted in W. Guthrie (1951), this book included an extended description of hand gestures considered appropriate to various themes of a speech.

6. John Walker's *Elements of Elocution* was the most popular English textbook used in American colleges in the early part of the nineteenth century.

7. The term "lyceum" was adopted from Aristotle's school, named for the park outside of Athens where it was located.

8. The program content was gradually broadened to include musicians, concerts, and other popular entertainment. However, drama was frowned upon until 1911, when some of Shakespeare's plays were produced. The peak year of the Chautauquas was 1924, when programs were presented in 10,000 communities, attended by over 40 million persons (Harrison 1958).

9. It is notable that the National Science Foundation still supports, through the Chautauqua foundation, "Chautauqua-type Short Courses," an annual series of forums throughout the United States in which scholars in various sciences can directly apprise college teachers of recent developments in their fields.

10. For an excellent exposition of these and related topics see Eiseley (1958).

11. In the next century other teachers of the deaf would also help stutterers. Outstanding among them were the Bells; see later in this chapter.

12. Grandfather of Charles Darwin and of Charles' cousin Francis Galton.

13. "Phonation" is a rather modern term. The process was called "voice" or "voicing" throughout the nineteenth century.

14. Although it seems obvious that the tongue is critical to articulate speech, its singular importance is severely qualified by those rare cases of individuals who speak well even though having a vestigial tongue, or none. Instances have been reported in relevant literature as early as the seventeenth century (see Goldstein 1940). In fact, Gibbon (1911: p. 705-706) documented reports of many persons who could speak intelligibly without a tongue. However, none of this evidence has been well disseminated, even in modern times.

15. Although Dieffenbach warned of the dangers of the operation he evidently did not actively dissuade potential patients from submitting to it.

16. The plausible basis for such claims will be considered in the last section of this chapter.

17. He also made a thoughtful, and generally supportive, review of the "Leigh method" (see below). Warren's "Remarks on Stammering" should be read by anyone seriously interested in the disorder. It should be readily available, having been reprinted late in the twentieth century, as cited in the References.

18. Itard is most famous for his work, *The Wild Boy of Aveyron*, which documents his remarkable efforts to teach a feral child. Anyone seriously interested in working with children, especially youngsters with learning problems, will be well rewarded for reading this little book.

19. No earlier account of devices has been found; except that the pebbles Demosthenes reportedly placed in his mouth might well be considered the original oral device.

20. Although its origin is unclear, it was variously attributed to an American physician (Yates) or to his daughter's governess, a Mrs. Leigh.

21. A valuable account of this method is to be found in Warren (1837, [1977]).

22. Potter (1882) identified Meigs as a physician on the faculty of the Jefferson Medical College who had developed an interest in speech defects. Potter himself, who stuttered, mentioned having used the devices but found them not to have a long-lasting effect.

23. Exchange of air to provide oxygen to the blood (lungs and pertinent musculature); protection of the lungs (vocal folds); ingestion and preparation of food (tongue, lips, teeth).

24. By a neurologist, Samuel Orton, who worked closely with Lee Travis. The contribution of these two men is noted in Chapters 5 and 6. Orton's inference regarding stuttering and language function is presented in Chapter 9.

25. Most sources that affirm many kinds of stuttering are satisfied to state the claim in general, nebulous terms. Among the few who attempted to identify various types, the champion appears to have been H. F. Rivers, a nineteenth-century English clergyman turned speech specialist, who claimed "innumerable species," twenty-two of which he gave separate names (Potter 1882).

26. See Wingate (1988: p. 10) for a review of pertinent evidence and discussion. The acts that are additional to the speech characteristics are best described as "accessory features" of a stutter event. This term has come into use only in recent times. The rationale for the classification of "accessories" is presented in Wingate (1964, and 1976: pp. 48-50).

27. Froeschels (1943) notes that in 1717 a David Bazin remarked on stutterers' difficulty "with one or another *letter*," and also that they do not "connect syllables."

28. A. Melville's brother, David C. Bell, was also prominent in the field of speech. Together they published, in 1860, *Bell's Standard Elocutionist*, which was reputed to have done more than any other agent on two continents "to make speech articulate."

29. Regarding rhythmus in speaking, see also Walker (1787). Thelwall's remarks on stuttering are contained in his 1805, 1806 and 1810 publications.

30. Regarding Colombat and his muthonome, see Wingate (1976: pp. 153-156). Any relationship to the metronome is uncertain. The metronome is recorded as having been invented in 1816, questionnably credited to Johann Maelzel.

31. Quite possibly the basis for E. W. Scripture's technique of "the octave twist." See Chapter 5.

32. Potter (1882: p. 58); Klingbeil (1939: p. 124).

33. Ninety-seven of the 110 persons cited wrote between 1800 and 1880.

34. The value of his work was recognized at the time; it received first prize at the fifty-seventh annual commencement of Jefferson Medical College, in Philadelphia.

35. It is notable that the shift to neurological accounts emerged in the era when physiology became a bona fide discipline, and when Sir Charles Bell and Francois Magendie reported the results of their discoveries of the sensory and motor systems.

36. The phrase "spasms of the glottis," brought up earlier in this chapter, appears occasionally in brief historical references of twentieth-century publications, though typically with a whimsical implication.

37. Also, some advertisements for stuttering treatment programs, seen for instance in *The Voice*, firmly assert, "No Electricity!"

38. One can make deductions about these matters from information contained in sources such as Hedley (1900, Part III, Chapter 1) or Jacoby (1901, Part V; Section II; Chapter 5), which give extended explanations of the many special instruments used and some general description of objective and procedure in their use. Evidently the fundamental purpose and rationale for medical electricity in general was the belief that it enhanced the body's inherent electrical forces. This belief was a vestige of the "animal magnetism" theory of Anton Mesmer, a German physician of the late eighteenth and early nineteenth century (whose work also led to European use of hypnotism).

39. The phrase "stuttering and stammering" represents a distinction between the clonic (stutter) and tonic (stammer) features of the disorder. As indicated in Chapter 1, the need for this distinction was questioned even in the nineteenth century.

40. Potter (1882) spoke well of Edgar Werner, who was one of only five authorities in the United States he recommended.

41. Gunther and A. Gutzmann, from Germany; Coen from Austria; Hammond, Potter, and Shuldham from England; Chervin from France.

42. It is of some interest to note that the *The Voice* was also adopted (in 1951, evidently unwittingly) by the California Speech and Hearing Association as the title of its journal.

43. Once appended with the conjecture that females receive "kinder treatment" than do males. This guess would be expanded into a hypothesis in the middle of the twentieth century (Schuell 1946). See Chapter 9.

CHAPTER 5

Early Twentieth Century

This chapter covers roughly the first third of the twentieth century, an era in which the number of cultural developments increased and the pace of social change quickened, especially in the United States.

Several broad developments of the later part of the nineteenth century, expanding into the early twentieth century, had varying degrees of indirect influence on the field of stuttering, especially through changes in education. Certain major sociocultural currents provided the groundswell of change. Legislation limiting child labor resulted in heavily increased school enrollments, which brought increased awareness of children with problems. The rapid expansion of new knowledge led to specialization of knowledge and to utilitarian concepts of the functions of education. In the United States the large influx of immigrants created additional recognition of educational needs. Women's suffrage and coeducation in high schools and colleges were moving toward reality. And then, midway through the second decade, came the First World War. This terrible event would, in a general sense, accelerate changes in social attitudes and thinking in the Western world, especially in the United States. It would also have many direct special effects: notably, for speech and hearing science, the need for speech rehabilitation of many war casualties.

One coincidental occurrence associated with the First World War is especially relevant to our topic. The song "K-K-K-Katy," written early in 1918 by Geoffrey O'Hara, was immensely popular among American (and other English-speaking) servicemen. It was widely popular for a number of years after the war and has remained a well-known favorite at summer camps and similar gatherings, apparently because of its catchy tune and homey lyrics. Significantly, all sources that mention it routinely describe it as "the stuttering song."[1]

DEVELOPMENTS HAVING MAJOR RELEVANCE TO STUTTERING

One can readily identify three major foci of development in the early twentieth century that would have great significance for the field of stuttering. The principal and most direct influence would come from developments within speech education. Because this topic leads easily into the discussion of stuttering, it will be considered last. The second most important influence on stuttering was the emergence of psychology as an independent area of study and inquiry. The third, closely related, influence devolved from changes in the field of anthropology.

Psychology

The very substantial influence of psychology on the field of stuttering would not become evident until well into the third decade of the twentieth century, by which time psychology itself had become soundly established as an independent discipline. An adequate appreciation of psychology's influence on stuttering, as well as the limitations and problems inherent in that influence, make necessary at least a brief overview of the history of psychology in the decades before and after the turn of the century.

Science Is Brought to Psychology. In the last quarter of the nineteenth century psychology began to clearly emerge from philosophy to become a separate discipline. Psychology became a viable entity primarily through the application of scientific methodology as the means of relevant inquiry. The beginnings of this approach that would mark psychology as a science were represented in the work of men such as Gustav Fechner, Hermann von Helmholtz, Wilhelm Wundt, and Francis Galton.

Actually, a scientific orientation in psychology can be traced back to the efforts made by Rene Descartes, in the seventeenth century, to bring psychological thinking into line with the rapid new developments in the physical sciences. However, Descartes' intent would lie unrealized for well over two centuries. Matters of "the mind" would remain a province of philosophy until some time after certain major advances in physiology, particularly in neurophysiology, paved the way for the development of psychology as a separate discipline. Physiology, which itself did not emerge as a separate discipline until 1833, provided a more appropriate model for psychology as a science than did the physical sciences. In addition, a considerable amount of the subject matter of physiology is pertinent to psychological interests. Most of those who were especially instrumental in the development of psychology as a science had some background in physiology, as had the men noted above.

Emergence of the "new" psychology, which meant experimental or laboratory-based psychology, is associated with the work of Wilhelm Wundt, a contemporary of Helmholtz. Wundt is recognized as the first modern psychologist. Trained in medicine, he was principally interested in physiology. In the course of pursuing laboratory research dealing with the effect of varied external stimulation on muscle action, he began to conceive of psychology as a unique area of scientific inquiry. In 1867 he introduced a course at the University of Heidelberg a course bearing the title "physiological psychology" — the first of its kind. In 1875, he established the first psychological laboratory, at the University of Leipzig.[2]

Academic and Laboratory Psychology. Psychology in the United States was at that time actively emerging from philosophy, largely through the writings and activities of William James. James' interests in psychology were wide-ranging, and his contributions to the field were extensive. They are difficult to encapsulate, primarily because of their breadth and variety. However, they need not concern us here since they are not especially relevant to the history of stuttering. It should be noted, however, that James was later considered to have been the first "true" psychologist in the United States, and that among the many dimensions of his psychologically relevant intellectual inquiry was an interest in physiology.[3] At the same time he retained a strong allegiance to philosophy, sufficiently so that he frequently denied his immersion in psychology, and even the existence of psychology as a discipline. In fact, he was recognized in the 1890s as America's leading philosopher.

The scientifically oriented psychology initiated by Wundt was quickly transported to the United States by men who eagerly went abroad to study its methods and bring its contributions to American psychology. I will note here only those individuals whose work and influence had reasonably direct relevance to trends and events important to the history of stuttering. In such context it is fitting to mention first the name of E. W. Scripture, a psychologist then at Yale University, who would later take an active interest in speech disorders, and especially stuttering (see Scripture 1912).

By 1880 rapid growth of psychology was under way in the United States, leading to dramatic changes in the next fifteen years. The first professorship of psychology anywhere in the world was instituted at the University of Pennsylvania in 1888. The American Psychological Association was established in 1892. By 1895 there were twenty-four psychological laboratories in American colleges and universities, and three professional journals.[4] This vigorous expansion continued into the early twentieth century.

The rapid growth in psychology, nurtured by its academic base, brought with it new ideas and differing points of view, which led to a certain amount of ideological grouping, or schools of thought. However, the two major conceptualizations of note in this early period were, first, *structuralism* and then *functionalism*.

Structuralism. The term "structuralism" came to refer to the concepts and methodology intrinsic to the original laboratory approach to psychological study established by Wundt. The term is descriptive of the fact that this approach was addressed to investigating the structure of the mind. For Wundt and his followers, the objective of psychology as a science was to investigate the dimensions of consciousness in order to understand the nature of the human mind. Consciousness was conceived to have basic states: sensation and perception, reaction, attention, feeling and association. These states were held to be directly observable and analyzable through the method of introspection. Importantly, the introspection to be employed by the experimental psychologist was not of the ingenuous, self-observing, reflective sort but, instead, a carefully controlled method following explicit rules for its proper use.

Structuralism influenced American psychology through the person of Wundt's most faithful pupil, Edward B. Titchener, an Englishman. Titchener had studied philosophy, the classics, and eventually physiology at Oxford, where he heard about psychology and went to study with Wundt. After receiving his degree from Leipzig in 1892, he accepted a position at Cornell University,[5] where he remained until his death in 1927. Diligent, industrious, and disciplined, he was the ideal person to carry on the Leipzig tradition. However, he was essentially its last descendent. Although he had many students, including fifty-eight doctorates done under his direction, no notable figure emerged to extend this line in psychology. In spite of Titchener's vigorous championing, structuralism did not develop a major importance in the field. At the same time, it did make a significant direct contribution to psychological study through its emphasis on rigorous and careful experimental method. Also, it indirectly helped to shape the field by serving as a clear counterpoint for other developments then taking form. These developments, which would become manifest in various areas of psychological inquiry, were encompassed under the designation "functionalism."

Functionalism. Functionalism referred to endeavors that were addressed to study of the mind as it functions or is used. In contrast to the delimited and narrow scope of structuralism, functionalism embraced a wide range of psychological interests and investigation. The hallmark of functionalism, as its name implies, was the concern with practical applications of psychology. The orientation common to individuals identifiable as functionalists, regardless of their widely varying interests and pursuits, was their conception of psychology as the study of the organism adapting and adjusting to its environment. This approach to psychological study, which featured a clear interest in practical application and a focus on individuals in relation to their surroundings, was particularly consonant with the American social and cultural ambience.

The foundations for functionalism had been laid by many predecessors, some of them, like Darwin, from relatively distant fields. More directly pertinent contributors on the contemporary scene were men like William James, noted above, and John Dewey, who became prominent in the field of education.

Other prominent figures soon emerged, including some who had gone to Leipzig to study under Wundt, like G. Stanley Hall and James McK. Cattell, the latter identified as Wundt's first bona fide American student.

Of the latter two men, Cattell was clearly the more influential in psychology over the long term. However, Hall deserves mention for his effect on American psychology through his skills as an organizer and administrator.[6] It was in the pursuit of these functions that he will probably be best remembered, and for which this short history has an interest in him. As president of the newly founded (1889) Clark University, he introduced Sigmund Freud to American awareness, both professional and lay, by inviting him to give a series of lectures at the university in 1909.

Cattell, independent of mind as well as of spirit, had done research in individual differences before he went to Leipzig, and while he was there began to question the value of introspection as the central methodology for psychology. After receiving his degree in 1886 he spent considerable time in England with Galton, who was a kindred spirit in respect to range of interests, all practical in nature, and flexibility of approach. Cattell returned to the United States in 1888 to accept the first professorship in psychology (as noted above) at the University of Pennsylvania. He was thereafter active and prominent in various aspects of the discipline: research, administration, publication and editing,[7] and the promotion of psychology as a profession as well as a science. He moved to Columbia University in 1891 as chair of the psychology department; during the years he was there, more aspiring psychologists came to study there than at any other institution in the United States. Soon after arriving at Columbia he was joined by another especially notable figure in the development of the field, Edward L. Thorndike.

Thorndike received his education as a psychologist under William James, at Harvard. While still a graduate student there he became interested in research with animals, beginning with chickens in a makeshift laboratory in James' basement. After taking the position at Columbia he shifted to working with kittens as experimental subjects. His studies of the behavior of kittens in a puzzle-box are classics in the field. His descriptions and analyses of their behavior in escaping from the box led him to speak of "trial and error learning," the concept for which he is best remembered. Within this concept Thorndike formulated two fundmental "laws" of learning: (1) the Law of Effect, which foreshadowed the principle of "reinforcement;" and (2) the Law of Exercise (in two parts), which, in invoking the idea of psychic "connections," set the stage for the persuasive appeal of behavioral descriptions couched in terms of stimulus and response and the hypothesized "bonds" between them.

It should be noted that although Thorndike's work was laboratory based and his treatment of it essentially objective, he did not make claims about the superior value of this form of experimental investigation. Although he did hope that much of psychology could be objectified, he did not abandon an interest in consciousness or repudiate inquiry into its dimensions. In this, as well as in other respects, he represents the tolerant attitude held by "functionalists" toward the many dimensions of psychological study being pursued within the broad range of functionalism.

Thorndike's introduction of the modern laboratory type of experiment with animals made a unique and innovative contribution to American psychology. At the same time it is a credit he shares with several other persons, the most prominent of whom were three Russian physiologists: Ivan M. Sechenov, Vladimir M. Bechterev and Ivan P. Pavlov.[8] It is important to recognize that all three of these men had in common, in their research, an interest in demonstrating that psychic processes are a function of the central nervous system, and therefore are physiological in nature. Of these three Russian physiologists, Pavlov is the best known, essentially because of his work that led to what he came to call "conditioning."[9]

The first half of Pavlov's career was devoted to work on the processes of digestion, for which, in fact, he eventually received the Nobel Prize in 1904. His research with conditioning resulted from a phase of his work on the digestive glands, of which one aspect was the study of salivary function in digestion. To obtain quantifiable data, a salivary duct of a dog was diverted, by operation, to deliver the fluid to an external container, thereby making it possible to measure the amount of saliva stimulated by meat powder introduced into the dog's mouth. Over the course of such study he observed that a dog began to salivate before the meat powder was actually in its mouth, and then at just the sight of the meat, and eventually at the sounds of the attendant approaching with the meat. Pavlov realized that an association had been established between the innate, reflexive process of salivary secretion and certain external conditions that were intrinsically unrelated to salivation. Initially he referred to these evident associations as "psychic reflexes." However, he soon decided to avoid becoming involved in psychological interpretations, a decision encouraged and strongly supported by his colleagues. Because the new occurrences of salivation were clearly linked to certain observable conditions, he settled upon a more objectively based referrent, calling the observed phenomenon a "conditioned reflex." The term first appeared in print in 1901.

The foregoing events and circumstances led to the eruption of a form of psychological orientation that was to have the most profound and widespread effect on psychology of any formulation yet devised: behaviorism.

Behaviorism. This orientation is best identified as primarily a revolutionary *movement* which, moreover, is properly considered as being an idea of what psychology should be *like* rather than a conceptualization itself. It was revolutionary in that it reacted against the forms of American psychology that had preceded it, especially structuralism. Its specification of what psychology should be like was couched in its absolute rejection of all mentalistic concepts, including attention, sensations, images, consciousness and the like, which were the essential substance of structuralism and also were accepted, or at least tolerated, within functionalism. In the same context, the method of introspection, even the exacting, rigorous type demanded by structuralist method, was decried as being fraught with subjectivism. Behaviorism insisted that the data of psychology must be *objective*, externally identifiable, and verifiable by several independent observers.

It is especially pertinent to the history of stuttering in the twentieth century to keep clearly in mind the fundamental principles of behaviorism reviewed in the preceding paragraph: specifically, its requirement of objective observation and, particularly, its absolute repudiation of the method of introspection, the procedure of observing and reporting on the working of one's own mind. This important issue will be brought into focus in Chapters 6 and 7.

John B. Watson is usually credited with initiating the behaviorism movement; he was clearly its prime mover at this time.[10] Watson was developing his position during the first decade of the century, during which he was heavily influenced by his experience and familiarity with animal research (which, at the time, a majority of psychologists actually considered to be of dubious relevance to psychology). Early statements of his position appeared from 1913 to 1915, the latter year marking his memorable presidential address to the American Psychological Association.[11] By that date he had read the work of Bechterev and Pavlov, and his first use of "conditioning" appeared in his presidential address.

Watson was a prolific writer, and he also lectured extensively. He pressed the concepts and claims of behaviorism vigorously and persuasively during the second and third decades of the twentieth century. Behaviorism was to be an objective psychology, to concern itself only with observable events, describable in terms of *stimulus* and *response*. The aim — as well as the claim — of behaviorism was to predict and control behavior. It was presumed that by knowing the stimulus, one should be able to predict the response. The dominant theme of behaviorism was *learning*, the acquisition and development of the individual's behavior (very broadly conceived) through the agency of stimulus-response "bonds." It was, thereby, preeminently environmentalistic.

Within a relatively short time behaviorism became the dominant movement in American psychology. In some measure its success reflected Watson's energetic advocacy. However, a major dimension of its appeal was that, having preempted the image of Pavlov's dog salivating to the sound of a bell,[12] behaviorism took on an aura of bona fide science. Moreover, it was undoubtedly popular because its theme of pragmatic environmentalism was inherently appealing to the American ethos. Watson's famous claim that he (the behaviorist) could shape the destiny of any given infant via manipulation of appropriate stimuli was an assertion readily accepted by a wide audience whose basic cultural tenets made such contentions credible.

Dynamic Psychology. Over the same period of time (the late nineteenth and early twentieth century) another quite different kind of psychology, dynamic psychology, was taking form. Dynamic psychology deals with concepts addressed to "inner" forces of the human mind, with the idea of conflicts and struggles that are conceived to exist and to be active below the level of consciousness, yet which influence the individual's overt behavior. Central to dynamic psychology is the theme that the life experiences of individuals are significant, if not in fact determinant, in the creation of their personalities and patterns of conduct.

Dynamic psychology originated within psychiatry, notably from the work of Jean Charcot (in France) and Joseph Breuer (in Austria) in their treatment of psychoneurosis, particularly hysteria. As had happened with academic psychology, noted above, various ideologies soon developed in dynamic psychology as well. Among these variant conceptions the most notorious and most influential was the set of formulations devised and espoused by Sigmund Freud, which, as should be commonly known, focused on sex.[13]

Throughout his lengthy career Freud insistently maintained that sexual confict is central to psychoneurosis. This contention was rejected by each of his early collaborators, who developed their own beliefs,[14] but he pressed this issue alone in his extensive writings, gaining many proselytes. Especially because his views were not well received on the European continent, it is of singular interest that they found much readier acceptance in the United States, especially following upon his visit to Clark University in 1909 at the invitation of G. Stanley Hall (see above). In fact, psychoanalysis, the term routinely reserved for Freud's brand of dynamic psychology, continued for many years to be more widely accepted in America than elsewhere (Sargent 1964).[15] Once again, the typical American attitudes and beliefs about the important role of life experiences in shaping the individual's personality and one's characteristic patterns of behavior, undoubtedly have underlain the favorable reception of Freud's notions in this country.

Anthropology

The rise of anthropology as a science coincided with the development of evolutionary thought, which had itself been evolving for many years prior to the publication of Darwin's *Origin of Species* in 1859. Both Darwin and Alfred R. Wallace, who shares with Darwin the insight of natural selection, were, among others, convinced of the validity of evolution considerably before that momentous date. Nonetheless, *Origin* excited new levels of interest and inquiry, especially in respect to possible long-term changes in humans as a species and, as well, in their societies and cultures.

The concepts of evolution drew particular attention to human heredity, expressly so in the work of Francis Galton, Charles Darwin's cousin.[16] Galton was a man of extraordinary intellect and many talents who made important contributions in a number of areas in the behavioral sciences, among them anthropometry, statistical analysis, mental imagery, mental association, and mental testing. Although Darwin had avoided discussing evolutionary implications for humans, Galton quickly affirmed the relevance of evolution to understanding human characteristics. From his studies of family pedigrees and of other data that gave evidence of variation in a wide range of human characteristics, he was led to the conviction that human abilities, and limitations, are inherited.[17]   He believed that further human evolution could be shaped positively by controlling which inherited characteristics were passed on to successive generations. For Galton, the objective was essentially to encourage propagation of better human stock, a proposed practice to which he gave the name "eugenics." However, as the concept of eugenics expanded to the level of a vigorous movement, the objective gradually became focused more heavily on diminishing the propagation of those who could be identified as "unfit."

Dramatic support for the belief that the major dimensions of human nature are hereditary came in the form of expansive claims from what has been called "criminal anthropology." The content of these claims reflected the more extreme hereditarian ideas that arose out of certain aspects of evolutionary thought. The essence of the claims was that criminal types and other deviants could be identified by various external physical characteristics. Since a person's physical features are demonstrably inherited, as seen regularly in family resemblances, the notion had a persuasive plausibility to many people. Originating largely in the writing of the French psychologist Benedict Morel in 1857, the claims were carried to notorious prominence some twenty years later following from the works of Caesare Lombroso, an Italian professor of legal medicine.

By the time Galton died in 1911, eugenics was fast becoming a worldwide movement, and it showed remarkable growth in the early twentieth century. Over the next twenty years its hereditarian (biological) precepts, espoused by Galton's retinue, would constitute one pole of the great "nature-nurture controversy," a vigorous and sometimes acrimonious debate over whether physical heredity or environmental factors were most important in determining human characteristics (see Pastore 1949). The pole directly opposite to the hereditarian was to be found in the tenets and convictions central to two mutually reinforcing positions that were rapidly expanding in the second decade of the century: behaviorism, propounded by John B. Watson (mentioned above) and cultural determinism, championed by Franz Boas (see below).

It should be noted that, in most countries, eugenics appealed primarily to certain segments of the upper classes and to many individuals in professions that dealt with persons presenting major social problems: the delinquent and the dependent. However, even at its high tide the eugenics movement was not widely popular in the United States, where an egalitarian attitude and belief in opportunity for individual achievement were widespread and well-established. Gradually the rationale for eugenics became increasingly suspect, and when, during the 1920s, the elitist and racist dimensions of the movement became more vociferous, it declined rapidly in prestige and acceptance. A major source of its eventual demise was the ultra-extremist use of its concepts by Nazi Germany.

The concept of eugenics had been compatible with the intellectual and social science climate of the latter part of the nineteenth century, in which anthropology was dominated by a "linear" conception of history, a point of view somewhat analogous to the "scale of being" concept prevalent in the biology of the seventeenth and eighteenth centuries. From this orientation human social development was thought to have passed through specifiable stages of cultural progress. According to this theme, humans had gradually developed from a state of savagery, through various levels of primitive culture, eventually attaining the societal level of "civilized" man — meaning the culture of western Europeans. Consistent with this point of view, extant non-European cultures that were less well developed materially and technologically were considered to represent various subordinate levels of attainment in human progression.

However, as the twentieth century unfolded, and following upon widening contact with many cultures and a more objective assessment of their uniqueness, the linear conception was gradually supplanted by a more relativistic orientation in which each culture was viewed as the particular product of its physical environment, cultural contacts, belief systems and other factors. The major figure in establishing this new orientation was Franz Boas, known as the founder of the "culture history" school of anthropology — the relativistic, culture-centered anthropological revolution that became predominant as the early decades of the twentieth century passed.

Franz Boas lived most of his adult life in America,[18] but he was born and educated in Germany. As a youth he was immersed in an atmosphere of revolutionary idealism regarding the human condition and its potential, a background that seems to have underlain his later absorbing interest in the relation between the actions of individuals and the traditions of their societies. The development of his concepts was markedly influenced by the anti-evolution school of German anthropology, and then by his own direct, lengthy participation in the cultures of the Baffin Island Eskimos and coastal tribes of British Columbia.

Boas was especially concerned with the question of racial differences, and his writings on the subject reflected a basic egalitarianism. Throughout his career he consistently emphasized the influence of cultural forms on the behavior and mental functions of individuals, and he maintained a prevailingly antagonistic posture to any concepts, including evolutionary theory, that affirmed biological pre-eminence in determining human characteristics.

The writings of Boas and his followers, notably Margaret Mead, Ruth Benedict, and Edward Sapir, had a profound influence not only in anthropology but on all the social sciences, and on the educated American public at large. The central theme espoused in the cultural anthropology of Boas and his retinue was the notion of "cultural determinism" — the contention that human behavior could be explained in purely cultural terms.

The reader will recognize that this supremely environmentalist doctrine was a counterpart of the beliefs and contentions intrinsic to the psychologies that emerged and flowered in this era: behaviorism and dynamic psychology. Like them, cultural anthropology was a doctrine that had great natural appeal to the American mind. The heavily environmentalist orientation of these three ideologies constituted an intellectual and social science background that grew in potency in the third and later decades of the twentieth century.

It is well worth noting that, of these three ideologies, cultural anthropology actually had the most sweeping influence. It can be said that, in several ways, cultural determinism provided the carrier substance for the other two. Clearly, anthropology has a broader scope, and conceptions devised for this arena could encompass or incorporate notions arising from both psychologies. In this particular instance, however, special circumstances provided support for the credibility of all three ideologies. Most important was the publication of *Coming of Age in Samoa*, a book by Margaret Mead that was based on her sojourn in Samoa.

Coming of Age in Samoa reported a study that was widely and thoroughly accepted as having been scientifically conducted and based on factually accurate data. In that guise it presented what was heralded as clear-cut evidence of cultural determinism. The book described an almost idyllic society in which a pervasive laissez-faire attitude occasioned the development of "easy, balanced human beings" from within a milieu that held "few situations for conflict."

Published in 1928, *Coming of Age in Samoa* appeared at a most opportune time for its widespread success. The American ethos, with its central focus on freedom, was in a fervid time, namely, the "roaring twenties," when freedom of expression was actively pursued and widely extolled. Mead's book was not only consonant with the spirit of the times but, moreover, served to justify and reinforce it. Once again sex helped sell. A major dimension of the Samoan laissez-faire, as reported by Mead, was the permissive and indulgent attitude about sexual activity, especially that of young women. This account struck a particular resonance with the mood of the roaring twenties. In this context the book was acclaimed by many lay intellectual leaders of the time. More important, it was ardently embraced by many social scientists. Coming as it did near the end of the lengthy nature-nurture struggle between the environmentalists and the hereditarians, *Coming of Age in Samoa* swept in to carry the day for environmentalism.

The social ambience near the close of the first third of the twentieth century, and particularly the frame of mind in social science circles, profoundly biased the field of stuttering. Such influence would expand in the period to follow. This matter will be dealt with in Part III.

THE PERENNIAL INTEREST IN SPEECH

In the midst of the major cultural developments noted at the beginning of this chapter, the well-established interest in speech and its problems would play a continuing and enlarging role, unspectacular yet fundamental in the encouragement and support of an emerging discipline and profession: speech and hearing science. Clinics for defects of speech began to appear in many countries, in most places supported by both educational and medical interest.[19]

On the European continent, particularly in Germany and Austria, the new specialty continued to remain within the purview of medicine (therefore the use of "logopedics" and "phoniatrics"). There, following the pattern set during the nineteenth century, the specialty was organized in the master-and-apprentice mode, in which practitioners acquired their knowledge under the tutelage of someone who had attained recognition. This arrangement fostered the development of "schools," in which the followers of any particular mentor maintained a deep-seated loyalty to their leader and his method. This situation, in turn, led to competition and contention among the disciples of different methods, and thus little interchange of ideas among them. The leading figures in the field had been Klencke, in Germany, whose mantle was passed to the Gutzmanns, father and son. Early in the twentieth century the focus shifted to Vienna, largely in the person of Emil Froeschels, who had established a speech and hearing clinic at a Viennese hospital. Expansion of interest in the field among some physicians in other European countries led to institution of the International Association of Logopedics and Phoniatry (IALP) in 1924. The main function of the association was to organize biennial congresses at which professional papers were presented. The membership, consisting mainly of physicians, grew slowly, and gradually included non-Europeans.[20] The journal *Folia Phoniatrica*, founded under partial patronage of the society in 1947, eventually provided a publication medium for exchange of professional information.

In England the situation was considerably different from that on the continent. Physicians in Great Britain, including John Wyllie, author of the well-known *Disorders of Speech*, did not consider the treatment of speech disorders to be a medical specialty. Instead, they sought assistance from persons who dealt professionally with voice and speech. Although the clinics dealing with speech problems were regularly housed in hospitals and were nominally under medical supervision, the practitioners who actually treated the speech disorders came from schools of speech and drama. Most likely because of this, schools of speech treatment method did not develop in Great Britain. About 1935 some members of the Association of Teachers of Speech and Drama who practiced as speech therapists formed a Remedial Section of the parent organization, then soon separated as the Association of Speech Therapists. Concurrently another group banded together as the Society of Speech Therapists. By 1945 the two groups had joined to form the College of Speech Therapists, and in that year adopted an existing journal, *Speech*, as its official publication.[21]

In the United States foundation of and support for the emerging discipline of speech science would come largely through higher education, which is undoubtedly the major reason that the new profession came to develop most vigorously in the United States. Around the turn of the century discipleship in the continental mold was brought to the United States by persons who had gone abroad to study. It then expanded to include others whose preparation for the field was suspect. The system had some success in the early years of the century, with the emergence of several "experts," particularly in stuttering, whom West (1959) referred to as the American "messiahs." The system began to dissipate during the second decade of the twentieth century; however, it did not pass entirely from the American scene until the end of the third decade, by which time a national professional association, founded in an academic background, had emerged and was becoming substantial.

It should be noted, however, that a rather comparable situation would obtain some years later, even though the "experts" of that period would be accepted as having professional credentials. This situation is exemplified in a book that presented individual views on the "nature and treatment of stuttering" by twenty five persons accepted as authorities, of whom eighteen were American (Hahn 1956). The editor noted in the introduction, "Each of these authorities has had a considerable number of followers."[22]

Elocution Modified

Changes in higher education in the United States, beginning in the late nineteenth century, had brought about a new system of academic preparation. Universities and colleges, previously not organized into separate departments, moved toward this arrangement in response to increases in specialization of knowledge. In the course of this change, elocution and the teaching of composition became, for a time, associated more closely with the study of literature and literary criticism. As a result, instruction in speech often was incorporated into departments of English. However, soon after the turn of the century separate departments of speech began to emerge. From the beginning, speech disorders were a significant dimension of their curriculum. The scientific study of speech gained momentum in the 1910s and soon became independent of its origins in elocution. It was from this academic base that a formal professional association, addressed specifically to disorders of speech, would eventually be realized in the mid-1920s.

It is of special interest that in November 1915 the National Council of Teachers of English developed a Committee on American Speech, which would reaffirm the position that adequate speech training of young Americans was of vital importance in our national culture. The committee recommended that attention be given first to tone ("shall be quiet, pleasant, clear") and then to distinctness. Next should come work on faults of dialect and provincialisms of word usage and pronunciation; then attention should be directed to variety in tone. These are noted here because the theme is so reminiscent of the passage from Sheridan's 1762 *Lectures on Elocution*, reproduced in Chapter 4.

It is also worth noting here that in September 1916 "Better Speech Week" was promoted by many highschools in the eastern United States. This movement spread throughout various parts of the nation in the next few years, and by 1924 had attracted a great deal of attention, particularly in related disciplines. An enlarging support, not only to speech improvement but to disorders of speech, was clearly reflected in the fact that, during the first two decades of the twentieth century public school systems in several cities undertook a census

of speech defects among school-age children and began to employ speech correctionists, reflecting greater attention to disorders of speech as well.

Several professional groups were actively involved in addressing problems of
speech during this twenty-year period. At the turn of the century the professional body was the National Education Association, from which developed the
National Council of Teachers of English, which was in turn the parent organization of the National Association of Teachers of Public Speaking. It was from
this latter organization that speech and hearing science began to emerge as a
separate discipline in the mid-1920s.

SPEECH AND HEARING SCIENCE: MIDWEST BEGINNINGS

Several members of the National Association of Teachers of Public Speaking
who were interested in speech disorders formally established a separate association in December 1925, during the annual convention of the parent group.
They saw a need for a professional organization to foster the reputation and
progress of speech science, which was threatened by the limited knowledge
and training of many practitioners and by the unscientific nature of many articles and books then being published in the field (see Paden 1970: p. 18ff.).

The new organization, named the American Academy of Speech Correction,
would eventually become (in 1947) the American Speech and Hearing Association.[23]   For the first five years membership in the organization remained
small, essentially limited to its twenty-five charter members. However, by the
mid-thirties the membership numbered over a hundred, and continued to grow
steadily thereafter (see Chapter 6). Its continued existence during the early
years and its eventual growth were due in large measure to the energy and leadership of Robert West of the University of Wisconsin (see Necrology, Robert W.
West [1968]).

Several colleges and universities began to offer coursework in speech correction in the second decade of the twentieth century. Interestingly, leadership
was initiated at institutions in the MidWest, notably Wisconsin and Iowa. The
first graduate program in speech pathology and the first speech clinic at an
institution of higher education were established in 1914 at the University of
Wisconsin, by John O'Neill. However, the major pioneering activity in the development of a speech pathology curriculum was under way at the University of
Iowa. It was initiated, promoted, and guided by Carl Emil Seashore, a psychologist out of Yale University.

Leadership at Iowa: Initiation

Seashore, a singular individual of outstanding ability, great energy, and remarkable foresight, had a wide range of interests uniquely suited to the developments he would initiate. Trained in "the new" (experimental) psychology, he
was interested in audition,[24] voice and speech, music, mental hygiene, and

child development. He was brought to Iowa in 1897 to be director of the psychological laboratory and — a mark of the times — professor of philosophy. Nonetheless, the University of Iowa was the first institution of higher learning in the United States to offer a course with the word "psychology" in its title.

In 1905, upon becoming head of the department, Seashore immediately set out upon his course of encouraging interdisciplinary study among his areas of interest, an endeavor made easier following his appointment as Dean of the Graduate College in 1908.

Seashore's fundamental commitment was to research as the basis for the applied aspects of his varied interests. He maintained a particular interest in the processes of speech, and in several ways over the next two decades, he was the central figure in laying the groundwork for what would become the Program in Speech Pathology at the University of Iowa. He also was indirectly responsible for engendering the professional organization. In the spring of 1925 he obtained funds to bring together young leaders in the field for a conference on speech disorders. The idea of a new professional association was first broached among participants in that conference who formalized the idea in December of that year, as noted earlier.

Early in the 1920s Seashore and Samuel Orton, a neurologist on the medical faculty,[25] decided that the emerging field needed a specially trained professional. They selected Lee Edward Travis, a promising senior in psychology, who would impressively justify his selection as the first person to be intentionally educated as a speech and hearing scientist at the doctoral level.

Leadership at Iowa: Continuation

Travis was another remarkable individual, truly in the Seashore mold during his years at the University of Iowa. He arrived at Iowa in 1921 with his wife and infant son, having had two years of college elsewhere. He earned the B.A. in 1922, the M.A. in 1923, and the Ph.D. in 1924. He stayed on at Iowa with a National Research Council fellowship, and by 1927 had published sixteen experimental studies dealing with motor coordination, reflex time, auditory acuity, speech, voice, and stuttering. He developed a particular interest in the study of stuttering, an endeavor for which he is, appropriately, best remembered.

STUTTERING IN THE EARLY TWENTIETH CENTURY

Stuttering has always attracted the lion's share of attention among the disorders of speech, a pattern evident also in this era, when increased interest in speech disorders of all kinds was so notable. The relative emphasis on stuttering during this period was manifest in several ways.

"Messiahs' " Schools

As reported by West (1959) and Paden (1970) speech science in America during the first two decades of the twentieth century was characterized by the European pattern of "schools," in which varying numbers of persons accepted, affirmed, and supported the teachings of a dominant central figure. West characterized these figures as "messiahs," and noted that it was especially in the field of stuttering that the messiahs thrived, each with his own account of the nature of stuttering, method of curing it, and retinue of followers. Interestingly, West's criticism was directed at certain persons who had managed to attain some level of notice in related fields, especially education. His complaint was not intended to impugn the kind of schools to be considered in the following section. It was directed at individuals who espoused a specific viewpoint, profered as the only true account and remedy for stuttering, for which the claimant presented himself as the originator and purveyor. Potter (1882) had referred to the same sort of practitioners as "semi-professional empirics."

The "Commercial Schools"

Another prominent sign of a substantial interest in stuttering was the development of private schools to treat stuttering, some of them residential centers. Some schools that offered aid for stutterers had a considerably wider interest, being concerned more broadly with instruction in speaking and training of the voice for singing (the type of school mentioned in discussion of *The Voice*, in Chapter 4).[26] However, of particular note at this point are schools whose only concern was the treatment of stuttering. Schools of this type also existed in Great Britain and on the continent, but evidently there were proportionately more of them in the United States. In many of these schools the founder and proprietor identified himself as a (former) stutterer who had overcome his stuttering. The treatment methods employed by these schools were those said to have been instrumental in effecting the recovery of their proprietors.

Clark (1964) identifies a dozen such schools that were operating in the east and midwest during this period (as well as some in Europe). The two centers likely to be most well known to speech pathologists were the Lewis School, in Detroit, established in 1894, and the Bogue Institute, in Indianapolis, established in 1901.[27]

Most likely the Bogue and Lewis centers were well known to speech pathologists because of what must be called a kind of notoriety, achieved through opprobrious references to them made by persons who had attended one or the other of these schools, and who later became prominent in the fledgling American professional association of speech pathology (ASHA). The centers exemplified by the Lewis School and the Bogue Institute were referred to by their detractors as "the commercial schools," with the implication or open contention that making money was their primary objective. The schools were derogated because they charged for their services, tried to keep their methods secret, and either promised or implied that cure could be achieved. (The latter aspect, although indefensible as stated, was not so blatant as the complainants implied.) The critics contended that the techniques employed by these schools were superficial; that the methods consisted of "tricks"; and that the treatment approach was "charlatanry," which yielded no improvement in speech — or even made the stuttering worse! Such contentions deserve at least as much criticism as they were intended to express. In addition to what in retrospect seems likely to have been marked overstatement, the complainants seem to have made no effort to understand the objective of the techniques used in these centers. The disparaging criticism of the "commercial schools" was vague and generalized, based principally in the personal reactions of their detractors.

It is unfortunate that the field of stuttering will probably never have pertinent objective, and broadly based data regarding the pattern of successes resulting from bona fide and sincere participation in the programs offered by these centers. There is, however, some evidence that these schools and their methods were not what their detractors within the profession contended. For instance, Mabel F. Gifford, an early and highly successful American speech therapist employed at the University of California Medical School in San Francisco from 1915 to 1940, overcame much of her own stuttering during her attendance at the Natural Instruction Institute in Buffalo some years earlier.

There are good things to say about the Bogue and Lewis schools as well. Another speech science professional, outstanding for his physiological research in the field, credited the Bogue Institute for helping him establish the basis for the fluency he achieved.[28] In 1973, I addressed inquiry to the Better Business Bureau of Indianapolis regarding the Bogue Institute. Reply from that agency stated that no record of complaint about the Institute could be found. In fact, the reply included a report[29] dated August 25, 1955, in which it was stated that "we do know there have been numerous occasions where much help has been obtained," and that "it has been definitely proven that where this approach was employed, unquestionable progress was made."

A compellingly favorable assessment of the Lewis school and its methods is presented in a long personal letter written by a man who had gone through that program and received considerable benefit from it (reproduced in Wingate 1976: pp. 141-148). The program described in the letter is very reminiscent of the method described by Klencke, the highly respected German practitioner of the nineteenth century. A synopsis of Klencke's method is presented in Chapter 4.

In contradiction to the complaint that such schools were secretive , a number of these schools offered correspondence instruction (see Clark 1964). It is of particular interest that Lewis had available a book (Lewis 1907) of substantial size (415 pages) that was addressed to treatment at home.

The major "trick" decried by derogators of the "commercial schools" was the use of rhythm. To consider the use of rhythm a trick is, at the least, cavalier. The complaint is also presumptive and dogmatic, since the nature of the well-known beneficial effect of rhythm is not understood and, moreover, has not been subjected to thoughtful investigation. Further, to contend that the use of rhythm was charlatanry reveals ignorance of pertinent history. As reviewed in Chapter 4, rhythm was used extensively, and to considerable advantage, throughout the nineteenth century, by some highly reputable professionals. From the limited information now available, rhythm seems to have been used in the programs of the commercial schools with a consideration and an objective comparable to its employ by respected professionals during the nineteenth century. Moreover, as will be brought out in Chapter 9, therapeutic use of rhythm surfaced once again later in the twentieth century, at which time its revival was met with apparently tolerant acceptance within the profession, even though with only casual and transient interest.

TWO NOTABLE PRACTITIONERS

E. W. Scripture and C. S. Bluemel were two figures in this era who, at least because of their credentials, were acceptable to leaders of what would become ASHA. Scripture, originally a psychologist at Yale University in the 1880s, had gone to Germany to study the "new psychology" and had stayed on to earn a medical degree. He developed an interest in disorders of speech, especially stuttering (see Scripture 1912), and studied with A. Gutzmann. His writings on speech defects were reasonably well received in America; however, he is probably best remembered only for the "octave twist," a rather unusual exercise he recommended for use with stutterers. The technique consisted in "pronouncing various words in such a way that the laryngeal tone passes over two octaves in the first important vowel" (p. 77). Scripture did not cite Klencke's work in this regard, but the octave twist might have been suggested by some of Klencke's exercises (see appropriate section in Chapter 4). Evidently the octave twist never was very popular; in fact, it seems to have met with the same off handed rejection as had rhythm. In the fleeting references made to the octave twist in later years, there is no trace of any recognition that Scripture intended its use simply as the means to an end, as an exercise of the vocal-gymnastics type. Scripture had emphasized that stutterers lack "melody" in their speech; the objective of the octave twist was to train the stutterer "to put melody and flexibility into his laryngeal tone" (1912: p. 74).

Bluemel, himself a stutterer, was born and raised in England. He came to the United States to attend the Lewis School, which he soon left in great disappointment (see Clark 1964; Wingate 1976, Chapter 6). He stayed in this country, earned a medical degree, and specialized in psychiatry. In his early contribution to stuttering (Bluemel 1913) he made the point, as had several authors in the previous century, that the difficulty in stuttering does not lie with the repeated or prolonged consonant but, instead, with the immediately sequential vowel. Bluemel spoke of the vowel as being "delayed," and he explained this delay as a "transitory auditory amnesia," meaning that the stutterer is temporarily unable to recall the auditory image of the appropriate vowel.

This particular contribution from Bluemel received hardly any serious consideration. In fact, what little attention it attracted led to it being dismissed as rather far-fetched. The objective analysis itself (*vowel*, not consonant) was ignored. Once again, calling attention to aspects of the criterial features of the stutter event — namely, the speech characteristics aroused no interest. In dramatic contrast, a subsequent contribution of Bluemel's, the "primary-secondary" scheme, which invoked psychological factors (see Chapter 6), was eagerly received by members of the young profession and was to have a long-term influence.

EMERGENCE OF EXPERIMENTATION

The early decades of the twentieth century also saw the sporadic beginnings of experimental study of stuttering. At the turn of the century two German investigators (Halle 1900; Ten Cate 1902) reported evidence that breathing patterns of stutterers differed markedly from those of normal speakers. Then, in the second decade John M. Fletcher (1914), an American, reported an extensive experimental study that clearly revealed many physiological irregularities in his stutterer subjects. Unfortunately, Fletcher, a psychologist who stuttered, offered the interpretation that these findings reflected the effect of negative emotions, especially fear.[30]

As noted in preceding chapters, fear is the long-term favorite, simple, but encompassing, explanation for stuttering; one that extends back to ancient times. It should be noted, however, that a number of writers in earlier centuries, when mentioning the effects of emotion, implicated positive as well as negative emotion. However, as attempts to explain stuttering unfolded in the twentieth century, the effects of positive emotion were routinely ignored; only emotions of a negative nature were invoked in the accounts developed. This matter receives particular notice in Chapters 7 and 8.

Near the end of the second decade, Robbins (1919) reported finding that stutterers showed differences from normal speakers in peripheral blood flow as one reaction to startle. Inferring blood-flow changes within the brain, he interpreted these findings as confirming Bluemel's idea regarding auditory amnesia, the "delay of the vowel." However, this line of inquiry was not pursued. At the same time, other physiologically oriented research was undertaken. Anderson (1923) reported evidence that stutterers differed from normal speakers not only in speech characteristics but also ". . .in reactions which have no apparent connection with speech," including certain acts described as "coordinative confusion."

Experimental evidence of physiological and coordinative anomalies among stutterers generally aroused little interest during this era, and only briefly in the period to follow, the years of Travis' outstanding work at the University of Iowa. The preference for a psychological account of stuttering was already emerging, and would expand substantially in ensuing years. Fletcher was instrumental in carrying this preference forward. More than a decade after publication of his 1914 report, mentioned above, he enlarged upon it in a book (Fletcher 1928) that was frequently cited thereafter. The book expanded the psychological interpretations he had made in the original report.

Fletcher is a notable personage for two main reasons. First, he was, evidently unintentionally, responsible for stuttering becoming a focus of inquiry in the budding speech and hearing science program at the University of Iowa (see below). Lee Travis, who was largely responsible for the program at Iowa becoming a highly regarded one, mentioned, in retrospect, that it was because of Fletcher that he (Travis) came to consider stuttering as a subject worth investigating. Second, Fletcher was the first of several individuals who would attain prominence in the field of stuttering and thereby materially influence its substance. Fletcher shared two determining attributes with the other figures who would later attain even greater prominence. First, they were stutterers themselves; and second, they were imbued, in varying intensity, with precepts from psychology. These two attributes are intimately related and interactive: the attraction of psychology and the heavy immersion in its precepts were based in the personal recollections and attitudes these individuals had accrued as stutterers; and their personal views became embellished by what they learned from a study of psychology. It has been consistently overlooked that these men could not speak for all stutterers; nevertheless, they presumed to do so.

Throughout the twentieth century many stutterers have attained professional status within the field. In fact, it is rather surprising to discover how large a number of stutterers are in the professional ranks, undoubtedly drawn into the field through their personal involvement. If a tally of these individuals were made one would find that most of them possess both of the attributes noted above. However, only a few can be said to stand out as major figures in this mold in terms of their influence. These few, listed in temporal sequence following Fletcher, would be Sidney Bluemel, Wendell Johnson, and Charles Van Riper. Of the three Johnson and Van Riper had by far the greatest impact. Bluemel's principal influence would find expression in the extended preoccupation with his proposal of "primary" and "secondary" stuttering. Van Riper's views had the considerable appeal of a rather homey, common-sense type of exposition interwoven with his own personal testimony. Presented largely from the perspective and experience of a clinical practitioner, his contributions have found widespread and continuing acceptance. In contrast, it was the views of Wendell Johnson, arranged in what would be called a "theory," that would have the most telling effect in the field. The influence of each of these men will be considered in later chapters (Johnson in Chapter 7; Van Riper in Chapter 9).

It is particularly germane to note here that, in the nineteenth century too, a number of persons who dealt with and wrote about stuttering were also themselves stutterers.   However, none of these individuals attained or even approached the extent of influence attained by Bluemel, Johnson, or Van Riper. The influence of these three men was grounded in and supported by several broadly based circumstances clearly unique to their time.

The influence of these personages was supported by two major circumstances. First, and fundamental, was the twentieth century Zeitgeist, which, set in motion by cultural changes around the turn of the century, was enlarged and embellished by the developments in anthropology and psychology in the second and third decades. Earlier sections of this chapter discussed these developments and their significance for what would unfold in the field of stuttering. The second major circumstance was the establishment and rapid growth of a professional association addressed to issues in speech and hearing science. The very existence of a professional association confers a mantle of authority on persons making a mark within it, especially if they are also charter members. Moreover, the burgeoning association membership represented a collateral increase in numbers of speech pathology programs, and thereby the numbers of people within these programs who received instruction from sources accepted as authoritative. This happenstance has had particular relevance in regard to the program at the University of Iowa.

Early Experimentation at Iowa

Early experimental study of stuttering is, quite justifiably, often associated with the University of Iowa, essentially because of the bona fide program[31] of research undertaken there by Lee Travis. The orientation of Travis' research was essentially neurophysiologic, reflecting his professional preparation and his close association with Samuel Orton, a neurologist. As evidence of Travis' capability and vigor his program of research, evidently begun the year he received his doctorate, resulted in nineteen publications over the thirteen years he remained at Iowa. Most of this work was addressed to assessing integrity of neuromotor function, particularly its relevance to speech. A series of five publications that appeared between 1927 and 1929,[32] head-titled "Studies in Stuttering," well represent the tenor of this program of research. By this time the concept of cerebral dominance had entered the picture, and Orton (1927) made clear reference to the substance of this concept in his introduction to Travis' "Studies in Stuttering" series.[33]

Travis and Cerebral Dominance

It is not clear when the concept of cerebral dominance was developed. Travis (1933a) mentioned that both Orton and M. W. Sachs, of Germany, espoused the concept. Nonetheless, the concept has been associated most closely with Travis, since he introduced it into the professional dialogue of the field and actively pursued research relative to it.

Cerebral dominance is a complex topic that cannot, and need not, be dealt with in much detail here. However, it seems appropriate to sketch its basic outlines, so that readers not already familiar with it can appreciate its essential substance. The concept is founded on a number of reliable observations and established facts, which are reviewed below. As a sort of preamble to the review, the reader's attention is directed to a commonly observable fact, that most people are right-handed. In fact, several reputable sources cite evidence that about 94 percent of general populations show a right-sided preference. It follows, then, that left-handedness is something of an anomaly.[34]

Evidently, linking cerebral dominance to stuttering originated from observations that some individuals who stuttered were also left-handed. Many such observations were reported in various literature sources in (at least) the early twentieth century, for example, Ballard (1912), Claiborne (1917), and Whipple (1911). The plausibility of cerebral dominance was especially enhanced by reports of instances in which stuttering appeared or subsided as a result of change in handedness usage.

The significant aspects of the cerebral dominance concept are the following. First, except for certain internal organs, the human body is structured bilaterally: it has two sides, identifiable simply as right and left. The significance of this arrangement relative to dominance is that the brain and the voluntarily controllable musculature of the body have right and left components (sides). Second, the movement repertoire of humans includes many unilateral acts, that is, activity that involves musculature on only one side of the body, for instance, picking up an object with either the right or the left hand. Third, in activities that involve only one side of the body, most individuals show a clear preference for the use of one side, as in picking up or throwing a small object. Fourth, one also performs many activities that involve, or may require, simultaneous activity of both sides of the body, for example, skiing. Fifth, in certain bilateral activities the two sides may perform with varying degrees of apparent independence, such as when typewriting or playing a guitar. Sixth, when the two sides are engaged in activity that has a single focus, the two sides must act in concord to produce the intended objective, such as playing golf or hitting a baseball. Nonetheless, in the performance of such activities, the preference for one side will be expressed (actually, required), with the preferred side "leading" in the bilateral performance.

The externally observable preference for using musculature on one side of the body, which is clearly evidenced in many unilateral activities and in single-focus bilateral activities, implies an internal preference inherent in the control system— the brain. Since the pertinent loci on each side of the brain are evidently capable of similar (and sometimes independent) activation of musculature on the side of the body they control, a preference for use of one side of the body suggests that one side in the control system is taking the lead (is *dominant*) over the other. Further, in particular consideration of single-focus bilateral activities, one can appreciate that such functions would not be performed smoothly, or readily, if both sides acted independently. For concerted activation that is well coordinated, it seems logical that one side of the control system must take the lead, that is, be dominant.

Cerebral dominance has particular relevance for speech because speaking involves, in substantial part, "midline" structures — lips, tongue, jaw — which are capable of, and often perform, unilateral action. In speaking, however, musculature of the two sides of the body must act in concert to produce very intricate and complex patterns and series of movements. In respect to speaking at least, effective cerebral control, describable in terms of dominance, is crucial.

Stuttering is uniquely amenable to explanation in terms of cerebral dominance, through the inference that the obvious incoordination represented in a stutter event reflects a lapse in cerebral dominance. Because such apparent lapses, inferred from their external manifestations (the stutter), are characteristic of the speech of certain individuals (stutterers), lack of, or incomplete, cerebral dominance is considered to be a neurologic *condition*, even though manifested with varying intermittency.

Linking cerebral dominance to speech, and thereby to stuttering, was aided by two other especially relevant matters that are closely related. First, while most neurons in the brain that are involved in control of body musculature "cross over," leading to expression on the opposite (contralateral) side of the body, some of these neurons remain on the side of origin (are ipsilateral). Although it seems abundantly clear that cortical control is predominantly contralateral (neural activation in certain reasonably specifiable loci of the left half of the brain controls the action of certain musculature on the right side of the body, and vice versa), a potential complication exists. Second, there is evidence, first reported by Paul Broca in 1861, that a certain area of the left cerebral cortex, situated near the loci responsible for the left hemisphere's contribution to activation of speech musculature, is most importantly involved in oral language expression. This finding was corroborated by Hughlings Jackson in 1864, and subsequently by many other investigators. Moreover, twentieth-century inquiry into cortical localization of the "speech function" indicates that, while certain loci of the left cerebral hemisphere are significantly involved in speech activity, there is very often representation in comparable sites in the right hemisphere as well, and that the extent of this participation probably varies among individuals.

We return, then, to the item mentioned above as the probable precipitant of the cerebral dominance concept, namely, that certain individuals with defective speech, especially stuttering, were also noted to be left-handed. Such evidence of left-side preference for muscular activity implies right-side cerebral dominance. This departure from the predominant neural control arrangement (right side preference, therefore *left*-hemisphere dominance) implies problems for control of speech functions.

As noted above, a number of sources in the early twentieth century reported a concurrence of stuttering and left-handedness, most frequently in children, especially youngsters in the early grades. With greater numbers of children beginning to enter school — and being taught to write — left-hand preference came under closer scrutiny. Very likely the extent of left-handedness, though still proportionately small, had become more noticeable with the increased influx of children. Left-handedness was often a cause for concern. Many educators and others believed that left-hand preference constituted a lifelong disadvantage,[35] and so efforts were made to change this preference. The most compelling reports of concurrence between stuttering and left-handedness involved instances of "forced" change in handedness. Often it was reported that a child began to stutter after being required to abandon his native left-hand preference and to learn right-hand usage. Further, many instances were reported in which a child stopped stuttering when allowed to return to his left-hand preference.

Travis' espousal of the cerebral dominance basis for stuttering evoked much professional excitement, stimulated a great deal of research, and aroused considerable controversy. Research addressed to some facet of the issue continued actively through the 1930s, yielding corroborative data, contradictory evidence, and findings that were equivocal. Then, by the early 1940s, attention to the issue subsided quite rapidly. This decline in interest may have resulted in part because of the equivocal and contradictory findings that had emerged. A major problem attending laterality research, not adequately recognized in this early work, is that laterality and its assessment are complex matters (see, for example, Annett 1978). However, the most likely reason was that, in 1938, Travis left Iowa, his laboratories, and his research program. After Travis' departure a much different ambience surfaced there.

Travis moved to southern California, where he held positions in several institutions until his death in 1987. However, after leaving Iowa his era of productive and stimulating research was over. In fact, some of his later writings (Travis 1940, 1957) were in the genre of dynamic psychology, in which he revealed a creative imagination and a verbal flair comparable to others who have written in that vein.[36] In shifting ground so dramatically, Travis implicitly repudiated his earlier outstanding research. Nonetheless, during the fifty years following his departure from Iowa, he never abandoned the "evidence of disturbed cerebral dominance in stutterers" (Moeller 1976: p. 75). In fact, late in life (Travis 1978a, 1978b) he reaffirmed his conviction that cerebral laterality is somehow involved in stuttering.

Since the time Travis left Iowa occasional expressions of interest in cerebral dominance have appeared, but only intermittently. Nonetheless, some sources continue to be impressed by evidence that indicates some link between laterality and stuttering (e.g., Blood 1985; Records et al. 1977; Sussman and MacNeilage 1975; Webster 1986; Wingate 1988.) However, beginning in approximately the mid-1930s, professional attention to this linkage was overwhelmed and deflected by a movement that even then was under way at the University of Iowa. The foundations and early developments of this movement are the major subject of Chapter 6.

NOTES

1. The source of O'Hara's inspiration remains obscure. A short-lived "reply" to "K-K-

K-Katy," which appeared in 1919, was "Thtop Your Thtuttering." The latter title
clearly implies a general recognition that both songs refer to speech defect.

2. Where, in the same year, he was appointed professor of *philosophy*.

3. There is evidence that he encouraged and supported the founding of a psychological laboratory at Harvard in the same year that Wundt set up his laboratory in Leipsig.
However, he did not pursue the project.

4. The first, in 1887, was the *American Journal of Psychology*, founded by G. Stanley Hall. The second, in 1891, the *Pedagogical Seminary* (later becoming the *Journal
of Genetic Psychology*), was also founded by Hall. The third, the *Psychological Review*, was founded by J. M. Baldwin and J. McK. Cattell in 1894.

5. Even though he would have preferred to return to Oxford. However, Oxford was
not ready for psychology. Oxford and Cambridge were only beginning to awaken to the
scientific spirit from the continent, and at that time psychology was hardly even on their
prestige lists of the sciences.

6. It was Hall's idea to establish the American Psychological Association, founded in
July 1892. He also began the first two professional journals; see note 4.

7. In addition to his collaboration in founding the *Psychological Review*, he acquired
from Alexander Graham Bell, in 1895, the weekly journal *Science*, which was then in
financial difficulty. Under his direction *Science* became the leading general scientific
publication in the United States, and in 1900 was made the official organ of the American Association for the Advancement of Science.

8. Bechterev and Pavlov, working late in the nineteenth century, were contemporaries. Their work was based on that of Sechenov (1829-1905), whose studies were first
published in 1863 under the title *Reflexes of the Brain.*

9. Bechterev did similar work with motor responses, which he called *"associated
reflexes."* His reports came to publication later than Pavlov's.

10. Although the position he articulated was presaged by strong objectivist attitudes
emerging in biology and psychology in the late nineteenth century.

11. The 1913 publication has been called "The Behaviorism Manifesto." His first
book appeared in 1914. His presidential address was published in an early issue of the
Psychological Review in 1916 (see Bibliography).

12. As noted in preceding paragraphs, Pavlov's famous experiment was intended, and
presented, as a demonstration in physiology, not psychology.

13. Freud's success has been explained as due largely to first, his emphasis on sex —
a topic that not only is of perennial interest but that most likely had uncommon appeal
in the stiff, suppressive Victorian culture of his time; and second, because of his prolific writings. The latter influence is captured in the adage that if something is said or
written often enough people will become inclined to believe it. Such influence has been
actively at work in the field of stuttering.

14. The variant beliefs of these original "theorists" can be seen to reflect their own
personal circumstances. Freud's central theme was the "Oedipus complex," a theme
that might well occur to an imaginative psychologist who happened to be the son of a
young mother and an old father—which Freud was. Similarly, Adler's major theme of
"inferiority" fits well with the fact that he was physically quite small. In Jung's mysti-
cal, quasi-religious "collective unconscious" theme one can discern the influences of a
childhood spent with a devout clergyman father; also, eight of his uncles were clergy-
men. It can been said, quite credibly, that much of the touted "genius" of these men
consisted largely of an active imagination and a gift for spinning a good yarn.

15. However, the fabric of these beliefs may finally be unraveling even in the United

States (Gray 1993).

16. Erasmus Darwin was their common grandfather.

17. In that time (circa 1869) the principles of genetics were still unknown. Although Gregor Mendel had presented his momentous findings, *twice*, to a scientific society in 1865 their significance was not recognized by members of his audience, and his findings were then forgotten. They were eventually discovered thirty-five years later, in 1900.

18. From 1886, at which time he was twenty-eight years old, until his death in 1942. Throughout most of this time he was on the faculty of Columbia University.

19. The first such clinic of record was established by G. Hudson Makuen at the Philadelphia Polyclinic Hospital in 1896. Similar facilities appeared in a number of European countries during the first decade of the twentieth century.

20. The membership has never been very large. Perello (1976) reported that the I.A.L.P. had 100 members in 1962 and 223 in 1974. For comparison, the American Speech and Hearing Association had over 6,000 members in 1962 and over 18,000 in 1974, and membership has grown proportionately since then.

21. This title was retained through 1957. The journal continued as *Speech Pathology and Therapy* (1958-1965), then as *British Journal of Disorders of Communication* (1966-1990), and since 1991 as *European Journal of Disorders of Communication*.

22. The persistence of many "viewpoints" about stuttering would be remarked some years later in a book by a recovering stutterer (Jonas 1977) who, hoping to gain from professional sources information about the disorder that would be meaningful to him, found instead "a grab-bag of competing theories."

23. The name by which the organization is most widely known (the word "Language" was added in 1979). The original name was succeeded first by the American Society for the Study of Disorders of Speech; and then became the American Speech Correction Association. Another earlier but abortive effort at organization was planned by a different group. Their association was to be called the National Society for the Study and Correction of Speech Disorders. This group planned to publish a professional journal, beginning in 1918; however, it did not materialize.

24. Seashore was instrumental in the development of the audiometer. He also built the first soundproof room (at Iowa).

25. Orton was interested in speech disorders, especially stuttering. He was also much interested in reading disability. The Orton Society (later, the Orton Dyslexia Society) was established in 1949 in his honor.

26. Such schools were similar to the schools of speech and drama in Great Britain, noted earlier in this chapter, some of whose practitioners began to specialize as speech therapists.

27. These centers, as did most others, bore their founders' names. Benjamin Bogue was a stutterer who, by his statement, had recovered using the methods employed in his institute. Evidently Lewis had normal speech. The Bogue Institute continued in operation until its founder's death in 1959. Termination date of the Lewis School is not known. These two schools are the topic of Chapter 6 in Wingate (1976).

28. Courtney Stromsta, personal conversation, July 1970. The interested reader should explore Stromsta's excellent book, *Elements of Stuttering* (1986).

29. Indianapolis Better Business Bureau report, author not identified.

30. Hill (1944a, 1944b) repeated this interpretive contention in his review of biochemical and physiological data extant at that time. The contention was stated again very recently by Bloodstein (1995: pp. 24-25) who claimed that physiological findings "are now generally understood to be the visceral correlations" of emotional arousal.

31. Actually, two M.A. theses done in the summer of 1924 at Iowa were the first studies addressed to stuttering on record there. It is of some interest that these were directed by John Fletcher, noted above, whom Seashore had invited to Iowa for the summer session. As might be expected, both studies were psychologically oriented; one dealt with suggestion, the other with word association.

32. Travis (1927a, 1927b); Travis and Fagan (1928); Orton and Travis (1929); Travis and Herren (1929).

33. He also mentioned "strephosymbolia," later to be called dyslexia. Orton had become intensely interested in this problem because his daughter evidenced the disorder.

34. See "sinistral" and "dextral" in the Glossary.

35. Which, in many respects, it is. As someone once noted, "the world is made for the right-handed," meaning that where accommodations are made for human use of machines, tools, and gadgets, the design typically addresses only right-hand use.   Several commercial sources now offer various tools and gadgets designed specifically for left-hand use, to assuage the problems posed by the tools of a predominantly right-handed world (a good example: use of scissors).

36. See section on psychodynamics in Chapter 9.

PART III

"MODERN TIMES"

CHAPTER 6

A Decade of Formative Transition

> There is a tide in the affairs of men,
> Which, taken at the flood, leads on to fortune.
> Shakespeare, *Julius Caesar*, IV, 3, 217

The fourth decade of the twentieth century brought considerable changes in the circumstances and conditions influencing the developing discipline of speech and hearing science, and especially the field of stuttering. The broad cultural trends of previous years had already made themselves felt. Other influences were emerging, some from preceding circumstances, others newly precipitated, particularly from distressing and threatening major contemporary events: the great economic depression in the United States and the impending disaster in Europe. These events bestirred an intellectual climate charged with a yearning to find ways to improve human affairs.

The promise embodied in environmentalism, the belief that appropriate control of external events affords a means for changing human behavior through shaping of the individual persona, was most encouraging. However, the molding of personalities takes a long time. There remained a need for some more immediate influence, one that was perhaps even more directly manageable. An apparent answer to this pressing need came in the form of an emphasis on the importance of attitudes and ways of thinking. Central to this emphasis was a focus on how the use of language affects one's view of the world and how one deals with it. A burgeoning movement of the mid-1930s, general semantics, had as its central claim that careless, improper word usage was not only intimately involved in human problems but a substantial cause of them. This focus would have, for a relatively brief time, considerable appeal for a sizeable portion of the general population. Although it held little import for speech and hearing science at large, it was to have a profound and extended impact on the field of stuttering.

The long-persisting interest in the art of speaking well, which had set the foundation for the profession of speech and hearing science, would continue henceforth in a separate domain, and as a rather remote background reference. Other academic areas of study, especially psychology and anthropology, became the major influences on speech and hearing science, especially the study of stuttering, where the tenets of these two disciplines would intertwine with the new focus on the use of language, especially the purported misdirection and distortion occasioned by improper word usage.

The appeal and vigor of the new discipline of speech and hearing science are reflected in its rapid development during the 1930s. Membership in the American Speech and Hearing Association more than doubled between 1930 and 1935; it doubled again by 1937, and yet again by 1941.[1] March 1936 saw the publication of the first issue of the Association's *Journal of Speech Disorders.*

STUTTERING: PATTERN AND PROMINENCE

The 1930s can be described as a period of formative transition in the study of stuttering, because the changes that occurred would solidify into a form that would remain dominant through the remainder of the century. The changes arose originally from influences in areas with which the study of stuttering had come into close proximity, particularly psychology, but anthropology as well. With these influences as a broad base, the course that would be followed in the field of stuttering was shaped largely from events within the field itself.

It has been mentioned previously that interest in disorders of speech has always been disproportionately focused on stuttering. Documentation of this historically apparent fact became possible following establishment of the professional organization. From the time of its inception, formal records of the American Speech and Hearing Association reveal the extent to which stuttering has indeed received the lion's share of attention. The first official effort at publication consisted of bound, mimeographed copies of the twenty-eight papers (totaling 200 pages) that made up the professional program of the 1930 meeting of the association. According to Paden (1970 p. 21) this publication[2] was "the first major contribution toward advancing knowledge within the profession to which it could lay claim." This event is significant in the history of stuttering in that all twenty-eight papers had been presented as a Symposium on Stuttering.

It is appropriate here to identify an early contribution on stuttering that would provide a widely used, although troublesome, reference in ensuing years. At the 1932 meeting of the association, Bluemel, himself a stutterer, introduced the concept of "primary stuttering." Bluemel believed it was necessary to reduce the number of "theories" of stuttering, and he thought the concept of primary stuttering could serve as a basic reference in the effort to understand the nature of the disorder. He saw, within the profession, "confusion of the primary speech disorder with the various complications and emotional reactions that associate themselves with the later stage of the disturbance" (Bluemel 1932). The essential point was that stuttering is, first and foremost, a speech disorder, and that other actions that sometimes accompany instances of stutter are secondary.

Bluemel offered the primary-secondary notion from retrospection of his own personal history, and in doing so began a tradition that would plague the study of stuttering through at least the remainder of the century; namely, that much of what has been said, written, elaborated, and believed about stuttering is built upon the personal testimonies of stutterers who have come into positions from which they could promulgate their views.

The crux of the primary-secondary notion was that, initially, stuttering is simply a disorder of speech, an anomaly characterized by the two symptoms that typify the speech of all stutterers—the iterations and perseverations—the classic features remarked upon throughout the history of the disorder and that eventually came to be called by the *mots justes* "clonic" and "tonic" over a century ago. Bluemel proposed that when the child becomes aware of his speech impediment, and then begins to react to it, he attempts to deal with it through certain other (nonspeech) acts many of which, though ineffective, become part of "well-developed" stuttering.[3]

Bluemel's proposal had considerable appeal. It is significant that although the profession had no interest in Bluemel's earlier description of the stutter event, which was couched in terms of speech variables, essentially phonetic ones (see Chapter 5), this later contribution, which featured psychological dimensions focusing on *reaction*, was accepted enthusiastically.

The primary-secondary scheme contains many flaws that have never received attention. First, it gives self-awareness of stutter a major, in fact critical, role in the supposed "development" of the disorder. However, it is impossible for an observer to determine if someone else is or is not aware of self, or of something about self, other than by asking the individual concerned. But to do so destroys, or at least severely contaminates, the credibility of the observation regarding the nature of his "awareness." Another serious limitation of this formulation is that it carries several assumptions within the notion of temporal sequence. A first assumption is that stuttering develops, that it begins as something simple (the "primary" stuttering) which invariably becomes more involved. A second assumption is that the acts supposedly marking "secondary" stuttering follow after, in fact are built upon, those called "primary." Third, these entities (primary and secondary) are assumed to characterize certain temporal periods, "early" and "later."

In this conception, then, early stuttering consists only of simple, although typical, disturbances in speech flow, something like "easy effortless repetitions."   In this scheme the nonspeech features do not occur in early stuttering but are "acquired" or "develop" in reaction to the speech difficulty, and are the hallmark of later stuttering. However, the formulation does not fit the facts as observed clinically. There are many cases in which nonspeech acts are observed in early stuttering, and an impressive number of instances in which long-term stutterers evidence quite a simple pattern.

Although the scheme had great appeal, it did not fare well practically, as one might have expected in view of the several contradictions noted in the preceding paragraph. For many practitioners it was not easy to distinguish objectively between "primary" and "secondary" stuttering. An attempt to focus on "awareness" as the means for making the distinction only served to enlarge the confusion. This confusion is not difficult to understand. If one reflects on the matter of "awareness," it should become evident that to objectively identify the presence, let alone the onset, of a child's awareness of stuttering is an unsolvable task.

Although the primary-secondary notion did not turn out to be useable in actual practice it continued to influence ways of thinking about stuttering. The individual terms themselves continued to be used, albeit not literally in the context of their origin, and they continued to carry the sense of their original formulation. This was especially true of the term "secondary," which, bearing its assumptions that the nonspeech acts are acquired, was readily assimilated into the rapidly developing conviction that stuttering is "learned behavior." Derived terms, such as "secondaries," "secondary mannerisms," and "acquired mannerisms," soon appeared, and these were widely used with a regularity and assurance that conveyed an unquestioning conviction of their validity.

Unfortunately, there was little evident realization that all of these terms, far from representing factual reality, were expressions of a conceptual bias. The source and nature of nonspeech acts that occur *in some instances* of stutter are not yet adequately understood or explained. In this regard it is entirely relevant to point out that any number of observed nonspeech acts are readily amenable to an account in neurologic terms.[4] Eventually it was suggested (Wingate 1964) that any nonspeech aspects of a stutter event are more properly identified as "accessory features." The term "accessory" is more appropriate on three counts: (1) it does not contain any implication of origin, nature, or temporal sequence; (2) these features can and do appear in cases of early stuttering; and (3) such features are not uniformly evident in cases of long-term stuttering. In a word, whatever their source, organic or psychological, they are "secondary" only in respect to importance. It is the speech features *alone* that identify the disorder. This fact, a matter for which there is continual compelling evidence, will be considered later.

One further unfortunate influence of the primary-secondary notion is that this conception gave unnecessary impetus to claims that stuttering "develops," and to related notions of "stages" of stuttering. The belief that stuttering develops has been a pervasive preoccupation in the field, principally from the time the professional association was established earlier in this century. The claim that stuttering regularly develops is continually reasserted in some form, essentially as an expression of a set of beliefs. Not only does the claim lack a body of convincing data, it also is contradicted by substantial evidence.[5]

Returning now to the disproportionate amount of professional attention stuttering has received, one finds clear evidence of it in long-term records from pertinent American Speech and Hearing Association sources. Table 6.1 shows the number of journal articles and convention papers addressed to eleven

Table 6.1
Level of Professional Interest in the Various Areas of Speech and Hearing Disorders, 1926-1957*

	Convention Papers	Journal Articles
Aphasia	67	47
Articulation Disorders	60	54
Audiometry	110	72
Cerebral Palsy	64	41
Cleft Palate	49	34
General Speech Pathol. & Therapy	129	81
Service Programs	118	0
Speech and Language Development	0	35
Stuttering	201	205
Voice Disorders	55	42
Average for all areas other than stuttering	70	44

*From Paden, E. (1970) A History of the American Speech and Hearing Association, 1925-1958. Washington: Am. Sp. Hrng. Assn. Table 3, p. 51.

different content areas during the first thirty years of ASHA records (from Paden, 1970, Table 3, p. 51). A quick computation will reveal that, compared to the average for the other ten categories, there were three times as many papers on stuttering and five times as many articles on stuttering. Table 6.2 presents a similar analysis for the next nineteen years,[6] here reporting separately the contents of the *Journal of Speech and Hearing Disorders* and the *Journal of Speech and Hearing Research*. In Table 6.2 the number of articles on stuttering is less disproportionate, due in large measure to the very substantial number of articles pertaining to hearing, or articles that one can assume have a technical base (audiology, psychoacoustics, speech and voice science). Still, the total number of "stuttering" entries is almost half again the average for the other nine categories.

Table 6.2
Level of   Professional Interest in the Various Areas of Speech and Hearing Disorders, 1958-1976

	JSHD	JSHR	Total
Aphasia	53	60	113
Articulation Disorders	121	89	210
Audiology/Audiometry	166	331	497
Education & Therapy (Hearing Dis.)	111	13	124
General Speech Pathol. & Therapy	53	5	58
Psychoacoustics	0	196	196
Speech and Language Development	89	147	236
Speech & Voice Science	0	235	235
Stuttering	103	186	289
Voice	104	37	141
Average for all areas other than stuttering	77	123	201

Table 6.3 extends this comparison over the next fourteen years.   Here, although there are a number of new categories, and fifteen in all, the number of articles dealing with stuttering is still substantially above the average.   Moreover, the tally should take account of another pertinent source.   The *Journal of Fluency Disorders* began publication in 1977, the first year covered in Table 6.3.   An average of about thirty-two articles a year are published in the *Journal of Fluency Disorders*, almost all of them addressed to stuttering.

Table 6.3
Level of Professional Interest in the Various Areas of Speech and Hearing Disorders, 1977-1990

	JSHD	JSHR	Total
Acoustic Immittance & Psychoacoustics	142	115	257
Aphasia, Apraxia & Agnosia	97	57	154
Articulation, Resonance and Phonological disorders	113	97	210
Assessment of Hearing	54	37	91
Assessment, Screening, Treatment & Diagnosis of Speech & Language	285	218	503
Audiology	116	241	357
Aural Rehabilitation, Habilitation Education and Conservation	83	85	168
Hearing loss, Deafness and Otic pathologies	172	180	352
Hearing aids, Prosthetics and Cochlear implants	102	51	153
Language disorders, Learning disabilities and Mental retardation	172	254	426
Other Disorders	83	112	195
Speech & Language Development, incl. anatomy and physiology	193	171	364
Speech Production & Perception and Auditory processing	187	138	325
Stuttering and Fluency disorders	237	73	310
Voice and Laryngeal disorders	75	91	166
Average for all areas other than stuttering	134	132	266

A Burgeoning Trend

Major dimensions of this predominant interest in stuttering are portrayed graphically in Figure 6.1. The data represented in this figure are of particular relevance to content in the remainder of this book. The two curves in Figure 6.1 represent the nature of research in stuttering over the period of almost sixty years between 1932 and 1990. Data for the first twenty years were compiled by Sortini (1955), who extracted from a broad base of relevant literature[7] articles reporting experimental research in stuttering. He separated the articles into seven content categories: genetics, laterality, neurophysiology, physiology, personality, psychology-behavior, and miscellaneous. For purposes of the comparison intended here, the first four categories were grouped under the heading "physiological" studies, and the fifth and sixth categories were combined to represent "psychological" research. Data for the remaining thirty-nine years incorporated in Figure 6.1 were extracted from the same source, using the same classificatory schema, by the present author (Wingate 1990).

It is clear from the curves of Figure 6.1 that during most of the 1930s research interest in stuttering was oriented much more to physiological than to psychological aspects. At the same time, interest in the latter showed a rather impressive increase during this period. Then, in a span of about seven years, the pattern of interest inverted and the pursuit of psychologically oriented research continued to gain in ascendancy. Note that the inversion took place in the early 1940s,[8] a matter whose significance will become more evident in Chapter 7.

The pattern of research interest in stuttering, wherein overweighting of stuttering research along psychological lines progressively overwhelmed research having a physiological orientation, reflects both the general ambience of the times and a special bias couched in that ambience. As brought out in Chapter 5, the early decades of the twentieth century had seen the development of three mutually supportive conceptual schemas that had attained, by the end of the 1920s, prominence, stature, and widening influence. These three schemas were *cultural determinism*, in anthropology; *behaviorism*, from academic psychology; and *dynamic psychology*, from psychiatry. The mutually reinforcing *leitmotif* common to these movements, especially the first two, is the belief that individual human characteristics and actions are determined by environmental, experiential, life-history circumstances, not by constitutional (physiological, genetic) ones.

As reviewed in Chapter 5, speech and hearing science emerged as a discipline, and as a professional specialty, in a context of intimate association with psychology. Moreover, especially in regard to a focus on speech disorders per se, vis-à-vis other aspects of speech and hearing science,[9] psychology has continued to be the major influence. Especially since the mid-1930s, speech pathology's concepts and formulations have shown a heavy dependence on psychological constructs. The area of stuttering, in particular, has not simply been influenced by tenets from psychology, it has engorged them.

Figure 6.1
Pattern of Research Interest in Stuttering, 1932-1990

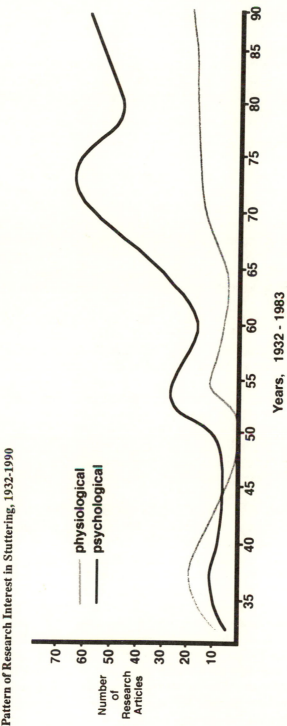

THE BACKGROUND REVISITED

Certain matters within the anthropological and psychological backgrounds are particularly pertinent to the developments in the field of stuttering in the middle 1930s and beyond. Because of the breadth of its scope and its seeming stability, the doctrine of cultural determinism, along with related matters, will be considered first.

Cultural Determinism

As summarized in Chapter 5, cultural determinism was held to be substantiated, and thereby established as valid, by the material contained in *Coming of Age in Samoa*. The contents of this book were accepted uncritically as a scientific report of Mead's research within a native culture. It was widely assumed that the research had been conducted properly, carefully, and in a professionally knowledgeable manner. For many years, well into the 1970s, the report continued to be not only cited, but praised and adulated even though, as the years went by, steadily mounting evidence contradicted both her findings and her analyses. Actually, substantial contradictory evidence existed even before Mead's sojourn (see Freeman 1983), but such evidence went unheeded. The extent of her inaccuracy, the circumstances contributing to it, and the motivations for structuring it were eventually brought together in a comprehensive assessment by Derek Freeman (1983).[10] Ten chapters of Freeman's book contain documentation revealing that many of the assertions that were made in *Coming of Age in Samoa* are fundamentally in error, some of them being clearly contradictory and others preposterously false.

The matter deserves at least a brief summary here, not only to present the essential outlines of this astounding misconstruction but to call attention to it as an example. The issue has general relevance to matters of scholarship and scientific inquiry, and particular pertinence to what has transpired in the study of stuttering.

Mead was not very well prepared to conduct research, even though it was especially important to have someone with adequate professional credentials undertake this particular study. She was a twenty-three-year-old graduate student, ill-suited in many ways to conduct this presumably pivotal study. Her training had not equipped her, either scientifically or procedurally, to investigate the subtle and complex interactions of biological and cultural variables that the endeavor demanded. In fact, she did not at any time carry out any systematic observations pertinent to a comparison of environmental and hereditary conditions, which was the crucial focus of the undertaking.

Mead had not had any experience in field work prior to leaving for Samoa, and while in Samoa she did not conduct the kind of field work that is routine in anthropological study. She did not live among the natives but, instead, in the familiar circumstances of an American household on a Navy base. In this setting she obtained her findings indirectly, through what she was told by a group of young native female informants who visited her regularly. She did not, therefore, make any direct, let alone careful, observations about the Samoans' activities, interactions, relationships, customs and other variables that are significant for responsible anthropological inquiry. In addition to her basic error of relying on informants, there is good reason to believe that her informants, perhaps playfully, intentionally misinformed her. Moreover, she had only minimal facility in the complex Samoan language, acquired in ten weeks or so after her arrival. Very likely this additional limitation further reduced the accuracy of the secondhand information she gathered.

Mead's basic and most crippling limitation carries the greatest significance as a scientific and scholarly moral. Again, the matter has direct pertinence to the history of stuttering, especially its recent history. This basic limitation was her abiding preoccupation with the doctrine of cultural determinism. An ardent devotee of her mentor, Boas, she was clearly motivated to confute biological explanations of human behavior by gathering, embellishing, and interpreting information to show that human conduct is solely the product of culture. Boas too must be considered culpable. Known to have been careful and scholarly in his own research, he must surely have been aware of the major faults in Mead's work. In fact, there is compelling indication that he was so aware, but took no action. Freeman makes the point (p. 282) that, by this time, cultural determinism had become "an ideology that, in an actively unscientific way, sought totally to exclude biology from the explanation of human behavior."

The real historical significance of Mead's report has several facets. First, it affords an outstanding example of the proselyting potential of doctrine and the distorting power of doctrinal conviction. Second, it points up the circumstantial potency of the *Zeitgeist*, the "tide in the affairs of men," the accepting (often eager) atmosphere of the times. Third, even people who ought to know better will help a myth along. Fourth, myths quickly acquire juggernaut momentum and easily crush isolated instances of reason or contradiction. Fifth, once a myth has been accepted, much time and effort must be expended to rescind it, particularly when it has been cloistered in an atmosphere that is impervious to rational criticism and logical analysis. These features have special relevance to the history of stuttering, and will be considered again in Chapter 8.

Behaviorism

Mead was not alone in making markedly biased and unsupported claims for environmentalism. John B. Watson had expressed such bias many times, in writing and in lecture, since having set behaviorism in motion in 1913. In his landmark book *Behaviorism*, he flatly asserted that there is "no such thing as an inheritance of capacity, talent, temperament, mental constitution and characteristics" (1924: p. 74). In many subsequent articles[11] he continued to proclaim that nurture, not nature, was the basis of human behavior. Watson's sweeping assertions were even more weakly founded than Mead's; they too were supported neither by relevant research nor, in fact, by any other substantial evidence. Nonetheless, their influence was in certain ways and in many circles even more profound than Mead's.

Watson had reported, in 1920, a study that had the same sort of appeal as had Mead's story, and it had received the same level of acclaim, albeit from a smaller audience. This study was the famous account of little Albert and the white rat, which purported to demonstrate stimulus generalization of fear as a learned response (Watson and Rayner 1920). This particular study would have special value for certain sources in stuttering, in that it brought together *fear*, the long-term favorite explanation for stuttering, and *learning*, which was to become an even more favored vehicle. However, the story of little Albert and the white rat, like Mead's story about Samoa, turned out to be another long-lived myth. In a thorough review of its lengthy history, Harris (1979) presents convincing documentation that, in the telling and retelling of this story, including the original version, there is as much fabrication and distortion as there is fact.

Undoubtedly the most eminent figure in the behaviorist tradition emerged during the rapid growth of behaviorism in the 1920s: Clark L. Hull. Hull stands out among other important figures in the era of "neobehaviorism"[12] because of the character of his formulation, developed according to the *hypothetico-deductive method*. Use of this method, he argued, was critical if psychology were to become an objective science on the order of other natural sciences. In fact, his formulation, with its theorems, constructs, and postulates, is the only one in the entire field of psychology (including, of course, dynamic psychology) that merits the designation "theory." Hull, uniquely, applied the precepts of mathematics and formal logic to psychological formulations.[13]

The primary focus of Hull's system was the conditioned reflex and the concept of reinforcement. During the 1930s he wrote, with colleagues, a number of articles describing how complex behavior could be explained in terms of conditioning. Hull is noted here for two reasons: first, because the level of his theoretical efforts enhanced the scientific image of psychology, and second, because of Kenneth Spence, a student of Hull and his closest associate.

Spence was intimately involved in the development of Hull's formulation, so much so that reference to the theory often includes his name as well. This connection is especially pertinent to the history of stuttering because, in 1938, Spence became a professor in the psychology department at the University of Iowa. There, through his research, writing and the many students influenced by him, he became a dominant figure in American psychology. Given the close association between psychology and speech-hearing science at Iowa, and especially the growing trend within speech pathology to draw substance from psychology, the themes of stimulus-response and conditioning were certain to show up in application to stuttering, and learning theory would soon take center stage.

In subsequent chapters of this book, reference will be made to several paradigms of the learning process developed from laboratory psychology. An explanation of each of the paradigms of learning seems out of place at this point; however it is pertinent to give a brief description of them.[14]

There are two main types of learning paradigm. The original type, known as classical conditioning, or S-R for stimulus-response, is exemplified in Pavlov's work. The salient distinction of this type of conditioning is that what the organism does (the response) is originally elicited by a stimulus (called the unconditioned stimulus) that is adequate to elicit the response, which is then reinforced (by relevant consequences). Then, a previously neutral (originally *in*adequate) stimulus, if paired often enough with the unconditioned stimulus, will come to evoke the response (now a *conditioned* response). In the other main learning paradigm, called instrumental conditioning, no adequate stimulus necessarily elicits the response, although the response may come to be linked to certain stimuli, and typically does; after which those stimuli can evoke the response. This type of learning is called "instrumental" because what the organism does (the act, "response") is *instrumental* in obtaining its reinforcement; that is, the act leads to or engenders its consequences. There are several forms of this paradigm: instrumental reward learning; instrumental escape learning; and instrumental avoidance learning (see Glossary, under "Learning; the paradigms"). Each of these paradigms has been invoked to create an explanation of stuttering, a matter to be addressed briefly in Chapter 8.

THE TROUBLE WITH WORDS

As mentioned at the beginning of this chapter, another conceptual focus emerged during this transition period that would have a profound effect on the field of stuttering: preoccupation with words and their use. Two sources, quite independent of each other, that gave rise to this focus were the writings of Alfred Korzybski, whose most influential work appeared in 1933, and those of Benjamin Whorf, who is best remembered for a series of articles that appeared in 1940. Both were essentially laymen in the fields of language use or linguistics; in fact, both had been educated as chemical engineers.

Korzybski and General Semantics

Alfred Korzybski[15] was born in 1879 into a family belonging to the nobility of Russian-dominated Poland. He grew up in a multilingual society of the intelligentsia, wherein he received the liberal education of a free intellectual in the era preceding the First World War. He studied mathematics, physics, and law in the course of his preparation as a chemical engineer. During the war he served as an officer in the Russian army, in which capacity he was sent on a mission to the United States and Canada. After the collapse of czarist Russia in 1917 he made his home in the United States, eventually becoming an American citizen in 1940. For a time during this period he served as a Polish military attache to the United States and to the League of Nations. Also during this period he wrote two books and a number of articles expressing a philosophy of life he had developed. His second book, *Science and Sanity*, would generate a considerable amount of interest and, among certain individuals, a devoted following.

Korzybski had matured intellectually during the period of active debate in Polish intellectual circles that concentrated on the nature of language and its function in the sciences vis-a-vis the arts. This content emerged in his postwar writings along with American influences derived from behaviorism and what has been called "engineering materialism." Korzybski believed that the serious problems in human affairs (wars and the like) were caused by the great disparity between the rate of progress in the social sciences and that in the natural and technological sciences. He believed that more sociocultural progress could be achieved by applying principles of engineering to human problems, which he thought could be best achieved through concentrating on the structure of language.

At base Korzybski's intended objective was the development of a new epistemology — the study of knowledge and how we know. In *Science and Sanity* (1933) he developed an epistemologic framework that he called "general semantics." General semantics was said to go beyond the study of words per se; beyond symbols, grammar, and related matters to a system for revamping knowledge, through which human lives could presumably be continually made better.

Korzybski's explanation of general semantics, its means of employ and expression, and the projected solutions said to be afforded by it are difficult to encapsulate. His own presentations of the concept and its dimensions were rather abstruse and in certain respects esoteric, often containing vocabulary and concepts from physics.[16] The term "general semantics" is itself potentially confusing in that he purportedly intended it to mean something quite different from the usual meaning of "semantics." At the same time, the issues on which he focused were consistently semantic ones.

One esoteric term that he used frequently as characterizing general semantics, the term "non-Aristotelian," offers a key to the core of his position. This term referred to the fact that one of Aristotle's great achievements (see Chapter 2) was his systems of classification, which have generally been considered an important contribution to Western thought. However, Korzybski complained that the mental orientation to the world that is reflected in such systems[17] underlies a "two-valued, either-or" way of evaluating what we experience, an orientation that prevents us from dealing with higher levels of abstraction and thereby from realizing our potentialities as humans. To illustrate such "either-or evaluations" he gave, as examples, that we speak of "day *or* night; land *or* water; hot *or* cold;" and the like.[18]

The rationale embodied in these examples was widely accepted as valid, and the examples were repeated or paraphrased in spite of their transparent misdirection. In contradiction to the claim that these examples represent a "two-valued system of evaluation" one need simply consider, in regard to only his first example, for instance, that we also regularly use the terms daybreak, dawn, sunup, early morning, mid-morning, late morning, noon, high noon, early afternoon, mid-afternoon, late afternoon, early evening, evening, dusk, twilight, gathering darkness, etc., which are gradations of, and stand between, the encompassing designations of "day" and "night." Kenneth Burke, an early critic of these fabrications, pointed out (Burke 1945) the hypocrisy of Korzybski's railing against a "two-valued system of evaluation" given that Korzybski's entire gospel was based on his construction of a "two-valued" opposition of Aristotelian versus non-Aristotelian.

Purportedly, Korzybski's attention to words as bearing the structure of language was largely a means-end concern. However, words were always his central focus and that of those who accepted and extended his position. Critical to his position was the issue he made regarding problems in word usage. This issue, well reflected in the illustrations reviewed above, was clearly represented in his frequent emphasis of the terms "extensional" versus "intensional"[19] and the word "evaluation."

In Korzybski's construction the word "extensional" referred to an intellectual orientation that focused on dealing with facts, matters that are observable and objective. In certain places he suggested that his sense and usage of this term were comparable to the concept of "operational definition" developed by the physicist P. W. Bridgman (1927) as an aid to clarifying technical discussion. This implication was certainly a loose association; "extensional" lacked the sophistication, the specificity, and the means for objectification contained within Bridgman's concept.

In contrast to the supposed highly objective intellectual attitude to be denoted by "extensional," the mental orientation identified as "intensional" was presented as being characterized by verbal constructions, internalized values, beliefs, and mental associations; in essence, it was said to be highly subjective and personalized. In Korzybski's view, humans are disposed to continually *evaluate* their experiences, and the character of their evaluations will, of course, depend upon the intellectual orientation with which they encounter those experiences. The intensional attitude, contaminated by internalized values and biases, was said to introduce error into the evaluation process. Clearly, adopting the extensional orientation, which purportedly was based in the *natural* order of evaluation, would be the road to intellectual and then societal salvation. Korzybski persistently contended that in order to improve the human condition it was necessary for people to adopt the extensional attitude.

The capstone indicator that words and word usage were central to Korzybski's notions was his coinage of the term "semantogenic." This neologism was intended to have a very literal meaning, namely, "caused by words." In fact, in *Science and Sanity* Korzybski boldly stated that various personal and professional maladjustments, many psychosomatic symptoms, and many emotional disturbances — "including even some neuroses and psychoses" —

have "a semantogenic, and therefore a neuro-semantic and neuro-linguistic origin." [20]

Whatever else one might find in Korzybski's writings, this central preoccupation with word usage was the feature that had the most widespread influence. In a very real sense, especially in efforts that were made to actually apply general semantics, the matter of words and the emphasis on potential problems inherent in their use quickly rose to major prominence. These claims soon had · a wide audience that extended well into the general public, particularly among the educated. This rapid expansion was due largely to the enthusiasm of certain authors who, caught up in the ferment of the movement, popularized it in books addressed to the lay audience. The first highly influential source of this kind was a book by Stuart Chase, a well-known and influential economist, social scientist, and author.[21] Bearing the catchy title *The Tyranny of Words* (1938), this little book carried general semantics dogma far afield. There soon followed the rather presumptuously titled *Language in Action: A Guide to Accurate Thinking, Reading and Writing* (1941) by S. I. Hayakawa. Then in a few years there appeared the ultimate advocacy, the expansive *People in Quandaries* (1946) by Wendell Johnson.[22]

For several years general semantics developed a kind of "cultism" (Carroll 1953: p. 163). Papers presented at early congresses on the subject (1935, 1941) attest that general semantics had shown up everywhere imaginable. For instance, formal papers presented at these meetings were addressed to the relevance of general semantics to such diverse disciplines as biology, dentistry, genetics, horticulture, music, and penology, as well as to many areas that would seem more likely, such as literature, philosophy, and psychology. By 1941 stuttering had shown up too, in the paper presented by Wendell Johnson to the Second International Congress, held in Denver, Colorado. By this time Johnson had begun to vigorously press the interpretation of stuttering that he saw general semantics could offer, and which he then expanded into a dogma that was actively disseminated and widely accepted. This major event in the history of stuttering is the subject of Chapter 7.

General semantics appealed to a wide audience through the 1940s and into the next decade, but then began to collapse inwardly with a rapidity that matched its original expansion. The collapse came about primarily because the substance supporting the movement had been inflated beyond its intrinsically limited capacity for support. The endless repetition of examples of its applications had reached satiation and had become trite and boring to many persons outside the believers' circle. As described in a recent review of the movement (Paulson 1983: p. 88), the remaining advocates "were increasingly speaking only to those already convinced or to each other." Collapse was hastened by a sobering realization of the essential superficiality of much that was embodied in the tenets of general semantics, a realization encouraged by thoughtful critics. One such critic, Lionel Trilling (1953: p. 189), deplored the rise of this "mythology . . . that we are betrayed by words." He noted that "the tyranny of words" had become a popular phrase which, however, was in most respects   grossly inaccurate and misleading. He pointed out that a century earlier Dickens had complained that he was tired of hearing this very phrase, "the tyranny of words," saying that he was less concerned with how words may abuse us than with the way we abuse words. Dickens emphasized that words cannot control us unless we wish to be controlled by them.

The general semantics movement began, crested, and faded in a span of about twenty years. Today its major remnants are found primarily in new editions of Hayakawa's book and in the activities of two societies established in those early years.[23] Its influence shriveled in all disciplines that had once been caught up in it, completely disappearing from most of them. However, its essence was nurtured and sustained in the field of stuttering, where it remains an active presence to this day. This matter is considered in Chapters 7 and 8.

It is pertinent to mention here that the field of linguistics itself was also in an era of transition during the 1930s. Leonard Bloomfield's *Language*, also published in 1933, is considered to be one of the outstanding landmarks in the development of structural linguistics. Prior to the early 1930s, the accepted view in linguistics had been that all languages are basically alike in most respects. The essential notion of structural linguistics, in contrast, was that all languages are different; therefore, each must be considered independently. It was characteristic of behavioral science in general during that era to place emphasis on objective description as the chief method of study. Structural linguistics, in keeping with the times, held that the scientific study of a language required analysis of the observable phenomena of that language, a position that resulted in many languages being analyzed in great detail. A few years later, in some respects due to such extensive analyses, it was realized that languages are not quite as unique as strict structuralist doctrine would contend; that there are, in fact, many features of different languages that are sufficiently similar to be considered "linguistic universals." (See, for instance, Greenberg 1963.)

However, preoccupation with the view that languages differ markedly, which implied related differences in thought and culture, persisted for some time. It is from within the context of this era of attention to perceived differences among languages that the contributions of Benjamin Whorf became particularly pertinent.

Whorf and Linguistic Relativity

Whorf, born in 1897, lived all his life in New England. He was educated as a chemical engineer, and he worked continuously and very successfully in that profession after his graduation from M.I.T. However, through various circumstances he developed an absorbing interest in linguistics, an interest he pursued vigorously during almost all of his spare time.

Whorf, an avid reader since an early age, had a wide range of interests, including botany, prehistoric Mexico, codes and ciphers, even astrology. His initial interest in linguistics was precipitated, around 1924, by a rather abstract concern — the marked difference between scientific and Biblical accounts of cosmology. This led him to a study of ancient Hebrew, during the course of which he came across, and studied thoroughly, an early nineteenth-century book by a French philologist and mystic, Antoine Fabret d'Olivet, who had claimed to have found hidden meanings in his phonetic-morphemic analysis of the Book of Genesis. Olivet's account intensified Whorf's interest in languages and energized the core of his long-term absorption in linguistics, namely, a search for inner meanings.

Whorf was a dedicated and tireless worker. Through his own study he developed a commendable competence in general linguistics and in linguistic field methods, and he began to correspond with various scholars of Mexican archeology and linguistics. This led to his undertaking the analysis of Aztec and certain related languages, an endeavor that resulted in highly acclaimed papers presented at professional meetings. His opportunity for directed study in linguistics came in 1931 after Edward Sapir joined the faculty of Yale University.[24] Whorf became a student and then an associate of Sapir, who encouraged him to study Hopi, a distant relative of Aztec. Whorf did so with his usual thoroughness, and it is for his work with Hopi that he is best known in linguistic circles.

It seems that the strange grammar of Hopi led him to seriously entertain the hypothesis that different languages lead the (native) speakers of that language to view the world differently from speakers of other languages.   This hypothesis, which came to be known as *linguistic relativity*, was not original with Whorf. It had been suggested by two German scholars in the eighteenth century, and was espoused by Sapir, who was a major influence in Whorf's linguistic sophistication. In fact, the extent of Sapir's influence is reflected in the fact that this notion is sometimes referred to as the "Sapir-Whorf hypothesis."   The reader should recognize Sapir as one of the prominent students of Franz Boas (Chapter 5). It seems that through Sapir and Whorf, cultural determinism had eventuated in linguistic relativity.

The hypothesis of linguistic relativity attained its most widespread influence through an article by Whorf (1940) that appeared in a publication addressed esentially to a lay audience. In the course of elaborating how "we dissect nature along lines laid down by our native languages" (p. 230), he gave as an example that, whereas English has only one "all-inclusive word" for snow, Eskimos have many different words for different forms of snow — forms that are, for Eskimos, "sensuously and operationally different." This example, along with the hypothesis it presumably elucidated, was quickly and offhandedly accepted as fact by many sources, and thereby acquired a reality. For over forty years this "fact" has been repeated and reprinted hundreds upon hundreds of times, in academic as well as lay sources. Moreover, as Pullam (1991) has documented, the number of purportedly different Eskimo words for snow has grown steadily over the years in the course of the telling and retelling of this particular myth.

Actually, Whorf had no direct knowledge to support this claim. The idea evidently occurred to him while reading Boas' *Handbook of North American*

Indians. In that source Boas discussed independent versus derivative words that might occur in different languages, his focus being the varying use of single versus separate word roots. Boas happened to use, as illustration, examples from Eskimo and English that included the words "water" and "snow." Whorf, primed mentally by his culture-language bias, saw something that was not there, and through his fabrication created another myth.

Pullam emphasizes — as did Martin (1986) before him — that the truth of the matter is that the Eskimos *do not* have lots of different words for different forms of snow, and that "no one who knows anything about Eskimo . . . has ever said they do" (Pullam 1991: p. 160). In support of this statement, Pullam cites C. W. Schultz-Lorentzen's *Dictionary of West Greenlandic Eskimo Language* as giving just two possibly relevant roots. However, even if Eskimos did have many different words for different forms of snow, this would hardly indicate that their perceptions are determined or controlled by the words. Rather, it would seem more rational to deduce that different forms of snow are important to them, which is why they have ready references for these forms. That is, careful perceptions are the basis for certain words, not the other way around.

Considering now the other part of Whorf's example, English is by no means impoverished in its references to "sensuously and operationally different" forms of snow. Commonly used terms include dry (or light) snow, wet (or heavy) snow, granular snow, corn snow, powdery snow ("powder"), packed snow, crusted snow — not to mention such clearly snow-form variants as slush, sleet, or even hail. Again, as with Korzybski's illustrations for his "two-valued" claim, it is very difficult to understand why some thoughtful speaker of English (at least among those living above the 40th parallel) did not challenge Whorf's myth by simply reflecting momentarily on his own personal experience with snow and the words for varying kinds of snow, as noted above, typically used by his friends, acquaintances, and most likely himself. A particularly relevant example here is the following: I have heard very young (monolingual English-speaking) children create some of their own designations for "sensuously and operationally different" forms of snow, for instance, fluffy snow, snowman snow, sledding snow, soaking snow.

Again, as with the little Albert myth, Whorf's notion had an appealing superficial credibility; to become established it only needed to be told and retold, especially when accompanied by the ring of authority.

The hypothesis of linguistic relativity aroused considerable interest, and was persuasive to many persons for a number of years after Whorf's 1940 publication. Although it is still a subject of some debate, interest in it has waned considerably. Efforts to test the notion experimentally have regularly yielded evidence credibly seen as disproving it, yet some have maintained that mounting a crucial test of the idea is very difficult (see McNeill 1987). To the contrary, it seems sensible to expect that, for a hypothesis that makes such a sweeping affirmation, tests of its credibility should reveal supporting evidence quite readily. However, none has been forthcoming.

At any rate, it is now widely recognized that although languages differ, some of them in many remarkable and unusual ways, there is, at the same time, little reason to suspect concomitant differences in perception or conception that are created through linguistic variations, especially via individual words.[25]

A Lingering Appeal

General semantics and "linguistic relativity," particularly the former, had intense appeal for a large number of people for many years. To some extent, the appeal continues to hold varying levels of attraction to the uninitiated. The source of the appeal seems clearly to be that these conceptions point to and emphasize a quality of words that substantially subverts our naive acceptance of their nature — a quality characterized in the comment that, in a certain sense, words are merely words. This characterization runs counter to the unspoken assumption that words are entities that have a meaning in substance.

Throughout recorded history, and almost certainly before recorded history, words have had a revered status. "In the beginning was the Word, and the Word was with God, and the Word was God."[26] Words have have been instrumental in reifying many entities of which we have not had, and cannot have, direct experience, such as goblins and gods, angels and devils, spirits and beasts, fanciful events and circumstances, imaginary places and things.[27] Over the centuries words have been major tools of sorcerers and other practitioners of magic, black and otherwise. An inherent belief in the power of words continues to be revealed in the conduct of various rituals that not only routinely include, but often center upon, some presumably significant verbalizations, many of which are formalized and esoteric, although some are quite spontaneous and casual.

In modern-day technologically advanced cultures, most persons recognize, at least superficially, that words do not possess true magical power. However, words implicitly retain that status in, for example, curses, casual supplications, formalized prayer, and benediction. Their role as magic also surfaces vividly in many lay superstitions, most pointedly in injunctions not to verbalize something that one fears might happen. In fact, the latter superstition shows up with surprising frequency. Although it may be expressed in apparent jest, in many instances there is good reason to suspect a barely obscured belief lying just below the verbal surface. A somewhat less obvious reflection of the same attitude is seen in the widespread use of euphemism.

When one is first made aware of the plausibility that "words are just words," it turns out to be quite a dramatic revelation, one that has two important aspects. First, careful objective analysis reveals that, at base, words are only patterns of sound. Although humans have devised methods of symbolizing these patterns in graphic, and thus seemingly concrete, form, their only substantive reality is as evanescent acoustic events. Moreover, in actual usage, words are simply *acts of reference*, and the large majority of them may seem, upon casual reflection, to have little apparent connection with whatever it is they refer to, signify, or "name." In large measure they appear, from reasonably careful direct inspection, to not bear or partake of the essence of what they identify. It is this apparent disconnection between words and their referents that underlies the description of words as "just words" or, more formally, as "arbitrary representations." From this standpoint words can be characterized, as Korzybski and his followers emphasized, as simply "labels." However, this appearance of superficiality is itself very misleading. Even though the ties between word and significate are frequently impalpable on the surface, most words are not so completely disconnected from their referents as the claim of arbitrariness suggests. The most compelling immediate evidence that many words have quite close connections to their referents is found in the many instances of onomatopoeia. Beyond such examples, however, explorations of word etymology reveal much additional compelling evidence that there are close connections between most words and what they signify. In fact, scholars of etymology estimate that only a small percentage of words are truly arbitrary (see, for instance, Householder 1946).[28]

At the same time, to the unsophisticated, the description of words as arbitrary is impressive and persuasive. When first faced with this seeming revelation regarding the apparently arbitrary nature of words, most individuals are nonplussed, initially incredulous, but eventually fascinated. Even so, for many it is a matter that is difficult to incorporate. Such lingering ambivalence and reservation were expressed openly by Stuart Chase: "I find it difficult to believe that words have no meaning in themselves, hard as I try. Habits of a lifetime are not lightly thrown aside."[29]

The second, corollary, aspect of this seeming revelation about words is the idea that, if words really are linked so loosely to their referents, perhaps they are not the accurate guides to reality that we have assumed them to be. Such reservation becomes more persuasive as one considers those dimensions of experience and knowledge that are abstract, that relate to matters beyond what is immediate and concrete. This apparent looseness of words has allowed the suspicion, and then the suggestion, that perhaps words may structure, or at least substantially influence, what we experience.

The reader should recognize this second aspect of the revelation about words as the essence of the linguistic relativity hypothesis. This notion is also cen- tral to at least the pragmatic expression of general semantics, wherein the ul- timate objective was to beneficently structure, or restructure, perceptions, attitudes, and beliefs through careful and appropriate use of words.

Although the underlying intent of both general semantics and linguistic relativity was generally benign, a creed that exploits the observation of a certain "looseness" between words and their referents can easily be oriented in a more sinister direction. A special case in point is the more recently developed attack on the word-meaning relationship known as "deconstruction." This undertaking represents an analytic method, applied particularly to literature and history, that questions the content of any written material. A crucial tenet of deconstruction is that the relationship between words and their meaning is arbitrary and indeterminate. Therefore, it is claimed, the accuracy and validity of any (or all) literary and historical sources is open to question—and therefore to repudiation. Happily, deconstruction, too, now seems to be collapsing of its own weight. (Readers interested in this special subject should see Rapaport 1989; McCarthy 1991.)

Specific to Stuttering

The focus on words that became energized during the period of transition covered in this chapter brought many people to a fuller realization that, in most aspects of human relations, thoughtful choice and use of words merit serious consideration. However, the aura surrounding the novelty of the general semantics movement faded, its crusade-like proportions gradually wore thin, and the large following it had attracted fell away. At the same time, a core of individuals remained committed to its precepts and carried on undaunted. Among these were a few whom the movement had led to a position regarding the power of words that is not far removed from the quasi-magic belief manifested in certain forms of superstition, such as not speaking of some undesirable event for fear it may happen.

This claim about the power of words, in its full quasi-magic form, was soon installed as the essential substance of a widely influential and incredibly durable explanation of stuttering. This account, known as the "semantogenic theory"[30] of stuttering, created by Wendell Johnson, is the essential focus of Chapter 7. Use of the term "semantogenic" was another direct borrowing from Korzybski's general semantics.

Students of stuttering, at least, should find it of great interest that, within a few years of its heyday in the 1940s, the influence of general semantics, the movement that had hailed the supposed power of words, would surface once more. This time it would show up in sociological anthropology, in the form of Lemert's (1951) concept of *secondary deviance*. The special relevance of this development for the history of stuttering is occasioned by the fact that Lemert's idea was based substantially on Johnson's claim of semantogenesis in stuttering. The unique set of events that led to Lemert's proposal of secondary deviance is described in Chapter 8.

NOTES

1. A trend that would continue; in 1992 membership stood at 65,049.
2. This publication and similar mimeographings over the next four years, were identified as a series: *Proceedings of the American Speech Correction Association.*
3. It is of particular interest in this regard that, at a later date, Bluemel (1957) made the point that although he was well aware of his stuttering at age five, he was "no more bothered by it than . . . about having dirty hands."

4.   Consider, for instance, the phenomena of tics.

5. See section on recovery in Chapter 9; also Van Riper's eventual position regarding this matter, also noted in Chapter 9.

6. The data for Tables 6.2 and 6.3 were compiled by the present author.

7. The source, *Psychological Abstracts*, covers publications that extend beyond those within the field of speech and hearing science.

8. In noting actual dates, one should take into account the lag time (interval) between the date research is undertaken and the date it appears in print.

9. Excluding, in this instance, topic areas within speech, such as phonetics, anatomy, speech process, etc.; and the various areas within audiology.

10.   In my view, Freeman's book, *Margaret Mead and Samoa: The Making and Unmaking of an Anthropological Myth*, should be required reading for all students in the social sciences, at least for the moral it provides on professional obligation and responsibility.

11. Compiled as a book, *The Ways of Behaviorism*, in 1928.

12. Notably E. R. Guthrie and E. C. Tolman.

13.   It is to B. F. Skinner's credit that he does not consider his own brand of behaviorism, operationism, to be a theory.

14. Primarily because direct reference to these paradigms is made in Chapter 8, the distinguishing characteristics of each type are presented in the Glossary. See under "Learning; the paradigms."

15.   Synoptic biographical material is contained in Paulson (1983). A personal recollection of the man by Van Riper (1992b: p. 83) strongly suggests eccentricity, which supports a similar impression gained from reading Korzybski's works.

16. See "general semantics" in the Glossary for several of Korzybski's own statements regarding the nature of this concept. Students interested in reasonably comprehensive, though relatively brief, accounts of general semantics should see Gorman (1962) or Paulson (1983).

17. Reportedly he used Aristotle essentially as the most exemplary reference of "the pre-scientific attitude" (which had certain other faults of thinking as well). However, his complaint centered on the matter of classification, for which Aristotle is noted, and its supposedly distorting mental influences. At the same time Korzybski acknowledged that the same orientation toward "classification" is found in peoples who have never been exposed to anything from Aristotle.

18. *Science and Sanity*, Preface to the third edition, p. vii.

19.   For Korzybski's own statements regarding these terms, see under "general semantics" in the Glossary.

20. *Science and Sanity*, Introduction to the second edition, p. xii.

21. His potential personal influence is reflected in the fact that he was for a time an advisor to President Franklin D. Roosevelt.

22. Only Hayakawa's book, with expanded title, has appeared in several editions, the latest as recently as 1989. The book by Johnson is considered in Chapter 7.

23.   The Institute of General Semantics (established by Korzybski) in Lakeville, Conn.; and the International Society for General Semantics, in San Francisco, Calif., of which Wendell Johnson was one founder.

24. Whorf lived and worked in Hartford, Connecticut. A synoptic biography of this remarkable man is contained in Carroll's (1956) introductory chapter.

25. Of course, language differences may influence or support certain differences in beliefs between cultures. But then, similar effects are notable within a language/culture as well: for example, Republican vis-a-vis Democrat,   Catholic vis-a-vis Southern Baptist, etc.

26. The Gospel According to St. John, 1:1.

27. For illustration see Page and Ingpen (1985); also Lum (1958)

28. It is important to recognize the extent of word origins from onomatopoeia, but also the evidence of an even more literal source: *phonetic symbolism*. See Hinton et al 1994.

29. This quotation appears at the head of Chapter 2 in the first version of Hayakawa's book (1941). Chase was among those few for whom general semantics evidently had a lingering appeal. His second book in this vein appeared in 1956, and a small book for children in 1969. See references.

30. Actually, as indicated elsewhere in this book, none of the explanations offered for stuttering merits the designation "theory," unless one is using the term with its common   lay connotation, meaning simply "guess."

CHAPTER 7

A View with Room

There is properly no history; only biography.
R.W. Emerson, *Essays: First Series*

Chapter 5 brought the history of stuttering to the middle 1930s, when the brief period of Travis' scientifically based program of research was coming to a close. Chapter 6 identified the major influences of that period external to stuttering that would profoundly affect its study from that point onward. This chapter will trace the development and expansion of a view of stuttering that would become widely accepted, well entrenched, and long-lived even though it was established, extended, and maintained on very questionable grounds.

As Chapters 5 and 6 show, influences from anthropology and psychology gave impetus and support to a nascent view of stuttering as a functional disorder. Moreover, appealing and persuasive — though faulty — "findings" from within these two disciplines provided room for this view to grow. Particularly influential were the appealing story generated by Margaret Mead and the attractive beliefs expounded by J. B. Watson. Furthermore, there emerged within this ambience a preoccupation with a belief in the power of words, propounded in the tenets of general semantics. This special focus was absorbed into a highly personalized formulation of stuttering that presented the disorder as a special kind of psychological problem.

By the late 1930s a movement based in this formulation was expanding in scope. It soon developed a large following, and became clearly overwhelming by the early 1940s. Although the background circumstances, reviewed earlier, might have carried the movement along, the vigor of its progression was due largely to the efforts of its originator, Wendell Johnson.

BACK TO IOWA

Imminent Change

Under Travis, the program in speech and hearing science at the University of Iowa had gained stature rapidly, attracting students who were interested in various aspects of the program. Travis' energy and innovations in his approach to the study of stuttering attracted hopeful patients as well, some of whom came also as students, or became students once there.

Two of the stutterers who came to the new program seeking help for their disorder were Wendell Johnson and Charles Van Riper, both of whom became involved in the academic program and earned advanced degrees in it. As noted in Chapter 5, among a few stutterers who would achieve prominence in the field of stuttering, these two men would become the most influential. Of these two, Wendell Johnson would have by far the greater impact in terms of what was widely accepted and believed about the nature of stuttering.

Both Johnson and Van Riper were students of Travis, were involved as subjects in some of his experimentation, and participated in the therapy efforts then being made. As mentioned previously, Travis' orientation was essentially neurophysiologic, and his own work was undertaken in that vein. However, in the spirit of free-ranging inquiry established at Iowa by Seashore and actively encouraged by Travis, students were allowed to pursue their individual persuasions.

With their personal recollections and suppositions as impetus, both Johnson and Van Riper were much more inclined to seek explanatory substance within the discipline of psychology. As the reader should recall, academic psychology was not only outstanding at Iowa but also had close ties with the program in speech and hearing science.

From the beginning, the writings of both Johnson and Van Riper were heavily infused with psychological precepts and notions, which usually offered a mix of unsophisticated lay notions and personal beliefs interwoven with more esoteric ideas from academic psychology.

It is of particular interest that, before going to Iowa, each of these men had majored in English (at separate institutions). Very likely this preparation underlay their later success with writing; both men wrote extensively in this special field. Johnson had transferred to Iowa from McPherson College as an English major. Van Riper had an M.A. degree in English from the University of Michigan when he arrived at Iowa in 1930, brought there by Bryngelson to work on his stuttering. Van Riper is undoubtedly the most widely known figure in speech pathology, largely because his writings addressed a wide range of speech disorders. His influence in stuttering, however, although substantial through the avenue of his essentially clinical contribution, was eclipsed by the impact of Wendell Johnson, which was both expansive and profound. Van Riper's influence in stuttering will be considered in Chapter 9. The present

chapter is addressed to the source, nature and extent of Johnson's singular influence on the field.

It is appropriate to present here a vignette that is both testimony to the spirit
of inquiry then encouraged at Iowa and, as well, the point of departure of a new
era. The spirit is clearly reflected in what Travis had to say in his introduction
to Johnson's partial autobiography, *Because I Stutter,* published in 1930.
Travis stated briefly that the study of stuttering pursued at Iowa up to that time
had been neurologically oriented, and was characterized by research that had
"sought and secured strictly objective instrumental determinations." He went
on to say that this approach had "not paid much attention to the so-called subjective or personal aspects of the stutterer's difficulty." He remarked that his
objective, instrumental method had yielded, by that time, sufficiently promising
results that the study of stuttering could then "take account profitably" of the
subjective aspects of the disorder. To provide this information, he felt "very
fortunate in having an ideal combination in Mr. Wendell Johnson, who is a
stutterer with training in psychology and in writing." He added that Johnson
had served as a subject in numerous objective studies at Iowa, and was one of a
large group of stutterers who had received treatment "based upon the concept
that stuttering is a definite neuromuscular derangement . . . in which there is a
general reduction in cortical activity." He noted further that over half of this
large group had recovered completely or shown marked improvement, and that
"at the present time Mr. Johnson enjoys a large measure of speech freedom" as
a result of this treatment.

Travis had encouraged Johnson's testimony and reflections regarding his personal history and experiences in the anticipation that a report of this kind
might offer a kind of grace note to the substantial findings already obtained
from Travis' objective research. However, matters would turn out quite differently. In his generous, open gesture of honest inquiry Travis had lifted the lid
of a Pandora's box.

A Different Drummer

A history of the field of stuttering from the 1930s to date must pivot on the
personage of Wendell Johnson. Although the quotation from Emerson at the
head of this chapter is, in a general sense, something of an overstatement, it
closely approximates the truth in this particular instance. No other individual
has had as much influence on the field of stuttering, or for so long a time, as
Wendell Johnson. The material covered in the present chapter and in Chapter
8 is crucial to an appreciation of the status and history of stuttering over the
past fifty years — and, undoubtedly, a shadow that will remain for many years
more.

Johnson was born and raised on a farm near Roxbury, Kansas, a small town
about fifty miles north of Wichita. Evidently the Johnson family had been successful as farmers, and also educated, since in his partial autobiography (see
below) Wendell referred to his father's library in their home. Little is known

about his early childhood or development, but the autobiography contains important information about him as a teenager. Evidently he stuttered from an early age, and reportedly was stuttering severely while attending McPherson College, a junior college located not far from his home town. There a sympathetic English teacher told him of Travis' research and encouraged him to go to Iowa. He entered the University of Iowa as a junior, in 1926, to major in English while working to improve his speech. He soon transferred to the speech pathology curriculum, in which he received his B.A. in 1928, his M.A. in 1929, and his Doctorate in 1931. He became a research assistant in 1930, later assumed administrative responsibilities for the Speech Clinic, and in 1937 became a member of the faculty. With a joint appointment in speech pathology and psychology, he remained at the University of Iowa until his death in 1965.

As the independent project for his M.A. degree Johnson prepared a personal case history, a partial autobiography that focused essentially on himself as a stutterer. It was published as a book the following year under the title *Because I Stutter* (Johnson 1930). Several selections from this source are reprinted here because they clearly reveal the nature and the intensity of Johnson's feelings about his stuttering, and also something of his personal outlook, which would profoundly affect the direction and substance of stuttering inquiry in the many years to follow.[1]

Johnson spoke of finding pleasure in his father's library from an early age, even "before stuttering meant anything in particular" to him. He "learned to read and to wonder at" what he read and, as he got older, developed a desire to become knowledgeable and well informed. He said:

Not able to talk adequately, I was forced to affirm what manner of stuff I was made of by some other means. In the first place, I had come to admire intelligence and learning, and to think of them as marks of superiority; I thought as highly of them as the so-called average person thinks of motor cars and pearl studs. There are, however, degrees in everything, and in Roxbury learning meant something quite different from what passes for learning in cultural centers. The sort of thing which I was taught to think of as intellectual superiority was of a relatively low standard. (p. 42)

He spoke several times of hating the farm and the "fatal clutch of the soil" that stifled his imagination and deadened his aesthetic sense.

Also, the farm offered no promise of glory, as I understood the term, no means of self-assertion or gratifying self-expression. Without those things, I should have been only a stutterer, an inferior person. The thought of that was always detestable. (p. 80)

He longed "to get on the other side of that basin horizon" to a world "preferable by far to my father's farm and Roxbury."

It seemed to me that there must be greater men somewhere else than the men I knew in the village; and it occurred to me that men who wanted to be superior in a great way did not belong in Roxbury. They didn't live there, and if they came, they left right away.

As the world became larger to my understanding and richer in possibilities, any kind of superiority at Roxbury came to mean less and less. . . .

Because I stuttered — largely. Granted that I had already formed studious inclinations before I began to stutter,[2] it was the incapacity to assume easily a place among my fellows that drove me to exertion. Without that exertion I was underrated, and no one can bear that indifferently. Without displaying a superiority gained by effort, I was an ordinary stutterer, a rather amusing sort of fellow, pathetic and not quite suited for the prevailing scheme of things. The though of being considered in that light was utterly repulsive to me; my innate restlessness plus my experience and training forced me to believe that I deserved better. My reaction was deliberate, almost desperate, ambition — an ambition that did not respect the encircling skyline, and the standards of Roxbury. I studied, my effort was determinate, and as I gained the objectives which I set up from time to time, my effort did not diminish; the momentum of it carried over every point that might have been a stopping place. Senior-class president, president of the student body in high school, captain of the football team, of the basketball team, of the baseball team, editor of an experimental high school paper, and valedictorian were only symbols of something, symbols that meant increasingly less to me as I won them one by one. I anticipated those little triumphs, found them momentarily satisfying, but found them insufficient.

So long as I stuttered, the fight was unrelentingly at hand. The moment I let up the struggle, I became nothing but a stutterer! (pp. 43-45)

End of an Era

In Johnson's several writings over the next few years, Travis' concepts were prominent in the texts or clearly significant to them. However, Johnson's preoccupation with the psychological aspect of stuttering was regularly evident. Soon, and quite rapidly, references to neurological concepts diminished, and the themes of reaction and attitude appeared more frequently. The pattern of this progression is revealed in the following synopsis of his early publications.

Johnson's doctoral dissertation reported his inquiry into "the influence of stuttering on the personality," which appeared with that title (Johnson 1932) in Iowa's Child Welfare series of publications. The methods of that study were largely survey, interview, and case history, but included one "mental hygiene inventory." In that paper he identified stuttering as "a disorder of rhythm in verbal expression . . . (that) . . . is most apparently characterized by tonic and clonic spasms, or both, in the neuro-muscular mechanisms for the production of sound and speech" (p. 11). In his narrative he noted how "the view that emotional disturbance is one of the prime causes of stuttering" had "become very popular," but he cautioned that "there is a big gap . . . between the emotion and the stuttering." Referring to the concept of central nervous system speech gradients developed through the research of Travis and co-workers, he remarked that "if emotion ever causes or aggravates stuttering it must evidently do so by virtue of its effect upon the gradients responsible for speech" (p. 93).

As late as 1936 he made reference to the neurological basis of stuttering. In a joint publication with M. D. Steer (Steer and Johnson 1936), reporting a study of psychological factors and severity of stuttering, the authors state:

It is obvious to any student of the subject that stuttering is a matter of organic function and that it is specifically a matter of the function of muscles, nerves and the brain. There is nothing in the results of this study which implies any contradiction of that statement.

Also:

It is necessary to distinguish between the instability of the stutterer's speech mechanism which is due entirely to fundamental constitutional factors, and the instability of the stutterer's speech mechanism which is due to superimposed and transitory emotional and psychological factors.

THE PERSONA EMERGES

The Voice From Within

Even before the foregoing publication (with Steer) was coming to print, changes in Johnson's outlook were clearly under way. In an article published in 1933 terms like "attitude" and "reaction" not only appeared but had acquired rather prominent roles. In this reflective narrative, based on his own introspective analysis, he described "three fairly distinct stages of the stuttering process." The core of the stutter, the actual stutter event identified as the muscular spasm itself, was designated as the *second* stage. In this scheme the first event, identified as the "pre-spasm" stage, was said to be the (negative) attitude with which the stutterer approaches the speech situation. The third, or "post-spasm" stage was cast as the stutterer's (negative) reaction to the spasm having occurred. Johnson acknowledged that the core of the stutter, the muscular spasm, was due (in part) to an instability of the speech gradient but contended that the frequency, intensity, and duration of the spasm also depended upon the pre-spasm and post-spasm emotional reactions of the stutterer.

A more elaborated proposal of a similar kind, developed in collaboration with John Knott, another stutterer, was set forth three years later (Johnson and Knott 1936). This interpretation, again based essentially on the authors' introspections, proposed that "four fairly distinct configurations" comprise "the moment of stuttering." This account still contained reference to the concept of the speech gradient and to emotional reactions said to interfere with it, but now the prominent explanatory terms forecast a clear change in theme: words like "expectation," "avoidance," "inhibition," "reactive inhibition," and "conflict." The latter three terms are borrowed from the psychological literature; the first two were based entirely on personal introspections.

Moeller (1975: p. 75) reported Knott to have said that this 1936 paper represented their break from a physiological conception of stuttering. He acknowledged that the "moment of stuttering" scheme was founded in conversations between Johnson and himself regarding their personal introspections. He also revealed that these conversations were the source of "the well-known paradox"[3] that stuttering is the attempt to avoid stuttering.

In another child welfare pamphlet, which appeared during the interim between the two foregoing ruminative narratives, Johnson (1934) spelled out a forecast of the view he would reiterate over many years, a view that would be embellished from time to time with other material that he would incorporate as purportedly supportive or corroborative evidence.

It seems that the message originally intended in this 1934 paper was to emphasize that a stuttering child is "not generally abnormal," or "an abnormal child," and that to permit a young stutterer to think so could lead to "a general sense of inferiority." This focus on "not abnormal" and "inferiority" seems clearly to echo the prominent theme in his autobiography. However, the pamphlet contained a good deal more than this particular message. In the course of the narrative he introduced claims and contentions that would be the core substance of his view as it was later embellished.

In his effort to explain how the stuttering child is not generally abnormal, he mentioned research addressed to the speech of normal children which showed that "one out of every four words figures in some kind of repetition." He also noted other research showing that children "when first regarded by their parents as stutterers" were not "more non-fluent" than other children whose speech was considered to be normal. He cited no sources for either of these statements. However, most likely the reference was to studies undertaken by Dorothy Davis, under Johnson's direction, that covered a period of several years and were eventually published at the end of the decade (Davis 1939, 1940). If so, the claims Johnson made here, as well as later, take substantial liberties with the results Davis obtained (see Wingate 1962a)—another dimension of his writing style that would recur often.

Style Is Everything

It is pertinent here to call the reader's attention to the quotations in the preceding paragraph, for they exemplify features of Johnson's verbal style that are found routinely in his writings. One feature is the skillful use of *gloss* terms or phrasing.[4] Thus "nonfluent," which is a very broad rubric, neatly obscures the fact that there are marked differences in the ways speakers, including children, are nonfluent; and these differences can be identified and described. Moreover, such differences turn out to be important and significant.

Another gloss, this one in phrase form—"some kind of repetition"— confounds the fact that there are also important differences among kinds of repetition. As was documented in the foregoing chapters of this book, *certain* kinds of repetition have, over the centuries, been sufficiently distinctive to have been recognized as unusual. They have been unusual enough to have not only repeatedly drawn attention but, additionally, to have elicited efforts at some form of treatment to manage them. Their particular uniqueness is unmistakably registered in the words for them in many different languages, which reveal a common character from language to language.

Another feature of Johnson's style is the ability to construct a statement that has a face value as fact when it is really no more than an inference. Thus, "when first regarded by their parents as stutterers" is something no one can reasonably claim to know in terms of either when that event may have occurred or what a child's speech was like at the time. This particular contention would subsequently be repeated—often—and later in the following form: "at the time of the original diagnosis." In this 1934 pamphlet Johnson made the claim, which he emphasized regularly thenceforth, that this "original diagnosis" would have been made by a (mistaken, because unsophisticated and overly judgmental) parent, not by "a speech expert." This claim contains several remarkable ironies that have never drawn appropriate criticism.

One crucial irony of this presumably impressive or persuasive complaint is that, over the years, pertinent research has provided evidence that lay persons are at least as able to identify stuttering as are the "experts." This significant finding is well represented in West's pithy observation that "everyone but the experts knows what stuttering is" (in West et al. 1957: p. 15). A further, related irony is that relevant research also has shown "speech experts" to report more stutters in a given sample of speech than have lay persons. The latter finding, in particular, contradicts the onus Johnson laid upon parents.

Perhaps the greatest irony involved in this claim is that the expertise of the "experts" was, and has remained, highly questionable. The experts, as touted by Johnson, have not given very persuasive evidence of being particularly knowledgeable about *speech* (oral language). The expertise typically offered has been limited to psychological notions. Moreover, their knowledge has been especially limited and superficial in regard to the very issue in focus—fluency! There was no established body of knowledge about fluency that the experts of that time could use as their frame of reference. There did not exist, until much later, any reference source describing the dimensions of fluency that the experts could cite. There was no source that would justify the implication that the knowledge about fluency of those to be called experts differed from that of the layman. Moreover, after such sources eventually did appear, in the mid-1950s—from research in the new discipline of psycholinguistics — their findings have been consistently ignored by the experts in stuttering. This policy has remained a signficant problem in the field; it has perpetuated and supported needless continuing controversy in place of efforts at logical resolution.

In this initial expression of his view (the 1934 pamphlet), Johnson happened to acknowledge that some children *do* stutter, and he also mentioned that some parents are rather indifferent to a child's stuttering. However, within a short time he would take the position that there really is no "early stuttering"; that what is mistakenly *called* stuttering is simply normal nonfluency.

Johnson cited no references in this 1934 pamphlet; therefore any possible external sources of contribution to his position[5] cannot be documented. However, it is highly likely that the claim regarding the course of early "repetitions" originated in a comment by Froeschels (in Froeschels et al. 1932), of which Johnson was almost certainly aware. The Froeschels reference is cited in one of the publications by Davis (1939), whose work, as noted above, was done in the early 1930s and was directed by Johnson.

Also, it is not clear whether Johnson had at this time been exposed to general semantics. Moeller (1975: p. 74) reports that Johnson was introduced to *Science and Sanity* and to Korzybski's Chicago institute in 1936. However, Korzybski's book was published in 1933, and the tenor of this 1934 narrative by Johnson had an unmistakable general semantics aura. He used the term "label" several times and made the point that parents' use of the label "stuttering" would sensitize their attention to the child's speech, increase their own concern about it, and energize their (misguided and complicating) efforts to help the child. Whatever the source of his ideas, he clearly felt sufficiently bold about the position he was constructing that he began this 1934 narrative with the following unwarranted contention:

It appears fairly certain that if parents and teachers could avoid certain mistakes in the training of children there would be very few stutterers. Contrary to beliefs that have persisted for centuries, modern scientific studies indicate that stuttering is not caused to a very significant degree by inherited physical abnormality, nor by injuries and diseases, but mainly by unfortunate policies and practices in home and school. (p. 3)

He went on to say that when a mother brings her child to the clinic for help with stuttering, the statements and general behavior of the mother are more important than those of the child, since "the causes of stuttering will usually be found in her."

The immediately preceding material stands as clear testimony to Johnson's remarkable presumption. There were absolutely no "modern scientific studies," then, nor have there been at any time since, to support any of these contentions. At best, he had probably seen, in the findings and notations being gathered by Davis (see above), certain bits of data that fit his preconceptions, which he then elaborated into these unfounded, doctrinaire assertions.

THE CALL OF THE WORD

Johnson first mentioned general semantics in a narrative "written late in 1936 or in the spring of 1937," but not published until 1955, when it appeared as Chapter 43 in *Stuttering in Children and Adults*, a compilation of papers associated almost entirely with his activity at Iowa.[6] He stated in a footnote that the content of Chapter 43 "reflects particularly the initial influence of general semantics on the writer's thinking about the clinical problem of stuttering, consequent to the study of Alfred Korzybski's *Science and Sanity*" (Johnson 1955: p. 432). This statement strongly suggests that he had studied Korzybski's work prior to 1936.

Then, in 1938, the term "evaluation" was introduced into his discourse on stuttering as a formal feature of the nomenclature (Johnson 1938). In this narrative, which reads more like a speech than a formal manuscript, there was again no citation of reference sources. However, the Korzybskian influence is clear; the reader should recall that "label" and "evaluation" were focal terms in Korzybski's writings. In this publication Johnson first gave some general account of how the evaluations a person makes of events or circumstances influence how he deals with them. Soon this theme became focused on speaking, and specifically on the claim that, via parental disapproval, the child comes to negatively evaluate his own hesitant speech—including evaluations of tongue pressure and the like [*sic*] — which leads to a "spiral effect" of continual worsening. Except for the introduction of and focus on the word "evaluation" this narrative clearly corresponds to the content in the 1934 pamphlet.

Actually it is relatively immaterial whether or not Johnson was familiar with general semantics by 1934. Its prominent features were at least consonant with what Johnson wished to believe, and he became completely absorbed in its catechism. As Moeller (1976) related, Johnson incorporated the tenets of general semantics into his courses as soon as he was named to the faculty in 1937. Moreover, he quickly developed an entire course devoted to general semantics (the first such course in any university), which he taught from 1939 until 1964, the year before his death. By this time he was among the few remaining advocates still left over from the days, almost twenty years earlier, when general semantics had bloomed and soon faded. Moeller summarizes:

From this time (1936-37) onward, through his entire academic career, Johnson brought coursework in general semantics to his students, and used a general semantics orientation in his counseling activities, public lectures, and writing. (p. 74)

His complete immersion[7] in the notions highlighted in general semantics, and in the claim embodied in linguistic relativity, is reflected succinctly in his remark that "we create our world linguistically, how else?" (p. 105)

General semantics had supplied Johnson with the means for dispelling his lifelong curse. Moreover, the curse could be made to vanish through a medium he had come to know well—the use of words. Armed with the notions of "evaluation" and that the world is structured through "labels," stuttering could be repudiated! One could explain that there is really no such thing as stuttering, certainly not in the sense of a constitutional condition, an organic anomaly, an abnormality! Stuttering would be simply a process product, occasioned by unfortunate external circumstances. The individual's role would be only that of faulty learning, which, moreover, was largely forced upon him by the untoward circumstances in which he was enmeshed. Thus, stuttering could be explained as essentially a psychological mistake.

The next step was to show that stuttering really *is* psychological in nature, that it is acquired by essentially normal individuals through a learning process.

ON TO S-R

In 1937 Johnson launched a series of articles head-titled "Studies in the Psychology of Stuttering." This head title clearly mimicked the Travis series (see earlier), yet at the same time announced that the purview of this series was to be psychological only. It was the harbinger of a more fundamental, but unspoken, change: thenceforth stuttering would no longer be considered a speech disorder but, instead, a psychological problem.[8] This material change in conception and emphasis, and its sweeping progression, are reflected dramatically in the two curves of Figure 6.1.

There were nineteen papers in this Johnson series, all done under his direction, most of them as M.A. theses. All were published in the *Journal of Speech Disorders* between 1937 and 1944. The significance of these studies lies in the fact that they are essentially position statements rather than instances of scientific inquiry. They have little scientific merit and, far from contributing any real substance to an understanding of stuttering, have served only to perpetuate questionable old claims or to generate new ones even more questionable. In most of these reports the methodology ranges from poor to suspect, and they are typically contaminated by unwarranted interpretations of results.

Among these studies four were addressed to the topic of "distraction" and another four to the claim of "expectancy." Both of these notions are derived directly from testimonials, which have little more than folklore status. In fact, the former is logically insupportable; the latter is readily contradictable by even simple clinical assessment. Four more of these reports were addressed to "(external) cues associated with stuttering," these studies being designed to yield findings amenable to claims for learning. The remainder of the reports in this series dealt with two topics that were to play a very substantial role in the subsequent history of stuttering: the "adaptation effect" and the so-called "consistency effect."

These "effects" refer to two dimensions of findings derived from the same experimental procedure. The data underpinning these two "phenomena" were obtained by having individual stutterers read the same material several times in succession, in the course of which a record was kept of the stutter occurrences in each successive reading.

One of these two phenomena, the "adaptation effect," reflected the observation that the amount of stuttering decreased over the course of the sequential readings. The other phenomenon, which was called the "consistency effect," was based on the observation that, from reading to reading in a series, there was a tendency for stutters to recur at the same places. *Tendency* is a most critical word in this description. That the noted recurrence[9] is only a tendency is regularly ignored in the substantial writings that have centered around this observation and its repeated demonstration. In these writings one never finds an admission that this tendency for stutter recurrence is intermittent, modest at best, and certainly far less frequent than one should expect if stimulus-response "bonds" are the basis for it.

Nevertheless, these two phenomena became the essential vehicles for making and pressing the claim that stuttering is "learned behavior." Both phenomena were reported in the first paper of the series (Johnson and Knott 1937), although the authors addressed relatively more attention to the matter of stutter recurrence. They explained this recurrence tendency "by assuming that at these loci there are stimuli to which the stutterer reacts, and that his reactions either precipitate, or are, the stuttering which results."

Stimulus-response had been inserted into stuttering and, in some form, it would be assiduously retained there for the rest of the century. From the time this first article in the series was published, both of these phenomena were touted as evidence that stuttering is learned. Moreover, the stature of these phenomena became aggrandized as time passed; they were acclaimed in many sources as "basic phenomena" in understanding the nature of stuttering. Although "adaptation" and "consistency," as they came to be known, were the fulcrum for leverage to claim that stuttering is learned, the other reports in this series played supporting, even though minor, roles.

The eventual massive edifice of stuttering as "learned behavior" was constructed from the base set up by this series of little studies; studies that were thin in rationale, design, method, results, and statistical treatment but, in contrast, very thick with conjecture, assumption, and interpretation.

The "Consistency" Effect

The observation of stutter recurrence, initially identified as a "tendency" for loci to be the same, soon became a "marked tendency." Then it was "consistent." Very soon thereafter it became "the consistency effect," and before long was fully reified as "consistency"! Clearly, the Korzybskian insistence on careful use of words was not going to be applied uniformly.[10] In fact, this label ("consistency") affords a prime example of how words were used in Johnson's formulations and in those of his followers. Recurrence of stuttering, even in the highly artificial circumstances of repeatedly reading the same material — which, it must be noted, is the ideal circumstance for engendering this phenomenon — did not show then, nor has it ever shown, the degree of regularity that one would expect when some event is described as "consistent." The phenomenon has never been more than an unclear *tendency* for recurrence. To have divined S-R bonds in these data was pure conjecture. To persist in claiming recurrence as "consistency," and to then carry this further by contending that it shows learning, is simply bland recitation of monolithic doctrine.

Introducing stimulus-response into the literature of stuttering via the recurrence findings was a verbal tour de force. To speak of stutter recurrence in terms of S-R lent this little report an aura of scientific inquiry, insinuating the brand of objective behavioral science verbalized by J. B. Watson. However, the foundation of Johnson's entire orientation was *introspection,* which, as pointed out in Chapter 5, was emphatically disavowed by S-R psychology. This contradiction was never even noted, let alone resolved, by those who have pressed the claim of stuttering as "learned behavior."

Contrary to what Johnson and his followers have contended, stuttering recurrence has no credible connection whatsoever with learning theory. The only connection — a very gossamer verbal one — is simply that Johnson called stuttering a response.[11] Of course, in an S-R formulation, if there is a response there must then also be a stimulus; and for any particular response there is a stimulus that is necessary and adequate to evoke that response. However, there was not then, nor has there ever been since that time, in any of the voluminous treatment of stuttering as "learned behavior," any demonstration or credible objective evidence of a repeatable stimulus that is necessary and adequate to elicit a stutter.

It is particularly relevant to note here that, prior to the time of this first report in the Studies in the Psychology of Stuttering series, Johnson had directed a study (Johnson and Brown 1935) whose findings not only bore directly on the matter of stutter recurrence but also were especially pertinent to the issue of stuttering as a response to stimuli. The essential objective of that study was to examine the frequency of stutter occurrence relative to the various phonemes of English, an inquiry mounted to study the notion of "difficult sounds." The notion of difficult sounds is also a direct expression of testimony, given by some stutterers, that they have particular trouble with certain sounds. Occasionally, although not routinely, a stutterer may express this claim in terms of fearing these sounds. Sometimes the complaint of difficulty is expressed in terms of certain words in which case the focus is actually on the initial sound of the words in complaint. The difficult sounds/words complaint is a testimony that is very often repeated in the literature and is highly favored in accounts of stuttering that emphasize the purported role of fear.

The data of the 1935 study by Johnson and Brown were obtained from seventy stutterers who individually read five different passages twice, with a time interval between the two readings. A major finding of the study, which received considerable attention in many later writings, was that the data compiled for these stutterers *as a group* revealed a clear overall rank order of "difficulty" of sounds. However, it was not recognized that these group-based data were not particularly relevant to the notion of "difficult sounds." The original publication, as well as many subsequent publications referring to this study as illustration, ignored the very important fact that the claim of "difficult sounds" is an entirely individual matter. Thus, data bearing on this issue are pertinent only for stutterers as individuals. Nonetheless, the group-based findings collected in this study were assumed to be, and accepted as, evidence supporting the "difficult sounds" belief.

Although these group-based data were not actually pertinent to the question they were presumed to answer, they did have other import for the study of stuttering. This matter will be considered briefly later in this chapter, in a section addressed to the evidence suggesting language factors in the disorder, and again more fully in Chapter 9.

The other major finding of this 1935 study, one that was highly pertinent to the matter of sound "difficulty" for individual stutterers, received only passing interest. This neglected finding was that the rank orderings of sound difficulty made by individual stutterers varied in certain important respects from the group-based results. Further, and of special pertinence to the beliefs regarding an individual stutterer's "difficult" or "feared" sounds, was the evidence that individual stutterers also varied in terms of their own "difficulty" rankings of sounds reported for the two separate readings (N.B., of the *same* material). That is, there was considerable individual variation in the consistency of "difficulty" ranking given various sounds, by the same individual, in the two readings — two readings in which the same sounds occurred in identical loci and proportions in the material read. These individually based findings, the only ones pertinent to the question raised, thus constituted evidence that clearly contradicted the belief in "difficult sounds," and especially in S-R terms.

Beyond the issue of difficult or feared sounds, the data for individual stutterers also bear pointedly on the belief that stuttering is credibly explained in terms of stimulus and response. If an S-R account is viable, one should expect that speech sounds would be foremost among the presumed stimuli for "the stuttering response." Now an S-R account of "difficult sounds" is plausible only in respect to individuals. However, the data from this study by Johnson and Brown gave no reason whatsoever to claim that the difficult sounds for any individual stutterer could be considered as stimuli for stutter occurrence. Not only did individual stutterers' rankings of sound difficulty differ in the two readings but, further, among the individual stutterers' rankings of those sounds that each stutterer did claim were "difficult," the median percentage of actual stuttering on one's "most difficult" sound (the sounds individual stutterers ranked highest in difficulty) was only 18.3 percent! An account in terms of S-R bonds would require that this value be at least close to, if not actually, 100 percent. As noted above, such matters have been consistently ignored, not only by Johnson but by many who have accepted and pursued the theme of stuttering as "learned behavior."

The Adaptation Effect

Johnson's interpretive treatment of this other phenomenon, the progressive decrease in stuttering over repeated readings of the same material, was as expansive and as flawed as his treatment of stutter recurrence. This phenomenon of decrease was first called the "adaptation effect" in the sixth report of the "Studies in the Psychology of Stuttering" series (Johnson and Millsapps 1937), and the term dominated the title of the thirteenth report (Johnson and Inness 1939). Its stature as an important phenomenon was thenceforth established.

From the beginning the adaptation effect was assumed to represent unlearning of the (stuttering) "response" and, in this literature on stuttering, "adaptation" has been used routinely with that assumption. However, the use of "adaptation" in this regard is not correct or appropriate. In the psychological literature this term is not synonymous with "unlearning," especially in regard to motor acts. Rather, it has the meaning of "habituation," "adjusting," "getting used to."[12]

Johnson's use of the term "adaptation" undoubtedly was borrowed directly from a pertinent source he well knew at the time, but did not credit. In 1934-1935 a study had been conducted at Iowa by Van Riper (Van Riper and Hull 1955)[13] that was designed to assess "the effect of certain situations" on stutter occurrence. Van Riper had found that the amount of stuttering decreased under several of the different circumstances investigated in that study, and these decreases were referred to as "adaptation." Here the term was used in its proper sense, as reflected in other phrases used by Van Riper, such as "familiarity with" and "adjusted to." Although this study was not cited by Johnson and Knott (1937)[14] as the origin of the "adaptation effect," Moeller (1975: p. 76) reported that many years later Knott had acknowledged it as the source.

It seems highly likely that Johnson, personally motivated to explain stuttering as an acquired problem, either had recalled or had clearly in mind the findings obtained two years earlier by Van Riper and Hull, especially that an adaptation curve plotted for their data had some resemblance to a typical extinction (unlearning) curve. Curves of the latter type were illustrated regularly in sources dealing with the psychology of learning. Evidently, noting the apparent similarity in the two graphic displays (Van Riper's adaptation curve, compared to the extinction curves plotted from results in the psychological laboratory),[15] Johnson inferred, or saw the opportunity to claim, that the processes represented by these curves were the same. Moreover, such linkage carried the prestige of associating stuttering adaptation studies with respectable, well-established laboratory research in psychology. In sources wherein Johnson thereafter recited his claim that stuttering is "learned behavior," he regularly referred to such similarity and, when doing so, invoked images of the psychological laboratory.[16]

The notion that stuttering is "learned behavior" had been set in motion. It would gain momentum in the next few years, pushed along vigorously by myrmidons of what Hamre (1992) has appropriately named "the Iowa school" (of stuttering). The contention would expand to juggernaut proportions within a decade. This topic merits a synoptic treatment of its own, to be covered in Chapter 8.

TO NULLIFY THE GENE

With the explanation of stuttering in terms of evaluation and learning now well under way, Johnson moved to address the issue of heredity in stuttering, a matter that had been raised in many sources prior to that time and that was also of contemporary interest. Under Johnson's direction, Marcella Gray (1940), another M.A. candidate, assessed the information available on two branches of a family in which there was a history of stuttering. One branch, living in Iowa, had considerably more stutterers in the fourth and fifth generation than did the branch living in Kansas. Fourth and fifth generation members of the Iowa branch were found to have more awareness of stuttering and used the word "stuttering" more often than did members of the Kansas branch. This finding was used to explain that the different incidence of stuttering in the two branches of the family represented a "social heredity." In this account, the occurrence of stuttering in family lines was explained as the result of (1) a persisting concern about fluency; (2) misevaluation of normal nonfluency; and (3) use of the label "stuttering." All of these presumed factors were said to be aspects of a family ambience that was passed on, essentially verbally, from one generation to the next, thereby explaining why stuttering recurred in family lines.

Space does not permit a review of the many limitations of this study by Gray, and especially the account of its findings. Among its astounding superficialities, a clear ignorance of the simplest genetic principles is only the most dramatic one. Yet, at least until well into the 1980s, many persons evidently continued to accept this account as credible and meaningful, as reflected in the number of letters that made a point of bringing the Gray reference to the attention of an outstanding human geneticist who had undertaken study of stuttering in family lines (Kidd 1977, 1984).[17]

GOING PUBLIC

A Letter Home

In 1941 Johnson carried forward the theme developed in his 1934 and 1938 publications,[18] expanding it into a lengthy "Open Letter to the Mother of a Stuttering Child." This missive, which is undoubtedly his most widely read publication, appeared initially in a lay magazine, *You and Your Child*. Soon thereafter "several hundred mimeographed copies were distributed chiefly to parents, teachers and speech correctionists."[19] In the next few years the letter appeared in several sources. It was printed in pamphlet form by Interstate Printers and Publishers — and remained continuously available through them from 1947 until 1986, the year their Speech and Hearing line was sold. The extent of the letter's dissemination is revealed in records available at Interstate press which show that between 1958 and 1986, 212,829 copies were printed by that source alone. The letter also was reproduced in all three editions of *Speech Handicapped School Children* (Johnson et al. 1948, 1956, 1967) and reprinted in the *Journal of Speech and Hearing Disorders* in 1949 (as the lead article;

Vol. 14, pp. 3-8) and in *Crippled Child Magazine* in 1950 (Vol. 28, pp. 7-9). It was also distributed by the National Society for Crippled Children and Adults.

In the "Open Letter" Johnson cast the content of the earlier two articles in a more personal form and laid particular emphasis on warning parents (of stutterers) of the dangers of *evaluation* of speech and the damaging effect of using *the label* "stuttering." Johnson spelled out in some detail his notion of how these errors were "the method used by parents . . . for making practically any child into a stutterer."[20] He closed with several suggestions for management which, although including a few that were pertinent, were generally either palliative or presumptuous. His last suggestion to parents — "Be as friendly and considerate toward your own child as you would be toward a house guest"[21] — conveys the general tenor of the letter. Although he acknowledged that the suggestion "may sound quite drastic," he nonetheless believed it to be "within the bounds of reason."

Certain sources have referred to this missive as "that famous letter," and in terms of the breadth of its dissemination and the extent to which it was touted, it might well be so described. However, in respect to its content and its effect, it is more properly described as "that *in*famous letter." Johnson's statements openly blamed parents (especially mothers) for the fact that their child stuttered. Such an accusation in itself, if justified, may not necessarily be reprehensible. But it was unconscionable to have presented this accusation as established, substantive fact based on a broad, sound base of research that had been scientifically executed, carefully analyzed, and objectively interpreted. This most certainly was not the case.

Not since the days of Dieffenbach (see Chapter 4) had supposition and assumption been so obtrusively imposed on the field of stuttering, or on the general public, as a sweeping answer to the question of stuttering. The surgery episode, however, was at least short-lived, due in part to the reaction, criticism, and denunciation that came from within the medical profession. In indelible contrast, no vigorous voice of reason was raised to object to the contentions in the "Open Letter" nor to seriously question the "evaluation" conjecture itself. Quite to the contrary, the letter and its message were widely distributed through the agency of many practitioners and leaders in the field. On those grounds alone many individuals must share in the calumny of that letter. Moreover, instead of being challenged, the "evaluation" conjecture was at least tacitly encouraged to live on, to gather momentum, to cast more shadows, and to extend its confusions.

Seek and You Will Find

About this time, one of Johnson's students, having been assigned the task of studying stuttering among the Bannock and Shoshone Indians of southern Idaho, reported being "unable to find any stuttering Indians." Subsequently, another student, J. Snidecor, was sent to continue the investigation. The ensuing report led to a pair of articles by Johnson (1944a, 1944b) head-titled "The

Indians Have No Word for It." The content of these articles soon reappeared, under the same title, as Chapter 17 in *People in Quandaries: The Semantics of Personal Adjustment* (Johnson 1946). This book, addressed essentially to a lay audience, was, so the author said, also "doubtless of professional interest to workers and students in the fields of psychiatry and clinical and abnormal psychology" (p. xi).

As revealed in the subtitle, this book was a general semantics statement. In the preface Johnson acknowledged the extensive influence of Korzybski, which is clearly reflected in every chapter.[22] The book has chapters on "analysis of the process of communication," "the language of maladjustment," and "methods of personality reeducation" — all from "a semantic point of view." In its early pages Johnson enlarged upon the Korzybski complaint about Aristotle and devoted considerable space to criticism of the purported problem of "either-or." However, later in the book (p. 451) he clearly was not concerned by the contradiction posed in his emphatic assertion that "a clear distinction must be made between non-fluency and stuttering."[23]

Johnson also had quite a bit to say about the nature of science and its methods, placing emphasis on such matters as careful observation, objectivity, lack of bias, and proper use of words. However, as revealed below, in discussion of stuttering among Indians in the same source, his expatiation on science and its methods was even more clearly an instance of doctrinaire hypocrisy.

Chapter 12 of *People in Quandaries*, "The Indians Have No Word for It," was presented as a showcase illustration of semantic potency, a compelling testimony to the formidable power of labels, revealed dramatically in a supposedly carefully implemented study of stuttering. In developing his discussion in this work, Johnson stated (p. 442) that, in all the sources of relevant information known to him[24] there were "for all practical purposes" no stutterers among North American Indians who lived in circumstances unaffected by "the white man's influence." He reported that in a "thorough investigation, interviewing several hundred Indians" Snidecor had

learned in the main two things. First, these Indians had *no word for stuttering* in their language. . . . Second, their standards of child care and training appeared to be extraordinarily lax in comparison with our own. With respect to speech in particular, it seemed to be that every Indian child was regarded as a satisfactory or normal speaker, regardless of the manner in which he spoke. (Johnson 1946: p. 443)

Actually, Snidecor (1945) listed as his first two findings (1) little effort to change native handedness, and (2) low incidence of birth injuries, and that the birth-injured did not survive. His third item was somewhat like the one Johnson listed as second, but phrased in more general terms. It was Snidecor's last item that Johnson not only put in first place, but also emphasized. Clearly, Johnson's persisting personal agenda on the nature of stuttering determined not only which findings would be reported but, even more remarkable, the degree of importance to be assigned to each finding that survived the sifting.

By 1954, at least, some pretty definitive information was at hand regarding stuttering in other cultures. Kluckhohn (1954: p. 944) reported that he had been unable to find any instances of a culture having no stutterers, which suggested to him that the disorder is "due to biological or idiosyncratic factors in all cultures." Although this observation was made by a prominent anthropologist and appeared in a source widely read at the time, it went unheeded by those who followed the Iowa school or were under its influence.

The claim about the creative potency of a word for stuttering would continue to be pursued, into the present day, by the devout of the Iowa school. It has also found acceptance among many others who are somehow unable to recognize the superficiality and hollowness of this contention. In addition, it would eventually turn up as the font for the sociological concepts of "secondary deviance," "societal reaction," and "labelling" theory. These matters will be addressed in Chapter 8.

EARLY "LANGUAGE FACTORS"

Having reached the mid-1940s in this historical review, it is appropriate to note an occurrence that would eventually offer something substantial in the groping toward an understanding of stuttering. Between 1935 and 1945 several studies, done by various investigators, yielded data pertinent to stutter occurrence in regard to various aspects of the spoken word.[25] The initial study in this line (Johnson and Brown 1935), addressed to phonetic factors, was discussed briefly earlier in this chapter because of its relevance to the stimulus-response context. Seven subsequent articles by Brown, published between 1937 and 1945, reported findings from his doctoral dissertation (at Iowa), which had extended this line of inquiry into other aspects of the spoken word. Among several other studies of "language factors" that appeared in this era, the reports by Brown are the most well known.

The findings of all these early studies (Brown's and the others) showed clearly that stutter occurrence is related to various readily identifiable features of oral language expression. However, the significance of these findings in terms of their own *linguistic* substance was ignored. The initial, and principal, authors reporting the study of language factors in stuttering (Brown, with Johnson)[26] were clearly eager to account for the findings in terms of stutterers' reactions. Therefore, proceeding from their assumptions that stuttering is based in apprehension and reaction, they developed the explanation that each of the linguistic features revealed in these works embodied some form of "prominence" for stutterers. The essence of this interpretation was that the stutterer evaluates these certain features of the language (those marked by stutter events) as especially important to communication; therefore they have prominence, which is why they are stuttered. Purportedly, the stutterer reacts to such prominences with apprehension, which causes him to struggle to perform them well. This apprehension and struggle, then, were claimed to be what was "called" stuttering.

Many years later it would eventually be determined that a linguistically relevant account of all these early (as well as later) findings offers a more parsimonious and credible analysis of the language factors (Wingate 1988). However, in this early period the interest in language factors in stuttering faded quickly, evidently because it was widely accepted as offering additional evidence of the psychological nature of stuttering. Interest in this area of inquiry would not surface again for twenty years. The later developments will be discussed in Chapter 9.

TO ENHANCE THE VIEW

The subsequent notable publications in which Johnson was importantly involved were published over ten years later (Johnson et al. 1959; Johnson 1961a).[27] The earlier of these two publications, titled *The Onset of Stuttering*, is the major work. In fact, as reported by Moeller (1975: p. 133), Johnson regarded this publication as his magnum opus.

The Onset of Stuttering is a report based on information collected from a number of sources (twelve associates are listed), but the interpretation of the findings and the narrative material in the book were written by Johnson.[28] The parameters of the study focused on comparisons of (initially) 150 "allegedly" stuttering and 150 "allegedly" nonstuttering children and their families. The former group of children were alleged (by parents) to have begun to stutter approximately eighteen months prior to the study. The objective of the undertaking is best summarized in the author's own words:

The program of research reported here has been concerned with this basic question: In what form, at what time, under what conditions, and for whom does the problem of stuttering arise? (p. 261)

To this end extensive data were collected on many psychological and sociological variables as well as some medical information relative to both groups. There was a heavy emphasis, of course, on matters relevant to speech, especially for the stuttering youngsters. The extent of the collected data is reflected in the fact that 308 of the book's 509 pages are taken up with appendices and tables. Most of these data were obtained through interview.

The general format of the study was to collect relevant data on two occasions: a first interview, and a follow-up, somewhat over two years later. On the second occasion certain direct records were obtained, most importantly samples of the children's speech.

As one proceeds through the generally ponderous, and often convoluted narrative, one is almost certain to gain the impression of being drawn inexorably toward an inescapable conclusion — one in which stuttering will be found to originate from negative parental "evaluation" and the unwarranted use of a label. This impression is confirmed in the author's final summation:

The data indicate that in the cases investigated the problem was to be described, at its point of origin, not primarily by reference to nonfluent speech, as such, but by reference mainly to an interaction between a listener and a speaker in which the listener made a distinctive perceptual and judgmental reaction to the speaker's nonfluencies. The speaker was characteristically a child between three and four years of age, and the listener was nearly always one of the child's parents, usually the mother. The nonfluencies, as reported, ranged from slight and decidedly ordinary to complex and unusual, and were in general impressively similar to those repetitions, hesitations, and other imperfections of fluency that were reported as having occurred in the speech of a control group of children of comparable age who were not regarded as stutterers. With few if any significant exceptions, the circumstances under which the parents first regarded these nonfluencies as stuttering appeared to be ordinary and unremarkable. What appears to have been crucial was the fact that the parents were motivated to evaluate the nonfluencies as unacceptable, or distressing, to classify them as "stuttering" and to react, nonverbally as a rule but verbally in some cases, to them and to the child accordingly. (p. 261)

However, a reasonably careful and objective reading of the text should lead one to quite a different conclusion. An overriding quality of the narrative is the pervasiveness of its presumption, an aura only hinted at by the frequency with which the word "presumably" is used.[29] But there are also more obvious faults; only the more dramatic need be noted here.

Characteristic of Johnson's writings are verbal maneuvers by which he could avoid confronting matters that contravened his position. One typical maneuver was the use of gloss references. For example, here, as elsewhere, he repeatedly used class terms in an apparent effort to avoid or ignore important distinctions that exist within the classes. This maneuver was pointedly evident especially in the regular use of "repetitions" and "hesitations"[30] to imply no difference in contexts wherein actual differences within these general categories clearly were found. In direct contrast to his misleading use of terms, Johnson felt free to dismiss certain aspects of parental report by questioning "the descriptive care exercised by the informants who used these words" (p. 137).

Other contradictions emerge in the narrative, often spaced at some distance. For example: "At the beginning of this period (the eighteen months before the first interview) the speech of the two groups of children was presumably more or less similar, so far as can be determined from the data presented" (p. 218). However, eleven pages later (p. 229) he revealed that the data showed sound repetitions, syllable repetitions, and prolongations to have been reported significantly more often for the stuttering children.

Sometimes either contradiction or confusion appeared in immediate sequence, as revealed in the following:

Once the parents had decided the child was beginning to stutter, about five months passed, in the average case, before they arrived at the judgment that the child had a "speech problem." The problem "came on gradually." . . .

In general, the beginning of the problem was reported as a perceptual and judgmental reaction to the child's speech, nearly always by one or both parents, usually the mother. (p. 230)

Transparent bias emerges in certain presumptions that lead to unsupportable interpretations. For instance: Johnson claimed (p. 218) that in the eighteen months prior to the initial interview, the "allegedly" stuttering children had been "subjected to varying degrees of negatively evaluative (parental) reactions to their speech." Some pages later he contended that these parental reactions colored the parent-child relations and that

while in most cases the effects seemed to be subtle, and some children were not affected in any clearly discernible ways, it appeared that in most cases the first slow turnings of a vicious circle had taken place by the time of the initial interview. (p. 231)

Thus recurs the "vicious spiral" theme so popular among those who want "reaction" to be a central feature in stuttering. According to the vicious spiral (or circle) theme, stuttering purportedly becomes progressively worse through a reaction-struggle-reaction process. However, there was certainly no evidence for it in the information collected in this study. At the time of the follow-up interview over two years later, only 4 of the 118 children (only 3 percent!) then participating were found to be worse. In contrast, 43 (36 percent) were no longer stuttering, and 61 (another 52 percent) had improved. Although Johnson implied that the improvement reflected the "counseling" that was (inexplicably) conveyed at the time of the very brief initial interview, this was an entirely presumptuous and unsupportable guess. It is of particular interest that (1) Johnson did not speak of this improvement as "recovery" or "remission;" (2) the evidence for spontaneous improvement was ignored, even though comments from at least 48 parents clearly indicated spontaneous remission; (3) the entire matter of improvement received minimal attention in the narrative; and (4) reference to either improvement or remission does not appear in the index.

Another major flaw overshadowing this study, as well as its companion piece, which would appear in 1961, is the list of fluency irregularities[31] used as the descriptive reference in both publications. This flaw, and its distorting influence, would be perpetuated indefinitely through the continued use of the list in many subsequent investigations, studies addressed not only to comparison of stuttered and normal speech samples but to normal speech as well. In these subsequent studies most of the authors have accepted the adequacy of the list without question or reservation. However, the list has a number of serious limitations, only the most fundamental of which will be noted here.[32]

This list, claimed by Johnson to be a "normative" reference, is by no means normative in the established, standard sense of the term. The list was not developed from the study of an *unselected* population. It was based on speech samples obtained from 100 adult normal speakers and 100 adult stutterers — the subjects who participated in the study that led to his 1961 publication addressed to "disfluency."[33] This supposedly normative reference is therefore grossly contaminated. One will not find, in any area of scientifically respectable investigation, a *normative* reference base built upon data obtained from a sample population that includes cases even suspected of being *ab*normal in some way that might vitiate a truly normative representation. In glaring contrast to such standard procedure, fully half of the purportedly normative population in this Johnson study had not only been determined to be abnormal, but abnormal specifically in regard to the very dimension under investigation!

The grossly improper population sampling that constituted the reference base for this study and the introduction of the term "disfluency" in his interpretation of its results, have created and perpetuated many unnecessary and obstructive problems and much controversy over the years since its publication. It is pertinent to note here that the word "disfluency" is a special-interest, ad hoc neologism that epitomizes the Johnson rhetoric. Standard, thoroughly comprehensive dictionaries, including the 12-volume Oxford English Dictionary, contain many words having the prefix "dis-," including some that are quite unusual, but "disfluency" is nowhere among them. The word was created by Johnson himself (Van Riper 1992b), almost certainly as a gloss under which "stuttering" could be obscured by melding it with the kinds of departures from literal fluency that typify normal speech. Many of the latter type were found, of course, in the two studies in focus here since they included normal speech samples and abnormal ones in the same base. With this contaminated "normative" population mixing abnormal with normal kinds of irregularities in fluency was made much easier. To extend and complete this distortion, the term "disfluency" has thenceforth been insinuated into the literature as the euphemistic substitute for "stuttering."[34]

Important findings relevant to the kinds of irregularities in fluency that are found in ordinary, normal speech were extant well before *Onset* was published. The new field of psycholinguistics had begun to emerge in the early 1950s, and findings specific to fluency were available in the early reports of Goldman-Eisler (1952, 1954, 1955, 1957) and Mahl (1956a, 1956b, 1956c). Even earlier, studies addressed to various aspects of spoken language contained relevant useful material (for instance: Baker 1948; Balken and Masserman 1940; Newman 1941; Sanford 1942). Moreover, data on certain dimensions of fluency (and these, significantly, were relative to children) had been in the literature for a long time (Adams 1932; Fisher 1932, 1934; McCarthy 1930). In fact, such data were yielded by a study reported even earlier (Smith 1926) that had been published, moreover, as a University of Iowa Child Welfare monograph!

Johnson's final publication in this line (Johnson 1961a) was, as mentioned above, actually an adult-level forerunner of the undertaking reported in *The Onset of Stuttering*. In the 1961 publication that reported the adult study, Johnson identified "three main purposes" of the study, the major one being "the further clarification of the fundamental nature of the problem called stuttering." As one could have predicted, he interpreted the findings to imply that stuttering "is not to be adequately identified or defined solely by reference to speech disfluency, as such" and that "variables associated with perceptual and evaluative reactions . . . are to be included." He arrived at this contention largely through two routine maneuvers. First, he minimized the highly significant differences found between stutterers and nonstutterers on the very kinds of "disfluency" that have always been the markers by which stuttering is identified: elemental repetitions and prolongations ("clonic" and "tonic"), a finding that had emerged once again in this very work. The second maneuver was to emphasize that stutterers and nonstutterers evidenced a certain amount of "overlap" in regard to several kinds of ordinary nonfluencies. This oblique, contorted interpretation of "similarity" was also emphasized in *Onset*. Of course, both of these maneuvers appear in his other writings as well.[35]

PRACTICALITIES

Johnson's position yielded little in the way of treatment principles or techniques having demonstrable merit. Here too one finds contradiction. Although in one source (Johnson 1956: p. 291) he recommended a form of voluntary easy repetition as a therapeutic goal, soon thereafter (Johnson 1957) he repudiated "the bounce," which was essentially identical.[36] In the former source (Johnson 1956) the commendable suggestions made for dealing directly with the stutter were simply techniques of long standing in stuttering therapy. His essential management objective, for all age levels, was to persuade stutterers, and parents, that the only actual problem lay in how they thought about speech. For older stutterers the approach focused on their "inferences" and "assumptions" about what was occurring at the times they *thought* they stuttered.[37] For child stutterers the method was to "counsel" parents and teachers. The invariant theme of such counseling was a reiteration of his standard interpretation, substance that has been highlighted in the present chapter.

EPILOGUE

It seems appropriate to end this chapter in the same contextual framework with which it was begun — in reference to the creator of this sophistic construction, the man himself.

Moeller (1972) tried to characterize Johnson in a kind of retrospective vignette. She referred to his "twin careers in speech pathology and general semantics, and in his activity as a clinical psychologist," and mentioned that Johnson, at least on one occasion, referred to himself as a communicologist. "Perhaps," said Moeller, "he was neither speech pathologist nor semanticist. Surely he was not primarily a clinician" (p. ix).

One must add to this characterization that he also was certainly not primarily a scientist. The extent of his direct participation in research is questionable[38] and, as exemplified in the course of this chapter, his writings consistently reveal characteristics that are fundamentally contrary to a truly scientific orientation, such as personal involvement, persistent bias, limited objectivity, imprecision, selective attention to findings, supposition, presumption, and unsupportable inferences and interpretation. The view he constructed was a highly personal one, created provincially at the far periphery of scientific inquiry.

Considering the nature of his writings, his skill in verbal structuring, the intent within his message, and his evident success in persuasion, he is probably best identified as an accomplished rhetorician. In concurrence with this description, the formulation he constructed is appropriately identified as an exemplary sophism.[39]

NOTES

1.   Someone well acquainted with Johnson during those early years at Iowa once told me that Johnson "just *hated* his stuttering." *Because I Stutter* was, in a quite literal sense, the *Mein Kampf* of stuttering, not only in terms of a personal report but also in regard to what it portended.

2.   Or "before stuttering meant anything in particular" to him. See earlier paragraph.

3.   More needs to be said about the role of paradoxes in the account of stuttering propounded by the Iowa school. To be taken up later, in Chapter 8.

4.   Johnson was undeniably a skillful as well as a prolific writer. In *Because I Stutter* (p. 47) he noted that "at an early age I found I could express the quality and quantity of my mind rather satisfactorily by writing." Also, note that his early preparation in college was as an English major.

5.   That is, sources other than his own predilections, which were based in his personal motivations.

6.   The bulk of which were theses done under his direction.

7.   His immersion is reflected principally in his unrelenting commitment to the movement which, beyond its continual application to stuttering, resulted also in his own sizeable book on the subject (Johnson 1946), his participation in establishing *ETC., A Review of General Semantics* in 1943, and service on its editorial board until 1958.

8.   Although it was to be presented as a rather everyday, normal, or surface kind of psychological problem; that is, not a psychodynamic type of disturbance, with its deep nonconscious stirrings, forbidden impulses, and conflicts.

9.   Was initially, and always has been in the many subsequent replications!

10.   Nor (the temptation is too great) consistently!

11.   The reader would soon tire of a notation made to every clear instance of Johnson's own use of "labels" that certainly did not meet the criteria of "extensional" form.

12. This error provides another instance of the hypocrisy underlying the claimed ideal of "careful use of words" touted in Johnson's writings.

13. The study finally appeared in print in the Johnson and Leutenegger (1955) compilation. In a brief historical footnote regarding the study (ibid., p. 199) Johnson tells that the Van Riper study "was probably the first investigation of adaptation in stuttering" that "anticipated later research." Although this statement implies a direct thematic relationship to Johnson's use, and meaning, of adaptation, Van Riper's work was in quite a different vein.

14. Nor at any later time. Although notation of the Van Riper and Hull study appeared as a reference in Johnson and Millsapps (1937) and in Johnson and Inness (1939), it was mentioned only in the sense that Van Riper and Hull had "also found" the adaptation effect.

15. Actually, there are a number of significant ways in which the typical stuttering adaptation curve and the extinction curve differ. (See Wingate 1966a, 1966b.)

16. See, for instance, *Speech Handicapped School Children*, p. 209 (Johnson et al. 1948).

17. Johnson repeated the "social heredity" notion in other places (e.g., Johnson et al. 1959; Johnson et al. 1967). The Gray study has been mentioned favorably in other sources; for instance, quite recently Bloodstein (1993) recounted it as though it had merit. For the reader interested in an extended criticism of the "social heredity" notion see Wingate (1986). The human geneticist noted here is K. K. Kidd of Yale University. In regard to the communications received in support of the Gray report, he wrote, in 1984, "Over the last twelve years I have continued to be confronted by this absurd paper" (personal correspondence).

18. See earlier in this chapter.

19. Quoted from the Editor's Note, *Journal of Speech and Hearing Disorders*, 14, 1949: p. 3.

20. In paragraph #21 of the "Open Letter."

21. From my personal and vicarious experience with parenting I would guess that anyone who has raised children should be able to appreciate what a formula for disaster this suggestion constitutes!

22. The spirit of Whorf also materializes.

23. This seems to be both the kind of hypocrisy noted by Burke (1945: Chapter 6, p. 112) and a maneuver to force an either-or choice in instances where an absolute distinction may be difficult to make. Bloodstein has noted, approvingly, in several places (e.g., 1981: p. 308) that Johnson insisted upon "a *categorical* distinction" between the two (italics added).

24. Evidently only very casual sources. Many years before, Sapir (1915) had reported stuttering as well as other speech disorders among Pacific Northwest Indians.

25. This work is summarized and discussed in Wingate 1988, Chapters 3 and 4.

26. "Authors" here refers essentially to Johnson and Brown. Johnson directed Brown's master's thesis and his doctoral dissertation, and he would almost certainly have led in the interpretation of its findings. Incidentally, Brown also stuttered.

27. *Stuttering in Children and Adults*, published in 1955 (with Leutenegger), was primarily a compilation of Iowa studies done to that time. Some of this material, relevant to the topic of *Onset*, was repeated in Johnson et al. (1959).

28. Although with the assistance of Dean Williams, a prominent figure of the Iowa school (also a stutterer) who "spent much time with the writer in discussion of the clini-

cal and theoretical implications of the data, read the manuscript critically, and contributed importantly to the point of view employed in interpretation of the findings" (W.
Johnson, *The Onset of Stuttering*, 1959: p. vi).

29. Sufficiently so that an operational definition of the presumption therein expressed
could be obtained from a tally of this word's use—especially if in regard to its appearance at points of critical issue.

30. The use of "repetitions and hesitations" in this way occurs persistently in the
writings of all associates of the Iowa school.

31. In the *Onset of Stuttering* these were called "nonfluencies." In the 1961 report
(Johnson 1961a), and from then on, the favored term was "disfluencies." See discussion
of nonfluency, disfluency, and dysfluency in Chapter 8.

32. The interested reader is referred to a detailed analysis of its inadequacies presented in Chapter 2 of Wingate 1988.

33. Johnson (1961a). This study was therefore done prior to the *Onset* study, although published later. See *The Onset of Stuttering*, p. 201.

34. Also, whether or not it was intended, additional confounding is provided by the
fact that the prefix "dis" is a homonyn of "dys," which is, significantly, its antonym.
Thus "*dis*fluency," the most general, all-inclusive reference, which by its nature incorporates all kinds of fluency irregularities, sounds the same as "*dys*fluency," which refers
only to a circumscribable subcategory consisting of fluency anomalies that are
"*ab*normal." The contrast between the two prefixes, a distinction that is made routinely
in standard dictionaries, is fully compromised in a dictionary specific to speech disorders (Nicolosi et al. 1978) wherein "disfluency" and "dysfluency" are cross-referenced
as equivalent terms. The latter distortion clearly reflects the confusion extant within the
field, wherein one not only finds, too often, "disfluency" substituted for "stuttering" but,
as well, instances of the glaringly self-contradictory "normal dysfluency."

35. In fact, they are a stock-in-trade of disciples of the Iowa school.

36. As this nickname for the technique indicates. The technique, under this name,
was actively advocated by others of his time, notably Bryngelson.

37. See "The Descriptional Principle and the Principle of Static Analysis," Chapter
43 in Johnson and Leutenegger 1955.

38. In the "Bibliography of Iowa Studies" that appears as the Appendix in Johnson
and Leutenegger (1955), Johnson's name appears in 78 references. Of these, 54 are solo
authorship; the remaining 24 are co-authored. Of the former: 1 is a letter to the editor;
2 represent his master's thesis and doctoral dissertation; 1 is a book (*Quandaries*); 26
are reviews, informational reports, reflections or philosphical statements that appear in
various sources; 24 are articles in lay magazines. Of the 24 co-authored entries; 2 are
textbooks; 2 are informational narratives; 3 are reports of research; 17 are M.A. theses
he directed. The research for the 1959 book (*Onset*), as noted within this chapter, was
done by the many "associates." The research for the 1961 publication, which bears
Johnson's name only, was evidently accomplished by several other individuals; at least a
quarter of it came from an M.A. thesis. This tally includes most of his writings; the
remainder would fit into the pattern revealed here.

39. Exemplary because it epitomizes the definition of sophism: "a clever and plausible but fallacious argument or form of reasoning, whether or not intended to deceive"
(*Webster's New World Dictionary*).

PART IV

STILL WANDERING

CHAPTER 8

The Legacy

Although Johnson's active involvement with stuttering ended in the early 1960s, his influence has persisted in a broad scope over the intervening thirty years and undoubtedly will continue into the next century. The present chapter is concerned with this legacy. There were, of course, events and developments during this era that were not, or were only minimally, influenced by the presence from Iowa; these matters will be addressed in Chapter 9.

As discussed in Chapter 6, the early decades of the century had seen, particularly in the United States, expanding claims regarding the crucial and salient role purportedly played by the environment in determining patterns of human behavior. The widening acceptance of these claims created a climate that was openly receptive to the kind of formulation devised and espoused by Johnson. It was a climate that in some circles would endure for many years.

Within this climate, as summarized in Chapter 7, Johnson's position was structured, given substance, and promulgated largely through his own efforts. Although he actively pressed these efforts personally until he died, "evaluation theory" might have faded within a reasonable length of time, as had its conceptual godfather general semantics, had it not been for several dimensions of influential support that Johnson's assertions had accrued. The most substantive source of support was the growing number of individuals within the field who came to accept his teachings to pass them on to others. The original cadre of followers consisted of graduate students who had studied under and been supervised by Johnson at Iowa. These early followers then went out into the field and carried his message abroad, gaining proselytes as the network enlarged.

Among the influences that helped to sustain and extend Johnson's beliefs, not the least was an intellectual atmosphere at Iowa that was based on pride in the uniqueness of the program and its history. This feeling, which was said to be especially keen during the 1940s and 1950s, evidently was heavy with not only a sense of achievement but of mission as well. William R. Tiffany,[1] describing in retrospect the several dimensions of this atmosphere, referred to it as "the Iowa mystique" (Moeller 1972: p. 151). Apparently Johnson, said to have been a charismatic individual, became something of a figurehead in this mystique.[2]

At the same time, Johnson's formulation itself, in substance and presentation, contained certain attractions of a kind that usually capture the credibility of at least a certain percentage of an audience. Undoubtedly the major attraction of Johnson's explanation is that it is simple in scope and structure. Overall, it makes minimal conceptual demands; anyone can quickly get the idea of the purported cause-and-effect relations and their supposed dimensions. Also, the vocabulary of its exposition undoubtedly has contributed significantly to the ease with which it has been communicated and thereby popularized. Much of the writing is vernacular in type, favoring ordinary words used casually (and cleverly, e.g., "repetitions and hesitations"). At the same time, it highlights specialized terms that not only are idiosyncratic but also have an impressively formalized ring, such as "diagnosogenic" and "semantogenic." It features claims ("at the time of the original diagnosis") that are vague, distant and un-verifiable and that, moreover, lie at the far periphery of plausibility and thereby are difficult to contradict objectively. The account offers an empathic lure, to wit: "Stuttering is what the speaker does when he (1) expects to stutter, (2) dreads doing it, and (3) reacts negatively . . . in an effort to avoid doing it" (Johnson et al. 1967: p. 240). Moreover, the appeal of this account is en-hanced by expressing it in the form of a brief, catchy, slogan-like expression: "Stuttering is what a person does trying not to stutter again." It also has a unique, impressively esoteric definition (an "anticipatory, apprehensive, hyper-tonic, avoidance reaction") that readily lends itself to abbreviation as an acro-nym — AAHAR (which, by the way, became another "famous" feature of the Johnson legacy). Moreover, a potent persuasive force is deeply embedded within the account: namely, the implied promise of a comprehensive solution for the disorder through the utilization of simple, easily implemented, and broadly applicable techniques. In brief, the appeal of the Johnson formulation itself lay largely in its being simple, prepossessive, and pollyannaish.

In addition, as noted earlier, the emphasis on learning was especially au cou-rant at the time. Further, this focus, which bore with it the esoteric nomencla-ture of the psychological laboratory, carried an aura of bona fide scientific in-quiry and analysis. Interlaced with such influence is the fact that much of the writing from the Iowa school is wordy and convoluted, with its inconsistencies and contradictions fairly well obscured under a surface plausibility, one that has hardly ever been seriously questioned.

In the years subsequent to Johnson's personal contributions, his construction remained afloat through the support provided by a retinue of followers who believed in his teachings. Some of them, quite active and vocal, have continued to produce material in the three overlapping areas that represent his position: (1) adaptation and consistency, (2) recourse to learning theory paradigms, and (3) evaluation and "the label." The latter dimension includes the provincial yet troublesome contention that stuttering is not reliably discriminable from normal nonfluency. Although soundly contradicted by much pertinent evidence, it continues to regenerate, like the Hydra of Greek mythology.

The major figure carrying forward the Johnson legacy is Oliver Bloodstein, a longtime student of Johnson[3] and his most active disciple. In the post-Johnson era Bloodstein has extended the essential theme of Johnson's position practically unaltered. Bloodstein's "anticipatory struggle hypothesis" is simply another way of expressing the old Johnson "expectancy-avoidance" claim. Similarly, Bloodstein's "continuity hypothesis" restates, in barely more specialized terms, the old Johnson contention that stuttering is really just exaggerated normal nonfluency. Bloodstein has maintained the Johnson heritage in many other ways as well, particularly in the form and style of his writings.

THE ADAPTATION EFFECT AND "CONSISTENCY"

Johnson's claim that the adaptation effect and the "consistency" effect show that stuttering is "learned behavior" was accepted literally and enthusiastically by a widely distributed audience. In fact, both in this country and abroad,[4] the two phenomena were touted as basic discoveries in the study of stuttering, acclaimed as phenomena that reveal the essential nature of the disorder.

The adaptation effect, in particular, was the object of much research effort over a long period of time. Most of this work was undertaken from an orientation in which it was already assumed that stuttering is learned behavior. Studies in this vein have appeared as late as 1980 (Brutten and Dancer 1980). Typically the narratives that have discussed and explicated the adaptation effect borrowed the vocabulary of the psychological laboratory—words like extinction, spontaneous recovery, reactive inhibition, and other terms. Further, this vocabulary was employed glibly, and quite inappropriately, as presumptive explanation. To the contrary, the basic distinction between adaptation and unlearning was never recognized in these writings. Crucial differences between the data obtained in stuttering adaptation and their presumed counterparts from the learning laboratory were overlooked. Moreover, a formal identification and explication of these important disparities (Wingate 1966a) was either pointedly rejected[5] or ignored. Clearly, there was little readiness within the profession to acknowledge a threat to the established belief system. To the contrary, the prevailing attitude has remained one of continuing to embrace the belief that stuttering is learned behavior.

Johnson had also hailed the adaptation effect as the prototypic model for therapy, and for some time this notion was duly accepted along with his other claims. However, the efforts made to pursue application of the adaptation effect to treatment were unrewarding, and gradually its essential irrelevance in at least this regard became evident.[6] However, recognition that the adaptation effect was a failure in treatment did not itself occasion any discernible modification of the belief that it constituted evidence that stuttering is learned behavior.

Preoccupation with the adaptation effect and its presumed expression of learning principles gradually lessened. This subsidence seems to have been at least encouraged by research whose findings yielded a more defensible interpretation of the nature of the adaptation effect (Wingate 1966c). Eventually, a comprehensive appraisal of the adaptation effect revealed it to have very little relation to a learning/unlearning process, certainly not in the way it was for so long claimed to be (Wingate 1986b, 1986c).

The phenomenon of the consistency effect (so-called) has had a rather different history. It was accorded a higher stature than the adaptation effect, largely by having been transmuted from a distorted observation into a pretentious concept. Then, persistently spoken of in certain sources as an actual process revealed by research, it has been invested with a fictitious reality and touted as an affirmed principle, reified with the label "consistency."

From its beginning the consistency effect has posed different, and much more serious, problems and limitations than has adaptation. Computation of the adaptation effect has been, from the beginning, an obvious and straightforward matter that raises no issue or question about the numerical values obtained. However, the measurement of "consistency" has had only faults. The standard formula, developed by Johnson, has for some time been known to yield inflated values as well as values that are obtainable simply by chance — hardly what is intrinsic to the meaning of "consistent." This inherent, variant distortion in measurement is clearly a crippling flaw in the very notion of "consistency." Moreover, this serious fault is compounded by the fact that even the inflated values thereby obtained are not enough to justify speaking of consistency. However, these limitations turn out to be of secondary significance in view of the fundamental error in the entire scheme: namely, that the formula itself is a misconstruction that does not at all represent what it purports to measure.[7] Nonetheless, reference to and claims for "consistency" have continued to appear in the literature. For instance, Bloodstein (1981, 1993), originator and principal advocate of "consistency" as reality, continues to accept the measurement, as well as the purported significance, of the consistency effect in its original (Johnson) form.

In the end, careful analysis of the phenomena called "the adaptation effect" and "consistency," separately and as a pair, reveals the contradictions, inconsistencies, and other critical faults within the extant literature addressed to them. Foremost among these limitations is the fact that, as phenomena, they are not independent of each other, as regularly implied, but are reciprocals. Of no less significance is the revelation that while some degree of stutter recurrence is evident, "consistency" of stuttering is a fabrication, a modern-day myth. The data relevant to "consistency" are only tangential to what is contended in this term.

The two phenomena, a decrease in stuttering and some amount of recurrence of stuttering, which occur under the special conditions described, have not deserved the attention, and certainly not the acclaim, they have received. Both phenomena can be explained adequately and parsimoniously in terms of quite mundane processes of increased familiarity, and practice (see Wingate 1986b, 1986c).

LEARNING THEORY PARADIGMS

Among the models available for casting stuttering in a learning theory mold, the escape learning paradigm would seem most suited to the supposed circumstances of stutter occurrence.[8] That is, in the instrumental escape paradigm an organism acquires a "behavior" that has relieved it (the organism) from an unpleasant state.

Although the escape learning model has a certain plausibility for an account of stuttering, the avoidance learning paradigm was the one selected and pursued by the proponents of a learning theory explanation. Almost certainly, preference for the avoidance model followed in literal association from Johnson's claim that stuttering is "an avoidant response." This claim, in turn, represents the widely accepted notion within the profession that nonspeech acts, which may occur during a stutter event, represent the stutterer's "avoidances" — another questionable maxim that is glibly expressed in the modern-day lore about stuttering.

However, the avoidance learning account soon faced serious dilemmas, in the general form of no clear agreement as to what it is that the stutterer is supposedly trying to avoid. The crux of Johnson's explanation—that stuttering is the effort to avoid stuttering—could not be applied literally because it provides no explanation for the *first* stutter (the presumably original "noxious stimulus") and how it arose. So, it was necessary to find something else that could be fit into the "noxious stimulus" slot. Prominent among the alternative agents that have been suggested for filling this (stimulus) role of "what the stutterer is attempting to avoid" were (a) the "label"; (b) nonfluency; (c) disapproval of nonfluency; (d) the original (parental) disapproval; (e) specific words; (f) specific sounds; and (g) perhaps any or all of the foregoing.

There seems to have been some occasional vague uneasiness among S-R proponents since all the conjectured parts do not fit quite as they should. In fact, it wasn't even very clear what all of the parts were. First of all, stuttering was only *assumed* to be a response (R). Second, no necessary and adequate (S) stimulus for the assumed response has ever been demonstrated. Third, no credible supposed reinforcement of it has come into clear view either.

So, with S-R formulations facing such evident limitations, considerable relief attended the introduction of the "operant" learning concept, through which at least one of the two missing links could be dismissed. In this framework there is no need to specify an eliciting stimulus; "operant behaviors" are said to be "emitted." However, according to the operant paradigm such behaviors are stabilized (acquired, learned) through some reinforcement that is contingent upon their occurrence. So here too, then, one of the missing links—the reinforcement assumption—still remains in limbo. But then, it is easier to explain away one missing link than to somehow have to account for two undiscernibles.

The operant concept, which permitted evasion of the serious missing-stimulus problem, was actively embraced and vigorously pursued in a new generation of explaining stuttering as "learned behavior." However, the deliverance from dilemma that was seemingly provided by the operant concept was only apparent. Those who gladly embraced the operant notion did not confront certain basic problems faced by the effort to invoke this seemingly "better" learning theory account.

Advocacy of the operant learning account of stuttering has failed to recognize the essential requirements for utilizing this model. If stuttering is to be credibly explained as an operant, then its occurrence must fit the sequence of events described for the operant pattern, for "operant behavior." According to the operant learning formulation, operants are acts (or "behaviors") that occur initially under some unspecified circumstances, and very likely at random. Operants become stabilized (acquired, learned) if they are attended by fortuitous reinforcement of their occurrence. Also, standardly, operants are acquired by being *rewarded*, that is, *positively* reinforced. In addition, they are best stabilized if the reinforcement is intermittent and if it is "delivered" considerably less frequently than 100 percent of the time. This means that (1) the behavior (operant; act) is not always reinforced, and (2) the behavior (operant; act) occurs much more often than it is reinforced.

So, for stuttering to be veridically explained as an "operant behavior," it must originally have been *emitted*; that is, it must have occurred as a *de novo* act of the individual, *before* it could then be reinforced. Moreover, the stutter would have to have occurred many times without being reinforced. That is, for stuttering to be subject to reinforcement, quite a few instances of this unique "emitted behavor" must have occurred, during only some proportion of which occurrences it was reinforced.

Now, the foregoing description does not at all match the conditions and events by which stuttering is supposedly learned. In accounts invoking learning theory, the question of the initial stutter(s) remains unaddressed. More important, in direct contrast to the operant model, the efforts to explain stuttering as "learned behavior" have, throughout, assigned the prominent role for its acquisition to some form of *punishment*, not reward. Moreover, the punishment is assumed to be steadily present, affecting each instance of stutter occurrence. So, the observations and the data relative to stuttering do not fit the model. Stuttering is no more credibly explained as "operant behavior" than as "avoidant behavior."

It has been something of an irony, then, that the rush to employ "operant technology" in the treatment of stuttering called for the use of negative reinforcement of the stuttering behavior to cause it to be "unlearned." Such procedure also contravenes the long-term, paramount proscription regarding how stuttering should be managed. The proscriptive "rule," which is basic to this formulation and well reflects its origin, is that this "behavior" should not be disapproved (punished).

Somewhat surprisingly, then, operant approaches to stuttering therapy have been associated with a certain amount of success. However, there is good reason to believe that whatever results have been achieved in such programs have had only a peripheral connection to the learning theory model proposed to account for it. To the contrary, it seems clear that the successes actually have been a function of two circumstances that typically have not been recognized, or at least acknowledged, by the practitioners. First, these "programs" (or studies) have regularly made use of some fluency-inducing procedure to "instate" fluency. Second, the real substance of any of the "contingent reinforcement" utilized is to be found in its cognitive aspect. Regarding the latter, there is good evidence from the relevant research that even little children quickly discern what is going on in the supposed reinforcement schemes. Also, they perform appropriately whether the supposed reinforcement is describable as positive, negative, or neutral. Moreover, they do even better if given initial instructions, that is, if they "know the rules" of the procedure beforehand rather than having to figure out the connection as the procedure unfolds. In other words, even children catch on to the scheme, which indicates that their "behavior" is based principally in a cognitive function rather than "controlled" by some schedule of reinforcement manipulated by an experimenter or practitioner.

It seems appropriate to mention here that, via the Iowa school's engorgement of psychology, particularly learning theory, the word "behavior" came into the speech pathology literature as an evidently adored byword. From stuttering as "learned behavior" came "stuttering behavior," and then increasingly the tiresomely redundant and superfluous use of "behavior" everywhere. Thus, "articulation behavior," "speech behavior," "language behavior," and on and on. The word seems to have the appeal of being a specialized, esoteric embellishment of otherwise mundane references, prized because it seems to lend to any statement a decidedly professional-sounding and scientific aura. In such usage the word takes on some of the quasi-magic value discussed in Chapter 6. Actually, matters were described at least as well in the many years before this term entered, and proliferated in, the literature. Adding the word "behavior" is not only unnecessary adornment that is pompously boring, it is fundamentally presumptive, prejudicial, and contaminating.

EVALUATION AND "THE LABEL"

These two residual dimensions of general semantics have continued to persist in one form or another over a broad range in the field of stuttering. As might be expected, this dissemination has been effected almost entirely through the purposeful action of followers of the Iowa school. The message continues to recur, in essentially original form, in both professional and lay sources.[9]

Before proceeding to a brief synopsis of the continued expression of these notions, it seems appropriate to raise certain general, rather basic considerations germane to their viability.

As reviewed earlier, especially in Chapter 7, these intimately interdependent notions, evaluation and the label, must be recognized as having been fundamentally introspective and ruminative in origin. They should have been acknowledged and dealt with as such. Yet in spite of the prideful claim that a spirit of questioning was a hallmark of speech and hearing science at Iowa in that early period, there is no evidence that any reasonable question was raised in regard to the evaluation conjecture. Also, there is no record of anyone wondering why the word "stutter" was evidently the only word in the world that had such purported power to create an abnormal condition. If the persuasive potency that was claimed for "stuttering" is somehow a potential capacity of any word or word use, it would have been appropriate to ask, for instance, if there had been only "fibbing" before someone began to use the word "lying" or only "sighing" before someone called it "moaning" or only "smiling" before someone said "grimacing" and on and on. Certainly no other illustrations out of even the general semantics literature itself could match this tale of the potency purportedly embodied in the single word "stuttering."

Professional inquiry regarding the purported power of words, or the supposed pernicious effect of drawing attention to some anomaly, could well have been limited to the area of speech alone. For instance: Is a process similar to the one claimed for stuttering to be found in other speech disorders or speech features? Do children who talk too fast begin to talk faster and faster because a parent told them they talked too fast? Do children evidencing a frontal lisp also begin to have a lateral lisp because a parent called the frontal one "lisping," or tried to show the child how to produce a proper /s/? Do children with several articulation errors originally have just one, but begin to have more because a parent made an issue of that error? Such examples could be multiplied many times.

Then too, particularly pertinent questions would have been: Where did the word "stutter" come from? How did those parents get the word? How did the word emerge in the language? Does the word have no ties whatsoever to reality? Doesn't the term "extensional" refer to observable features, and do not the observable speech features called "stutter" fit the character of the word? Has anyone ever heard of onomatopoeia? What about those long-established, widely used terms "clonic" and "tonic?" Does the etymology of the word "stutter" have any bearing?

Also, in specific regard to the Indians or to linguistic relativity in general, and the presence or absence of any particular word, isn't it rather extreme, or at least naive and simplistic, to claim that something exists because there is a word for it? Do the words for real-world things, events, and processes exist before the appearance of what they designate, and then actually operate to create their referents? Isn't it, rather, an axiom in the study of cultures and languages that when something exists, occurs, or is brought into a culture, a reference (name) for it will *then* be devised? Even if it were not an axiom, isn't it at least considerably more rational and credible than putting it the other way around?

THE "SECONDARY DEVIANCE" EPISODE

The evaluation conjecture made a unique contribution to at least the spirit of linguistic relativity through the sociological concept of "secondary deviance" (Lemert 1951, 1972) and its derivative, "labeling theory." These concepts emerged from studies of social deviance, originally crime and delinquency, and were intended to introduce the variables of self-concept and interpersonal relationships into an account of deviant conduct.

Purportedly, secondary deviance occurs when a person learns the role and accepts the identity of a deviant as the basis of his lifestyle. This is said to occur when "significant others" refer to the individual as a deviant and, through this assessment and attendant negative reactions, reinforce and stabilize the behavior they have identified and labeled. Thus, according to this claim, a young person who is labeled a juvenile delinquent may then encounter sequences of circumstances that lead eventually to his becoming a criminal. The concept of secondary deviance came to be applied to a variety of social problems, including various criminal categories, alcoholism, persons partially sighted who are legally blind, mental retardation, and severe mental illness (specifically, schizophrenia).

Initially, Lemert's idea of secondary deviance was prompted by a supposition advanced by A. L. Smith, a criminologist at the University of Indiana, that heroin addiction involved a cognitive dimension. However, the essential substance of the concept of secondary deviance was actually derived from Johnson's conjectures about stuttering, which came to Lemert's attention quite by happenstance.[10] At the time he developed the concept, Lemert was on the faculty at Western Michigan University, where he had become well acquainted socially with Van Riper. Their acquaintance included casual conversations about the content and concepts in each other's fields. In the course of one such conversation, in which Lemert described Smith's idea of a cognitive dimension in deviant conduct, Van Riper mentioned Johnson's semantogenic notion as having a somewhat similar theme.

Lemert was acquainted with the hypothesis of linguistic relativity, but the formulation created by Johnson appeared to him as a ready-made model of what was coalescing in his mind. He saw Johnson's claim as representing the isolated instance of "the pure case" that illustrated actual societal *generation* of deviance. The concept of secondary deviance, in contrast, clearly implies that a certain amount of actual deviance already exists (has already occurred), for example, the use of alcohol or drugs, significant loss of vision, acts of thievery, etc. Taking Johnson's position at face value, Lemert saw it as the "pure case" in that within it the primary deviance was said to be simply normal variations or "only minor abnormalities"; societal reaction, through the use of a "label," was posited as the genuine cause of this deviance (stuttering).

Within a short time certain sources began to apply labeling theory in "pure case" form to severe mental illness, especially schizophrenia. This notion was pursued quite vigorously in certain quarters; it also was criticized severely by others, and considerable controversy over the matter ensued for a number of years. Societal reaction/labeling theory reached its zenith in the late 1960s and early 1970s and went into decline shortly thereafter.

It is of particular relevance to a history of stuttering that the endeavor to apply "pure case" labeling theory to mental illness unraveled as the result of a line of careful research addressed to the issue. Pertinent investigation, undertaken in regard to widely divergent cultures, yielded findings that consistently refuted the claims arising from the concept of secondary deviance and the associated notion of labeling theory, which soon led to their demise.[11]

So, secondary deviance arose, attained substance, then faded away. Labeling theory blossomed, flowered, then shriveled. However, evaluation and "the label" in stuttering, the font of all this moribund intellectualizing, continued on untouched, unscathed, unchanged.

THE DEFINITION STRUGGLE

The matter of defining stuttering has become a problem only in modern times, in fact, not until well into the twentieth century. Two happenings in the nineteenth century might appear to have involved the issue of definition, but they did not present a parallel to the current problem. One was the evident need to clarify the distinction between "stutter" and "stammer" that arose intermittently (see Chapter 1). The other was the transient interest in cataloguing many supposed "symptoms" of stuttering (see Chapter 4). However, the intended clarification or elaboration of stuttering undertaken in those times was simply in reference to observational description. In those considerations of over a century ago there was no evidence of any impulsion to *define* the disorder.

The twentieth-century issue of the definition of stuttering is a very different matter, and it embodies a serious, although unnecessary, problem. The *fact* of the problem is represented in the existence of so many differing definitions;[12] the *crux* of the problem is the prevalence with which these definitions center in an assertion regarding etiology.

The authors of these various definitions minimize recognition that stuttering is a disorder of speech and, instead, emphasize an etiological statement that reflects their particular predilections. Routinely, any mention of the classic characteristics of stuttering is omitted, in many cases carefully avoided. Although some such definitions do make reference to speech, this dimension of the statement is cast in terms that are unclear or ambiguous (for example, "fluency failure"). Actually, a number of the definitions consist entirely of an etiologic claim! Typically these etiologic statements feature negative emotionality, which stands as the prominent part of the definition. Particularly in definitions of the purely etiologic type, if one were to read the definition out of context and with the lead word "stuttering" obscured, one would have no idea what the author was talking about!

Definitions of stuttering that incorporate some statement of etiology are patently indefensible, especially if offered with the pretension of being scientific. Definitions of stuttering that either are, feature, or include an etiological statement reflect a particularly blatant presumption and contradiction, inasmuch as it is widely acknowledged that the source of stuttering is unknown. At the same time, ironically, etiologic definitions carry an important acknowledgment by default: in omitting mention of the descriptive characteristics of stuttering, they reveal an unspoken admission that these ubiquitous features should be well known to anyone.[13]

Etiologic definitions have arisen readily out of orientations that attempt to account for stuttering as a psychological problem. Statements asserting cause of the disorder have been generated not only from psychodynamic formulations but also from less exotic systems of belief, such as learning theory, or even the more plebeian psychology of essentially lay origin. Some definitions of the etiologic type appeared earlier in this century, particularly from within psychodynamic beliefs. However, the era of the definitions that feature an etiologic statement is concurrent with the injection of psychological preoccupations into the literature and discourse on stuttering. As reviewed in preceding chapters, this ambience was set in motion largely through events at the University of Iowa beginning in the late 1930s.

The influence the increasingly pervasive psychological presence had on definitions of stuttering is reflected in what happened to a good definition of the disorder that was presented by West in the early days of the profession. This statement (West 1933), is still defensible as the most lucid, instructive, and accurate among extant definitions to be found within the literature of the field. Necessarily of moderate length,[14] it was intentionally descriptive and included illustration of pertinent specific features. The definition was repeated in another book published four years later (West et al. 1937); however, it subsequently disappeared from the literature in a relatively short time. Evidently West's statement was not very widely accepted over any appreciable period, and in a revised edition of the book (West et al. 1957) the definition had not only shrunk considerably but included, as a sizeable portion of it, a purely psychological dimension. By this time, of course, the belief that stuttering is a psychological problem had been expressed extensively and had become even more widely accepted. Preoccupation with assumptions regarding the nature of the disorder led various authors to formalize their preoccupations in some special "definition" of stuttering which, routinely, at least emphasizes an assertion of etiology.

Undoubtedly the most influential of the etiologic definitions was the one propounded by Wendell Johnson, namely, that stuttering is "an anticipatory, apprehensive, hypertonic, avoidance reaction." Its appeal is reflected in the frequent reference to it by acronym: "the AAHAR definition." In one respect this "famous" definition epitomizes the purely etiologic type, inasmuch as it is exclusively a contention of cause and does not even mention speech. At the same time, it is unique in that, whereas in other such etiological definitions the descriptive features characteristic of stuttering were evidently omitted as givens, there is no doubt that in the Johnson definition descriptive specification was intentionally avoided.

On the subject of etiological definitions based in personal preoccupation, it is especially pertinent to note that before Johnson became immersed in general semantics his statements about stuttering were considerably more objective and empirically supported. The following quotation appears, although in a footnote, in the 1935 report on phonetic factors in stuttering (Johnson and Brown 1935: p. 484). It is quite an adequate descriptive statement of the essential features of a stutter.

A stuttering spasm was taken to be any interruption of the normal rhythm of the reading. It might take the form of a complete block, undue prolongation of a sound, a repetition of the initial sound of a word or syllable, saying "uh-uh-uh," repetition of the previous word or words, or a complete cessation of all attempts to speak for a moment.[15]

In recent years the Johnson AAHAR definition has less often been stated so boldly in its full etiologic contention. However, some sources still propound the definition and its message in their original presumptive form.   For instance, a recent booklet (Selmar 1991) "written for parents and teachers of school-age children who stutter" restates the definition verbatim and presents it as "a comprehensive description [of stuttering, which] when examined word by word, enables us to understand why stuttering occurs" (Selmar 1991: p. 3).

For a number of years acolytes of the Iowa school have attempted to capitalize on the definition struggle, using it as the rationale for a nihilistic argument epitomized in the claim that "there is no such thing as stuttering!" The contention from this position is that disagreements about the definition of stuttering must mean that there is no acceptable definition of it, which is then hurriedly assumed to mean that, therefore, there is really nothing to define.

The contention that lack of agreement about the definition of stuttering somehow nullifies or makes questionable the reality of stuttering or the ability to identify it is a thoroughly contrived issue. There are other academic and professional disciplines that face problems of definition, but within which there is no evidence of a call for surrender. A particularly relevant comparison is to be found in linguistics. Linguists have long acknowledged that completely objective definitions of the terms "consonant," "vowel," "syllable," "morpheme," and "word" has not been achieved,[16] yet no clan of linguists spends time and effort elaborating this fact into a denial that any of these entities exist, nor is this fact seized upon as the basis for a contention that such entities cannot be reliably identified.

Defining stuttering is actually a much simpler task than the one faced by linguists. The whole issue of defining stuttering could be made to disappear under a sincere common effort to address the matter through standard scientific methodology, namely, by centering on empirical observation and objective data. At the present time some sources within the field, beyond the Iowa legacy, have made some progress in this direction. There seems to be a gradually broadening acceptance of an effort to emphasize the objectively discernible criterial features of stuttering and to recognize that various ancillary and associated features should be considered in properly subsidiary roles (see Wingate 1964a; 1976, Chapter 4; 1988, Part I).

At the same time the definition struggle, founded and nurtured in provincialism, continues on in the literature of stuttering. The most defensible definition of the disorder currently in print is not to be found in the literature of the field (a sobering commentary on the divisiveness within it) but in *Churchill's Medical Dictionary*; it is reproduced in the Glossary (under Stuttering, Definition). Note that this definition is very much like the one first offered by West sixty years ago (also reproduced in the Glossary).

KEEPING THE FAITH

There are a number of ways, other than those covered earlier in this chapter, in which the Iowa school has worked at perpetuating the Johnson position. It is not difficult to discern a basic policy that carries on the pervasive Johnson effort to manipulate reality through word selection, usage, and style of expression. To this end a number of techniques are evident, the main ones being to homogenize, evade, avoid, and ignore.

Homogenize

It seems that a cardinal tenet is to do whatever is necessary to keep stuttering all mixed in with normal nonfluency. Procedures for accomplishing this objective feature the following.

1. The use of general terms of classification and reference, for example:
    a. The persistent use of "repetitions and hesitations" is the classic instance. As noted earlier, these words are glosses of an exemplary form. Both words are *class* terms, general rubrics that incorporate, without distinction, subsidiary

terms among which certain ones are critical in descriptive differentiation be-tween stuttering and normal nonfluencies.[17]

b. The encroaching use of "disfluency." This grandest gloss of all could have found serviceable employ if used properly and carefully as the broad ru-bric denoted by its etymological structure. Such usage requires that there be the clear intention of using the term objectively, carefully, and *only* to refer comprehensively to *all* aspects of speech that depart from literal, absolute flu-ency. However, it has been used only infrequently and casually in this proper, generalized sense. In serious contrast, it has much too frequently been em-ployed as the equivalent of "stuttering." It appears in this guise in many jour-nal articles, pamphlets and books. A particularly pointed example is found in a dictionary compiled specifically for speech and hearing science (Nicolosi et al. 1978) where "disfluency" is cross-referenced with "dysfluency," with accompa-nying notations stating that the two words mean the same thing. The state-ment, or acceptance, of synonymity of "dis" and "dys" reflects, at best, not only ignorance of etymology but also of the well-established usage of both prefixes in their proper references: "dis" having an umbrella connotation of "not;" "dys" meaning "abnormal," "bad," "difficult." The confusion in use of the gen-eral term has spread to lay sources as well, as revealed in an article, Spotting and Stopping Stuttering, in the popular publication *Changing Times* (1983) which advises the reader that "the technical [*sic*] term for it is 'disfluency'. "

For other instances of the confusion created by the use of this term, see Win-gate (1984a). The suspicion, noted in that source, that "disfluency" is an Iowa school neologism created by Johnson, evidently for its obscurant properties, was later confirmed in a recollection by Van Riper (1992b). It is pertinent to record Van Riper's assessment of the term, which is revealed in his note of having once told Johnson that "disfluency" is a "garbage-can word." The specially designed ad hoc nature of the term is well reflected in the fact that it does not appear in any standard dictionary, including the Oxford English Dictionary, even though that reference source contains many other quite remarkable entries of "dis-" prefix words, such as disbranch, dispauper, and disrudder.[18]

2. Emphasize the "overlap" in disfluency between samples of stuttered speech and samples of normal speech.

This maneuver is taken whole from Johnson's original manipulations. This "final redoubt" kind of defense should be easily breached by average intellect employing common sense, let alone by an attitude of scientific inquiry. A rea-sonably careful look at Johnson's bases for emphasizing "overlap" should be sobering.[19] Additionally, however, one is well reminded that all kinds of things or events that appear similar show considerably more overlapping of features than are found for stuttered and normal speech. For instance, examples of ex-tensive overlap are readily found in descriptions of many ordinary comparisons wherein significant differences are easily remarked, vans vs buses, peaches vs nectarines, thunderhead vs high cumulus, basil vs tarragon, coyotes vs wolves, and so on. In fact, there is considerably more overlap in the describable features of male and female of a species than in the comparisons to be made regarding certain kinds of departures from literal fluency.

The matter of overlap is a chimera that is easily dispelled if one is actually interested in noting differences, rather than, in contrast, being happy that a differentiation may not, in certain instances, be readily made. An outstanding illustration can be found within the field of speech itself. Sweet, over a century ago, made an observation that has been made repeatedly since then, namely that "the boundary between vowel and consonant, like that between the different kingdoms of nature, cannot be drawn with absolute definiteness" (Sweet 1887: p. 51). Yet the literature of phonetics is not continually plagued with contentions that consonant and vowel cannot be reliably discriminated.

In the final analysis, if the matter of overlap were a meaningful issue, it could be somewhat vexing, and a scientific orientation to it would require that it be resolved. However, the Iowa school gives no evidence of any such interest. Rather, one finds a sturdy attitude of contentment with this little burble in the data, and an equally clear resolve to make the most of this apparent windfall for the defense structure.

3. Make an issue of the fact that listeners do not invariably agree about all stutter events in speech samples and, furthermore, do not always agree when asked to discriminate stutters from normal nonfluencies. One can thereby claim that "judgments" of stuttering are "unreliable." This will permit the further claim that listeners can't really tell the difference between stuttering and normal nonfluency, which will in turn allow the grander contention of "continuity" in character of "disfluencies" and, therefore, that stuttering is just exaggerated normal nonfluency.

The crux of contention embodied in this maneuver is the requirement that, before it can be accepted that stuttering is differentiable from normal nonfluency one must demonstrate that listeners can agree on every (or almost every) instance of stutter. This is without doubt the most clever ploy among the maneuvers of the Iowa school, for it poses a challenge that is practically incapable of resolution. As noted by S. S. Stevens (1955), who does represent truly scientific endeavor, "One can always plague the taxonomist with the borderline case." However, as Stevens emphasized, such instances do not mean that the system of classification is suspect. Certainly they do not dispel the reality represented by that classification system. In a similar vein, Edmund Burke (1945) remarked that knowing the difference between night and day is a simple judgment made regularly by everyone, yet just when day becomes night, and vice versa, can pose insurmountable problems.

In many ways the "unreliability" issue is a tempest in a teapot. Even if it were a serious matter the only persons who should show much concern about correctly identifying every instance of stutter are those who would undertake to "control" stuttering via reinforcements delivered contingently upon occurrence of the "response." However, the operant fad crested in the early 1970s and has declined considerably since then (see Prins and Hubbard 1988), so even in that arena this particular little concern is essentially passe.

If one penetrates the fragile crust of this "unreliability" issue one finds a tangle of (perhaps unrecognized, certainly unheeded) contradictions within the constructions of the Iowa school. The demand of absolute identification of stuttering has its roots in Johnson's insistence that stuttering and normal nonfluency be *categorically* distinct. It is a demand that Bloodstein applauds and continues to affirm. This maneuver forces the opposition to adopt an either-or classification, with no place for an "uncertain" category. As noted in Chapter 7, this position clearly contradicts Johnson's own expressed repudiation of either-or classifications, revealing the same kind of hypocrisy that Kenneth Burke observed in Korzybski's writings (see Chapter 6). But there are many other contradictions as well. In his "Open Letter," Johnson defied "any expert" to pick out the stutterers in a group of people if specific information about how those persons speak (or spoke) were withheld. Not only does this requirement reveal that he recognized stuttering to be a *speech* problem, it also clearly reveals recognition and acceptance of the fact that there is something discriminable in the speech of certain persons that is the essence for identifying stuttering.

Again, in the compilation of studies published in 1955 Johnson noted[20] that "what we think of as stuttering reduces . . . to stutterings—and that stutterings can be counted." Now, one cannot very well count instances of something that one cannot perceive and identify. Further, in other places he and many others of the Iowa school make the point that some normal speakers are more nonfluent than some stutterers. How is it possible to make such an analysis if one cannot distinguish stuttering from normal nonfluency with at least reasonable reliability? Another contradiction is found in the counsel these sources recommend be given to parents of stuttering youngsters, namely, that the parents should listen for the child's *normal* nonfluencies *also*, since the child's speech can be expected to contain more fluency departures of the normal type.

It is in the area of research itself that the more patent contradictions regarding "unreliability" emerge. It is standard procedure in comparative research to select subjects for assignment to either the stutterer group or the normal-speaker group on the basis of speech characteristics. Moreover, the investigator must demonstrate through the statistical appraisal of independent judgments that the selection was reliably made. Ironically, this standard procedure has been followed in those studies claiming to show unreliability of stutter judgments. Further, in a preponderance of stuttering research the data are based on instances of stutter, the identification of which must also pass a reliability check. Significantly, the values of such reliability checks are regularly well above .80 and typically above .90. These values raise the image of another major contradiction within Iowa school contentions: namely, that even the lower of these two figures is markedly above the values that have been reported, readily accepted, and in fact claimed as evidence for "consistency."

The area of therapy contains another set of contradictions. Acceptance for, and certainly retention in, therapy depends upon reliable identification that the individual stutters. Persons are not referred for, nor accepted in, therapy because they are "disfluent"; otherwise everyone would be seen for treatment. Recommendations regarding therapy are made in reference to certain *kinds* of irregularities in fluency. These featues are also the basis for (1) the assessment that the person has or has not improved; (2) dismissal from therapy; and (3) readmission if there has been a relapse.

Evade

The objective here is to not seriously consider any findings that are incompatible with any aspect of the position. Two standard techniques are the following.

1. Ignore those findings that are outright contradictory.
A long-term example is that the literature of the Iowa school has shown no discernible inclination to take into consideration the contents of a three-article series published in 1962 that pointed to many limitations, inconsistencies and contradictions of Johnson's position.[21]   Those analyses remain pertinent to any extensions of the Johnson position as they continue to find expression in the works of the Iowa school.

2. Neutralize those findings that cannot be ignored but are inconsistent with the position and potentially damaging.
An outstanding example of this technique is how Bloodstein (1981) deals with the matter of recovery from stuttering. As discussed earlier, recovery from stuttering clearly contradicts the Iowa school position that stuttering develops through the supposed reaction-struggle-reaction scheme. Bloodstein therefore contends that

the necessary and irreducible factor common to all recoveries . . . is to be found in the observation that if stutterers could forget that they were stutterers, and in so doing forget to do all of the things that stutterers think they have to do in order to talk, they would have no further difficulty with their speech. (p. 393)

This quintessentially armchair kind of statement incorporates a number of ingenuous and indefensible contentions, including the notion of "the label," a belief in "distraction," and the idea of "role." It also completely ignores several very critical matters, including the following. First, not even testimonies from individual stutterers have implied this kind of effect. In fact, testimonies have included a variety of other content, all considerably different from anything like the above. Second, much recovery occurs among children when they are quite young, and when the notion of "stutterer" is quite vague, if existent at all.[22]   Third, but most important,   if stuttering represents what the stutterer "thinks he has to do in order to talk," why doesn't he stutter much more of the time—why not, in fact, all of the time? Moreover, this particular claim by Bloodstein completely disregards the considerable evidence that, as a general average, only about 10 percent of a stutterer's words are stuttered.[23]

Avoid

The objective here is to not deal with even relevant content if it could disturb the status quo.

A prime example of this maneuver is the persistence with which the Iowa school has let alone the findings regarding fluency and irregularities of fluency that have resulted from a range of reputable studies in psycholinguistics, highly relevant research that is based on speech samples from persons with normal speech. As noted earlier, especially in Chapter 7, such important information has been available in the literature for a long time, and particularly since the middle 1950s. Although certain writings from within the Iowa school have given token recognition that some of these studies exist, the findings from psy-cholinguistic research have been carefully left in place. The structures dependent upon Johnson's highly inadequate "normative study of fluency" would be at least threatened by not only the evidence from the psycholinguistic studies but the quality of their analyses and discussions as well.

Ignore

The principal objective in this maneuver is to overlook potential paradoxes within the position. However, if a paradox is likely to be obvious, pretend that it reflects insight.

Among the many paradoxes in the constructions of the Iowa school that have already been identified, one in particular deserves further comment. This one is, as Knott (Moeller 1975: p. 76) described it, "that well known paradox"—the explanation devised by Johnson and Knott that stuttering is the effort to avoid stuttering.

In the world of science, paradoxes do occasionally arise, as represented in the following examples. In astronomy, planetary retrograde motion was once a paradox. In metallurgy, it was observed that metals, when burned, increased rather than decreased in weight. In psychology, paradoxical cold and warmth were once troublesome, as was Humphrey's paradox. However, these and other paradoxes are discovered from observation and experimentation; they are not generated through reflection. Moreover, once identified, efforts are made to resolve them, not to enjoy them. Most certainly they are not received gladly as revelation and then established as the basis for explanation.

A similar critical and investigative attitude toward paradox is maintained in nonscientific disciplines as well. A case in point is the "paradox of analysis" which, interestingly, involves a semantic issue. In this case, as in others like it, the paradox is resolved by realizing that the question underlying it is a mis-leading one (see Langford 1942).

However, followers of the Iowa school are as comfortable with paradox as with contradiction and inconsistency. This lack of intellectual discipline seems clearly to be driven by the constraints of a system of belief that is often repre-sented in free-wheeling expressions characterized by bombast and flummery. Occasionally the inherent paradoxes, contradictions and/or inconsistencies in such expressions are more discernible than at other times because in such in-stances open absurdity surfaces. A few choice examples should suffice.

Bloodstein (1990) tells readers that he can only define stuttering if someone tells him what they mean by it. However, he has defined it in at least one source (Bloodstein 1958: p. 5), to wit: "In a word, stuttering is the speech diffi-culty of a person who tries to speak not wisely but too well."[24] If one is to ac-cept his 1990 statement at face value, does he mean that (in recent times any-way) he will define stuttering from whatever statement anyone would give him? Looking at his claim from another direction: routinely, if a person can define something, one can assume that the person has knowledge of what it is that he is defining; and, conversely, if he cannot give a definition of something, then very likely he does not know what it is. Does Bloodstein, then, have no idea of what stuttering is, or is like, or how to identify it?

An article by Perkins, Kent, and Curlee (1991), purporting to present a theory of neurolinguistic function in stuttering, contains a number of the kind of anomalies under consideration here; only the more focal ones need be re-viewed. Within their extended narrative it soon becomes clear that the authors are intent on melding stuttering with normal nonfluency. They disavow "perceptual" (observational) identification of stuttering. Instead, they define stuttering as "disruption of speech that is experienced by the speaker as loss of control." It results "when the speaker is under time pressure and is relatively unaware of the cause of dyssynchrony." Both *time pressure and relative un-awareness* "are necessary for the identification . . . of stuttering."

I doubt that anyone (else) would fail to see that there is absolutely nothing even potentially objective about these dimensions. They are entirely introspec-tive.[25] Actually, "relative unawareness" indicates even a sort of part-time intro-spection, and who can tell when or for how long the introspection is on or off? However, a more critical matter here is their specification that the two criteria noted above are what *identify* stuttering. In fact, they purport that nonstut-tered "disfluency" differs from stuttered "disfluency" only if the speaker is *not* under time pressure. So now the assessment of time pressure becomes critical!

Without continuing further into this morass, it should suffice to point out that these claims are at least contradictory to the findings of a good deal of psy-cholinguistic research addressed specifically to this matter — which, as noted earlier, is standardly avoided by Iowa school minions. Even more important, these contentions are fundamentally contradictory to basic scientific procedure.

Their argument reaches a pinnacle of absurdity in their claim that "nonstuttered disfluency is abnormal, as well as normal sounding disfluency not experienced as loss of control." In simpler terms this has to mean that any, or all, disfluency is abnormal — especially since normal speakers are unaware of their normal, and normal-sounding, nonfluencies, which therefore are not experienced as loss of control. Now there are a lot of clear-thinking persons in a variety of different disciplines who would find a great deal of analytic slippage in such a contention. This claim too reveals either ignorance or cavalier dismissal of consistent findings from a substantial amount of pertinent research. But this contention, in particular, raises another questionable issue. If all disfluency is abnormal, then why all the fuss about something "called" stuttering, and why the furor over whether it can be reliably identified?[26]

One further point about this particular article. It exemplifies a type in which Iowa school beliefs are embedded or woven into other content that, by itself, may be credible and possibly have scientific merit. Within such a context the Johnson catechism, by simply being present under some penumbra of apparent scientific respectability, stands to take on a little of the coloration.

A CURRENT CLAIM: PREVENTION

A recent excrescence of the Johnson legacy is found in the presumptive programs for the prevention of stuttering. This area of venture has its own blend of paradox, contradiction, and inconsistency. Fundamentally, these proposals have been generated and proceed either in ignorance of or in a willingness to ignore certain dimensions of knowledge about stuttering that are critically relevant to the expressed intent of the proposals.

Most important, the two major presumptions underlying these programs are contradicted by directly pertinent evidence, or lack thereof. The major presumptions are (1) that the source of stuttering is understood, and (2) that stuttering "develops"—that is, that it regularly gets worse. Within this presumptive context parental attitude and management continue to be assigned a substantial role.[27]

First of all, it should be widely known that (1) the source of stuttering is unknown, and (2) that any attribution of source is, at best, hypothetical — but most likely conjectural. Second, the best information available regarding the course of early stuttering — and there is now a considerable amount of such information — clearly indicates that early stuttering typically *does not* "develop." Johnson's own (ignored) data[28] provide evidence that instances in which stuttering "develops" are quite rare. In that report, of 118 stuttering youngsters seen for follow-up after twenty-eight months (during which time they received no special attention), only four were worse; ten were the same; sixty-one were better; and forty-three were no longer stuttering.[29]

A third dimension of contradiction is posed by the fact that, in spite of many efforts to determine parental "role" in stuttering, there is no credible evidence whatsoever that parental attitudes or management have contributed in any demonstrable way to the generation, maintenance, or worsening of stuttering in young children. In fact, there is, to the contrary, credible evidence that parental actions have been either innocuous or beneficial. Continuing to point an accusing finger at parents is a signal vestige of the Johnson position—and it is still as unsubstantiated, and as reprehensible, as when it was first devised and promulgated.

One striking inconsistency to be found within these purported programs for stuttering prevention is that persons who pursue or support such ventures are among those who press the claim that stuttering is not reliably discriminable from normal nonfluency, or that the two are "continuous." How then is it possible to identify children who are at risk for "developing" stuttering if, in fact, one cannot tell the difference between stuttering and normal nonfluency? That is, how can they identify the dimensions of "risk" prediction, or know whether or not the "risk" is actualized?

Another presumption inherent in these programs is that, supposedly by virtue of certain maneuvers of intervention, the "development" of stuttering will be dissipated or deflected. On what grounds can anyone make or imply such claims? This position casually ignores the very substantial evidence that stuttering typically does not "develop." Such well-documented evidence should be familiar to anyone knowledgeable about the literature of stuttering.[30]

Further, it is widely recognized that, regardless of claims made for them, all treatment approaches have a questionable outlook for success — for any age level and any level of stuttering "severity."[31] How, then, can anyone expect to translate such a dismal record into laudable — in fact, any — success with supposedly "beginning" stuttering? And again, if the identification of stuttering is so unreliable, or so uncertain vis-a-vis normal nonfluency, how will the pretentious preventers know when what is what?

There is another compelling reservation about claims regarding prevention of stuttering, namely, that no clear prognostic indicators have ever been discerned.[32] The impressive evidence regarding remission and the reasons to which remission is attributed have all been acquired post hoc. Thus, at this time prediction regarding remission is entirely actuarial; that is, one can predict only that more than 50 percent of stuttering youngsters will recover, but no readily implemented guidelines exist for identifying those who will be among that favored percentage.

A further critical matter yielded in the study of stuttering remission is that not only does most stuttering in young children subside, it does so *without* professional attention or intervention.[33] This finding strongly suggests that a maturational factor is responsible. A serious question to put to the prevention purveyors is: "What can these ventures honestly offer, from a defensible data base, that one can seriously expect will be any improvement upon letting nature take its course?" In like vein, there is reason to wonder if the "prevention" movement is anything more than opportunism — taking advantage of the opportunity to capitalize on an evidently maturational effect. After all, the pertinent research gives reason to expect that over half of these youngsters will recover without anyone doing anything.

One might well require of the purveyors of prevention that, until they can reliably differentiate those youngsters who will recover spontaneously from those few who perhaps will not, they should not burden the field of stuttering, and especially not a trusting public, with indefensible assumptions, unwarranted statements of explanation, implied assurances, and dubious claims of achievement.

A particularly alarming dimension of the prevention schema is its extreme expression in the claim that essentially all children need to acquire "a feeling of fluency control." This incredible contention assumes that all children are, at least in some measure, lacking this sense. Actually, one source (Cooper and Cooper 1991) contends that "many, if not most, school age children feel discomfiture, even fear, at the thought of experiencing fluency failures" Here is another of those armchair ruminations, free-floating from any pertinent reality base in either research, relevant fact, or historical awareness.

There is a body of literature addressed to the matter of fear about speaking but it deals essentially with what has been called "stage fright," the apprehension of speaking before a group. The more extreme among such cases, identified as "reticents," have received special attention over recent decades (see Muir 1964; Phillips 1968; Phillips et al. 1991; Daly et al. 1984). However, the fear experienced by even these special cases is not in respect to *how* they speak. In particular, there is no extant literature that identifies or even suggests a condition, among normal speakers, of personal individual concerns that focus on fluency.

The particular fantasy presenting the image of childhood fear about fluency serves as the basis for a prevention-type program with which school systems can be invaded, bearing an attached offer to provide specialized professional services that, as far as can be demonstrated, are both unnecessary and unjustifiable. This type of venture draws its substance from the "anxiety about fluency" overdraft of the Johnson legacy and reflects the same fabrications, the same narrow messianic zeal and broad unsubstantiated claims of the original formulation, and its continued irresponsible repetition.[34]

RETROSPECTIVE SUMMATION

Viewed from the perspective of content covered in earlier chapters, the Iowa school represents a modern day analogue of the "physicians after Galen" (see Chapter 3) who for so long continued to espouse and argue the teachings passed down to them, remaining disinterested in, impervious to, or actually defensive against the knowledge and reason accessible to them. The tangle of notions expressed in "evaluation/expectancy/anxiety/reaction/avoidance/learning" is the current day *rete mirabile* of the Iowa school. Also, comparable to the kind of explanations routinely given in those eras of past history peopled by the Doctors of Physick, the formulation and expressions of vested interest and persisting convictions may shift slightly from time to time, but the answer always comes out the same in the end.

The orientation of the Iowa school, as with its originator, continues to be more rhetorical and forensic than scientific. In an analogue from a more recent time, Freeman's criticism of cultural determinism, interestingly, can be applied verbatim to the thrust of the Iowa school: "An ideology that, in an actively unscientific way, sought totally to exclude biology from the explanation of human behavior" (1983: p. 282).

Freeman's quotation appeared earlier in this book (Chapter 6). The paragraph following that quotation contained five points reflecting the actual historical value of Margaret Mead's report. Inasmuch as those points have similar import in regard to the writings of Wendell Johnson and those of his legatees as well, they bear restatement here.

First, Johnson's writings, as did Mead's, afford an outstanding example of the proselyting potential of doctrine and the distorting power of doctrinal conviction. Second, they point up the circumstantial potency of the *Zeitgeist,* the "tide in the affairs of men," the accepting—if not eagerly adulating—atmosphere of the times. Third, even people who ought to know better will help a myth along. Fourth, myths quickly acquire juggernaut momentum and easily crush isolated instances of reason or contradiction. Fifth, once a myth has been accepted, much time and effort must be expended to rescind it, particularly when it has been cloistered in an attitude that is impervious to contradictory evidence, rational criticism, and logical analysis.

Some of Johnson's followers, and perhaps some others speaking as apologists, have made the point that his view stimulated a considerable amount of research. This claim overlooks the fact that such research was mounted in regard to a *cause* Johnson initiated and pursued. The research has not represented inquiry that extends from a foundation of careful observation and objective, unbiased exploration. The bulk of this research has been undertaken to demonstrate, not to investigate; and it continues to be pursued in this vein.[35] Research conducted under such constraints encourages confounding, not understanding.

One must also take note of how the management of stuttering has been influenced. In substantial measure the management of stuttering from this position has continued on the treadmill set in motion by Johnson's view. Unfortunately this condition is most explicit in respect to children — and their parents — as is alarmingly represented in the recent flurry of "prevention" assertions, all of which are founded in a melange of presumption, inconsistency, contradiction, and questionable motivation.

NOTES

1. Tiffany, well known in the field of audiology, received his doctorate at Iowa in 1951.

2. If one takes account of the belief he engendered, the devotion of his followers, their adherence to his teachings, and the extent to which his influence has been spread, he might be called, to borrow West's simile (Chapter 5), the *true* messiah of stuttering.

3. Bloodstein's master's thesis was the final publication in Johnson's "Studies in the Psychology of Stuttering" series (Bloodstein 1944). He completed the doctoral degree, directed by Johnson, in 1948.

4. See, for instance, the book by Beech and Fransella (1968), two British professionals, in which adaptation and "consistency" are presented as "basic phenomena of stuttering."

5. For instance, see Adams, Webster, and Maxwell (1967); Brookshire (1967).

6. See, for instance, Prins (1968).

7. The insurmountable problems with "consistency" are discussed in Wingate 1984, 1986b, and 1986c.

8. However, this model does not offer a good fit to stuttering either. The limitations of these several models are discussed in Wingate 1966b and Wingate 1976: p. 14ff.

9. Professional sources are numerous. A good illustration of its appearance in a lay source is found in restatements of the Johnson position that appeared in 1988, 1990, and 1992 issues of *Letting Go* (Vol. 8, #6; Vol. 10, #9; Vol. 12, #1), the monthly newsletter of the National Stuttering Project, an active self-help group for stutterers. In fact, the title of one of these articles was "Don't Use 'Stutterer!' "

10. Personal conversation with Dr. Lemert, May 1995.

11. For a comprehensive summary of this significant research, see Murphy (1976). Comparably pertinent evidence refuting Johnson's notions (see Wingate 1962a, 1962b, 1962c) has been steadfastly disregarded.

12. Which, typically reflecting their author's bias, led Gerald Jonas, a "recovered" stutterer intent on learning something about the disorder, to remark that what he found was "a grab-bag of competing theories" (Jonas 1977).

13. Another testimony to West's remark that "everyone but the experts knows what stuttering is" (in West et al. 1957: p. 15).

14. Because of its significance in content, as well as its historical value, it should be recorded in the present work. However, in view of its length and because its content is not in specific focus here, it is reproduced in the Glossary, under "West, Robert." Another early contribution made by West, also soon passed over, was his effort to establish a system of classification of speech disorders employing technical terms. In this endeavor stuttering, as "spasmophemia" was one of four types of "dysphemia," the other three being "aphemia," "paraphemia," and "tachyphemia."

15. Note use of the word "spasm." See also his statement in the 1932 *University of Iowa Studies in Child Welfare*, Vol. 5, No. 5, reproduced here in Chapter 7. Further, in the 1935 statement, he emphasized that these "various interruptions" should be considered in regard to "the type of stuttering characteristic of each stutterer," noting that in some instances certain of these interruptions might not be actual stutters.

16. See, for instance, Greenberg (1965), Labov (1973), Lenneberg (1967), Quinting (1971), Studdert-Kennedy (1975), Sweet (1877).

17. See Wingate 1962a; 1976, Chapter 4; 1988, Chapters 1 and 2.

18. For some time in his earlier writings Johnson had used the term "nonfluency" as a general rubric. For instance, in *The Onset of Stuttering* (1959) the index contains 21 separate entries under "nonfluency"; the word "disfluency" does not appear at all. In keeping with Johnson's characteristic maneuvering with words, it seems highly likely

that he purposefully coined the much more obscurantic "disfluency" simply because it is a homophone of "dysfluency." It is pertinent to note here that West (1958) was critical even of Johnson's use of "*non* fluency;" in fact, he raised serious, logical questions about the whole notion of semantogenesis. Evidently, few took note.

19. See Wingate 1962a; 1962c; Wingate 1988, Chapter 2.

20. *Stuttering in Children and Adults*, p. 198. This acknowledgment appeared in other places as well; see, for instance, Steer and Johnson (1936).

21. Wingate, 1962a; 1962b; 1962c. The only clear sign that the criticisms had been noted was a weak and inaccurate reply from Johnson himself (Johnson 1962).

22. See Johnson's own personal statement, early in Chapter 7.

23. Most computations of this proportion vary between 7 and 12 percent. See, as examples, Johnson and Brown (1935), Hejna (1955), and Soderberg (1962).

24. This is another instance of an etiologic definition. This one is in latter-day form, in which speech is mentioned but the description is so broad as to have no definitive value. For instance, this particular statement could well describe a contrite drunk.

25. "Theory" has been marking time for over fifty years. (As discussed in Chapter 7, introspection is the essential substance of Johnson's notions.)

26. The substance of these two sources (Bloodstein and Perkins et al.) exemplify con-cerns raised by Andreski (1972) in *Social Sciences as Sorcery*.

27. Although the contribution of "the label" is not now so pointedly emphasized, the dogma and its radii are clearly present (see Starkweather et al. 1990).

28. See Chapter 7. Also see the section on recovery in Chapter 9.

29. Johnson et al. 1959, Tables 56 and 57, p. 171. Incidentally, the interviewers and the parents evidently agreed well (Table 58).

30. The least well known evidence (because it was ignored) has already been re-viewed, in Chapter 7, and noted above. The readily available evidence (because point-edly emphasized) will be presented in Chapter 9.

31. The most impressive and convincing evidence of this fact is that whenever a "new" treatment method is announced, usually with extravagant claims, the method is greeted within the profession with universal suspicion and doubt. Such reception is couched in the implicit assurance that this "new" method too will soon be shown to have the mediocrity of the others.

32. The prognostic inadequacy of any observable features was highlighted in some recent excellent research reported by Yairi (1995). At the same time, certain spectro-graphic features show promise. Originally described by Stromsta (1965; and 1986, Appendix II) they were noted again recently by Kowalczyk and Yairi (1995).

33. In fact, consistent with the dismal record for stuttering therapy, very few recov-ered stutterers who have had therapy give it much credit for their improvement. For a summary of studies dealing with recovery from stuttering, see Wingate 1976, Chapter 5.

34. With perhaps an eye to drumming up business.

35. Well represented currently in the persisting efforts to demonstrate "unreliability" of stuttering identification.

CHAPTER 9

Other Dimensions

The span of time encompassed in this chapter is roughly the same fifty-odd years covered in Chapters 7 and 8. However, Chapter 9 is addressed to major events and developments occurring during this period that were largely independent of the Iowa school and not in any substantial sense directly influenced by its precepts. In addressing these other developments the effort will be made to present them in essentially chronological order.

SOMEWHERE DEEP IN THE MIND

As noted in earlier chapters, psychological explanations of stuttering had been proffered long before the twentieth century, usually as unsophisticated surmises — in many ways the sorts of inferences made regularly even today by members of the laity as well as by some persons of professional status. Attempts to explain stuttering in psychological terms increased substantially in the twentieth century, due essentially to two highly pertinent major events that took shape around the turn of the century: the burgeoning development of psychology as a discipline, and the emergence of dynamic psychological concepts within psychiatry. Efforts to apply psychological concepts to stuttering soon came to be vigorously pursued, particularly in the fifty-odd years covered in this chapter and the two preceding chapters. The extent of this movement is reflected graphically in Figure 6.1.

Once the various disciplines of psychology began to flourish, as the early decades of the twentieth century passed, the widespread readiness to accept psychological formulations provided fertile ground for the emergence and flowering of a variety of such accounts. Homespun varieties of psychological explanation[1] found avenues for expansion in several directions.

As suggested in the early pages of Chapter 5, it is understandable that psychological explanations of stuttering should find favor and wide acceptance in the United States, especially since so many such explanations have been based on, or derived in reference to, case histories and the testimonials of individuals. The heritage of our cultural ideology supports and encourages the notion that the individual's personal experiences and milieu hold the key to human behavior. The American *political* ideal, and presumed moral tenet, that all men are created equal has, at many levels, been extended and incorporated into the assumption that all persons have essentially comparable inherent capacities, and that differences among individuals, clearly evident to even casual observation, are simply products of environmental forces — those unique circumstances that are presumed to have molded each individual during the course of his or her development.

Moreover, casual everyday observation of stuttering occurrence readily leads to the inference that the disorder is "something psychological" or "something emotional."[2] The fact that stuttering seems to occur or to become exacerbated in circumstances perceived or interpreted as "emotional" readily suggests, or at least encourages, this assumption. Even more important as a source of such belief are the complaints and claims made by many stutterers themselves. In fact, some of the more compelling personal statements from individual stutterers at least imply that the major source of the disorder lies in circumstances that originate in external conditions. Such claims have been accepted as essentially valid by most sources within the profession and have then been featured in the relevant literature, professional and lay. It should also be recognized that the belief that stuttering is "something psychological" gains support through the sympathy that the disorder tends to elicit in normally speaking persons. Further, a substantial amount of support for the assumption derives from the fact that a certain degree of misguided empathy is also elicited in many listeners. That is, normal speakers, recognizing that they are likely to be (normally) nonfluent under conditions of stress, are thereby well prepared to assume that stuttering is caused by emotional arousal.

"Something psychological" is quite a broad rubric that spans a wide range of explanations from, at one limit, accounts that would be considered to be truly psychodynamic to, at the other limit, those that embody the vernacular, everyday appreciation of psychological matters common to the lay person. Somewhere between these limits are the formulations that espouse the principles of learning theory borrowed from the psychological laboratory. In the professional literature, of course, one finds a preoccupation with some variant of either of the esoteric accounts — dynamic psychology or learning theory. Within this range of more or less sophisticated explanatory effort one finds formulations that employ, in varying degree, certain specially favored concepts.

The various expressions of formal psychological explanation, as noted above, are not quite as different as they might appear to be. All of them attempt to link what is directly observable—the stuttering—to certain hypothesized underlying processes that are assumed to be the source of what occurs outwardly. Moreover, all of these accounts are based, in varying proportion, in two essential variables: emotion, and learning. The essential differences among these accounts are to be found only in respect to (1) the emphasis placed on one or the other of these two variables, and (2) the interpretation of the relationship said to exist between underlying process and overt acts.

In psychodynamic accounts, on the one hand, the overt acts, the so-called symptoms, are believed to afford the key to understanding the underlying personal dynamics (conflicts, etc.) that are supposedly the source of the symptoms, and how the dynamics and the symptoms are interrelated. Learning theory explanations, on the other hand, begin with the hypothesized underlying process(es), the "principles of learning," that are believed to provide the key to understanding the acts and how they were "acquired."[3]

The truly psychodynamic formulations emphasize the emotional forces that are presumed to be active in the subconscious "mind," representing conflicts and stresses of which the individual is unaware and with which he presumably cannot deal openly. These forces are said to be the font of the overtly expressed "symptoms" (the overt acts; in this case, stutters). However, learning also plays an important role in such explanations, since the acts (the symptoms) are assumed to have been acquired via the agency of the psychodynamic pressures.

At the other limit, idealized learning theory accounts place emphasis on the process(es) by which certain acts are presumably acquired and stabilized. These processes also are assumed to occur below the individual's conscious awareness, but this unawareness does not have the aura of "forbidden" impulses that must be kept from conscious awareness (which are salient in psychodynamic accounts). At the same time, emotion also plays an important part in learning theory formulations, albeit in a much less dramatic guise, in the form of "motivation," "feelings," or "reinforcement." Although this form of emotion is not often presented as such, it is actually the central aspect in learning accounts, inasmuch as it is the source that is said to energize the process of acquisition.

It is especially important to recognize that all purely psychological accounts of stuttering have another dimension in common. All of them contain the implicit assumption that stuttering is not really, in essence, a disorder of speech. A major dimension of this assumption is that the linguistic, neurological, and motor systems underlying, and involved in, production of the eventual acoustic signal are essentially and fundamentally normal. Accordingly, the stuttering that one observes is believed to be the result of events and circumstances of the individual's personal history that operate, within his[4] "mind," to distort expression of the final product, namely, normally fluent speech — the ordinary external expression of a person's intent to communicate verbally.

Although learning theory concepts have come to occupy, in fact dominate, center stage in attempts to explain the nature of stuttering, psychodynamic and personality "theories" of stuttering came into prominence earlier. This sequence in priority can be explained simply by noting that Sigmund Freud arrived on the scene before John B. Watson did and, moreover, that Freud had a much more enthralling story to tell. Freud's influence began with his visit to Clark University in 1909, and it spread quickly throughout both professions and the lay public in the United States.[5] Although Watson's "behaviorist manifesto" was delivered only a few years later, in 1913, it was hardly as sensational a message as the one conveyed by Freud. Also, Watson's communication was addressed originally to a more staid audience, members of a professional organization concerned primarily with what was then largely an academic issue. Watson's views had a relatively limited sphere of influence until well into the 1920s, after which time they came to have a rapidly widening impact. The burgeoning acceptance of behaviorism resulted largely from two circumstances. First, Watson's own expanding writings were now addressed in considerable measure to the lay public. Second, his position fit hand-in-glove with Mead's *Coming of Age in Samoa*, which, proclaiming the validity of cultural determinism, was being so enthusiastically accepted at the time (see Chapter 6). By the 1930s behaviorism had attracted a considerable following which would expand rapidly within the next decade and continue to grow apace in ensuing years.

Deep and Dark

Psychodynamic accounts of how people act and of the reasons for the things they do have always had an inherent appeal. They contain an air of mystery, intrigue, excitement, and suspense, a fascination with the unknown, a strong hint of the forbidden, the promise of discovery and revelation. From direct personal experience, we all have evidence of what we can accept as a nonconscious dimension of "the mind," if only through recollection of our dreams, or simply the awareness that we dream. It is the sort of evidence corroborated by reports of similar experience from others. We are also aware, both directly and vicariously, that some of our dreams reflect certain wishes, or feelings of fear, or anger, or longing.

Just as lay ideas about "bad habit" underlie the preoccupaton with stuttering as "learned behavior," so the homespun notions that link stuttering to fear, embarrassment, self-image, and related circumstances have provided the underpinning for a variety of psychological explanations of the disorder proposed in professional sources. Some of these accounts are hardly more sophisticated than lay notions. However, some of them have invoked quite esoteric ideas from extant psychodynamic theorizing which are then applied to stuttering.

The most arcane of such accounts are the psychodynamic interpretations that, through one avenue or another, owe their substance to notions arising from writings in psychoanalysis — the works of Freud and his original followers, and the contributions of neo-Freudians as well. Applied to stuttering, such accounts start from the assumption that the stutter is a symptom of some significant inadmissible internal conflict which, held to be threatening to the integrity of the personality, is actively submerged into the nonconscious. Further, expression of the ineffable conflict is said to be diverted from the patient's conscious awareness, and from revelation to others, through the development of a "symptom," which is linked symbolically to the nature of the conflict.

The following descriptions exemplify the application to stuttering of certain well-known features of the Freudian account of psychological ("psychosexual") development. Two of the very early sequences in personality development, according to Freud, are oral dependency and then oral aggressivity. So, the obvious fact that stuttering involves oral activity readily invited conjectures purporting to explain the nonconscious "hidden" significance of the acts that occur in the course of a stutter. Thus, in some accounts stuttering has been interpreted as the symbolic expression of an inadmissable, and therefore repressed, need to be dependent. In this account the oral activity of a stutter event is supposedly the literal representation of a non-conscious wish to once again be a suckling. Of course, a viewpoint based on a theoretical preference for the oral aggressive stage would yield a different interpretation, and this belief also has been advanced. In this version the stutter "symptom" is held to represent repressed impulses of hostility and aggression. Accordingly, the oral activity occurring in stutter is said to represent an inadmissible desire to bite, lacerate, and otherwise cause damage with the mouth.

A milder version of the latter interpretation was expressed in the contention that the stutterer actually succeeds in expressing his presumed underlying hostility merely through the occurrence of his stuttering. That is, his auditor is reputed to be effectively trapped in an uncomfortable position, a social and emotional dilemma wherein he is caught between a compassionate wish to help and at the same time a felt obligation to feign unawareness — and overall, a pressing desire to flee from the encounter.

In Chapter 5 it was noted that, following his departure from Iowa, Travis had shifted his talents to addressing stuttering in psychodynamic terms. He justified this change in orientation as occasioned by the fact that his new facilities were limited to clinical rather than experimental support and that, feeling an obligation to "get results" with stutterers, he thought that adopting an essentially psychoanalytic approach seemed indicated. Actually, this rationale was contradicted by the literature that was even then available, since reports from eminent psychoanalysts of the time[6] had revealed independently that their efforts with stutterers had been disappointing. Nonetheless, Travis undertook to work and write in this medium with a creative imagination and verbal flair comparable to others writing in that vein.

Because Travis is clearly a major figure in the history of stuttering and because his expositions in the psychodynamic line fully represent the character of such interpretations, it seems appropriate here to introduce some exemplary quotations from his best-known statement of such content (Travis 1957), as follows.

In capturing the essence of the psychodynamic position in general, as presented above, Travis said:

A symptom is a remark about the culture in which that symptom developed. It is a reflection upon the nurturing influences of the home and the community in which the person was reared . . . the patient . . . found along the way that to react symptomatically reduced drives and tensions. His symptom was thus rewarded or reinforced, and in this sense learned. (p. 918)

The final sentence of this part of his statement invokes the substance of learning theory, for which he made a pertinent reference to a well-known literature source on psychodynamics (Dollard and Miller 1950). Travis went on to apply this form of analysis to stuttering, saying, "Stuttering may be conceptualized then as a final defense or block against the threatening revelation through spoken words of unspeakable thoughts and feelings." (p. 934) Applying this formulation to his diagnostic assessment of an individual stutterer yielded the following description:

His fear and anxiety were not over the possibility of stuttering speech. They were over the threat of the telling in talking, of giving himself away in his words. He was never afraid of his stuttering per se. Really, he was afraid that his stuttering, as a defense, would not hold. He was afraid of possible loopholes in his stuttering and the consequent probability that his blocking utterances were not capable of fulfilling their purposes of defending against words conveying unspeakable feelings and thoughts. (p. 936)[7]

Consistent with the belief regarding the nature of stuttering, personality "theory" positions contend that the treatment of stuttering must deal with the forces presumed to be responsible for the disorder. Treatment must work to remove, minimize, or neutralize the influences within the stutterer's mind that are believed to evoke the "symptoms" that are seen overtly as stuttering. From this position, to work directly with speech is "only symptomatic" treatment. That is, therapy addressed to speech processes is considered to deal only with what are believed to be the symptoms, not the cause, of the problem and therefore cannot be expected to yield cure or even substantial improvement.

The various themes in this line of explanation have had their own spheres of influence, which varied in size, effect and duration. Some of these views have persisted, and undoubtedly at least certain of their tenets will continue to find acceptance in some quarters for some time to come. However, the heavy surge of this kind of "theory" crested during the 1950s and has been slowly subsiding thereafter. Personality accounts of stuttering gradually lost their appeal as it slowly became evident that treatment from this orientation was lengthy, tedious, expensive — and unsuccessful. However, an even more telling basis for disillusion with such accounts was that pertinent research consistently yielded negative or unsupportive evidence. By the late 1950s psychodynamically based "theories" of stuttering were in clear decline (see Wingate 1976, Chapter 2).

Other formulations have fallen somewhere between the heavily psychodynamic, on one hand, and those attempting to adopt a clear learning theory paradigm on the other hand. A variety of such positions have taken form, but little would be gained from a comparative review of them. However, brief attention to a representative of this group seems appropriate.

Explanatory efforts that have attempted to combine ideas from psychodynamics and learning theory are exemplified in the "conflict theory of stuttering" proposed by Sheehan (1958), another stutterer with a background in psychology. This account was constructed on the schema of the "double approach-avoidance conflict," one of the motivational conflict paradigms described by Miller (1944). It also incorporated contributions from Freud's writings on anxiety (Freud 1936), the "two-factor theory of learning" proposed by O. H. Mowrer (1956),[8] and Sheehan's own personal experiences and reflections. The crucial, although unrecognized, fault of this construction was that the major dimensions presented as the analogues, for stuttering, of the double approach-avoidance conflict paradigm, could not logically be fitted to the hypothetical model.

In Miller's paradigm the organism, initially in a neutral circumstance, becomes motivated to move toward either of two "goals," both of which have attractive and repellant "valences." The attractive dimensions of either goal are initially ascendant, eliciting approach. However, as the goal is neared its repellant features become more potent than its attraction, causing the organism to then move toward the other goal. However, upon approaching the second goal the events that transpired relative to the first goal recur, and the organism is then caught in a vacillation between the two alternatives. In Sheehan's use of this paradigm stuttering is explained as representing a vacillation between the opposing "goals" of *speech* and *silence*. However, this intended application of Miller's paradigm contains a critical hiatus not recognized by its author or by many others who have accepted this account. The critical, nullifying element in this transposition is that, in contrast to the model it supposedly matches, there is no neutral starting point from which to move toward either presumed valence (of speech or silence). There is no separate, neutral, initial condition from which an individual proceeds to begin speaking or to begin being silent. One is either silent, or speaking!

This serious discrepancy did not, however, limit the range of speculation and interpretation through which the "conflict theory" formulation was spelled out. In fact, it should be noted in passing that this construction also contained certain other damaging limitations, in the form of various assumptions and inconsistencies. Beyond these, the overall nature of the formulation is well reflected in the treatment of several instances of paradox that arise. Here, as in the Iowa school "evaluation" theme, paradox was not only tolerated but presented as explanatory. The most flagrant of the paradoxes in the "conflict theory" account is the following. As a summary statement of a section that purports to explain how his "fear-reduction hypothesis" clarifies "a number of relationships," Sheehan writes: "Hence we have a paradoxical relation — the stuttering produces the fluency and the fluency produces the stuttering" (1958: p. 133). As noted previously (Chapter 8) in regard to the matter of paradox, the rational and scientific treatment of paradoxes endeavors to resolve them, not to offer them as explanation.

Many explanations of stuttering that contain some mixture of personality variables and learning principles do not attempt so formal a structure as does the preceding account. In these less formalized views, ideas from the two conceptual sources are casually intermingled and not differentiated. As could be expected, then, the presumably relevant treatment approaches incorporate some mix of counseling and instructional dimensions.

The explanatory accounts that focus on or exclusively feature ideas borrowed from learning theory have been considered in the two previous chapters and need only be noted here. However, this is a good point at which to include an example of how various funds of data of great potential significance for stuttering can be shaped to conform to a psychological account of their pertinence.

It was noted in Chapter 4 that in the nineteenth century several writers had remarked that stuttering occurs more often in males than in females. By the 1930s this observation had been made sufficiently often to become accepted as a fact about stuttering. One nineteenth century writer had conjectured that this advantage to females might reflect that girls receive "kinder treatment" than do boys. In the middle of the twentieth century this kinder treatment notion would serve as the core of an hypothesis offered to explain the sex difference in stuttering prevalence in terms of environmental influence and learning.

By the middle of the twentieth century a considerable amount of research dealing with children, undertaken within a range of disciplines, had yielded data on many variables relative to comparisons between boys and girls. Schuell (1946, 1947) endeavored to account for the sex difference in stuttering in reference to these data. Her extensive review of the studies on boy-girl comparisons contained compelling documentation that on many dimensions of comparison (physiologic, medical, maturational, developmental, behavioral, scholastic, linguistic) boys evidenced more intrinsic limitations than did girls. Schuell posited that, in specific reference to stuttering, the greater frequency of stuttering in boys than in girls did not reflect the various limitations themselves, but instead resulted from the psychological pressures generated by an unsympathetic environment. In developing this interpretation Schuell invoked three sources of explanation: the oft-repeated folklore regarding the supposed differential treatment of boys versus girls; something from "evaluation theory" claims; and reference to the presumed pertinence of learning principles.[9]

In closing this section it is pertinent to note again that, from the simple and mundane to the intricate and esoteric, whether dynamically oriented or reflecting learning theory, psychological accounts of stuttering are structured around a network of assumptions that are rarely recognized. The central assumption is that stutterers have the inherent ability to speak normally. An implicit companion assumption is that the actual neural systems underlying speech are intact and functioning normally. It is further assumed that this normal capability is somehow affected by adverse forces or influences within the psyche, most of which supposedly have an external origin and, as well, a persisting connection of some sort with those external factors. In such schemes, both the speech and the nonspeech (accessory) aspects of a stutter event are believed to be merely symptoms of an underlying psychological disturbance. These beliefs carry the further assumption that, once the deleterious influences creating the disturbance are removed or neutralized — the treatment objective — normal speech will ensue.

One other, actually more profound, assumption underlies the beliefs outlined in the preceding paragraph, namely, the assumption that normal speech is automatic. This assumption surfaces openly in statements to the effect that the goal of therapy is to return a stutterer's speech to "automaticity." This particular assumption reflects an appallingly casual and uneducated conception of the nature of speech.

The Matter of Symptoms

Psychodynamic accounts of stuttering regularly refer to the "symptoms" of stuttering. Use of the term in these formulations reflects their background in medicine, wherein symptoms are signs of some underlying disorder. Reference to symptoms is especially intrinsic to psychodynamic positions, inasmuch as symptoms are integral to the overall scheme of explanation. That is, in these accounts symptoms are not simply, as in their medical model, "signs" of some underlying disturbance; they are held to be interwoven with and symbolic of that disturbance. That is, in such conceptions symptoms not only have reference to *cause,* they are also believed to have a *significance* and an *economy.*[10]

It is important to recognize that psychologically based accounts of stuttering other than those linked to a medical model also speak of the "symptoms" of stuttering. However, in such accounts a reference to symptoms is inappropriate, essentially because no underlying disorder is hypothesized.[11] Nonetheless, many such accounts not only speak of symptoms but refer to "the variety" of supposed symptoms. Of course, the variety that is claimed has to consist predominantly of *non*speech events — the accessory features — since the speech features[12] are very limited in number (just two). Although it is seldom acknowledged, or even recognized, the nonspeech aspects are not at all distinctive of stuttering (as symptoms should be). First, accessory features are not present in many cases of stuttering. Second, to the contrary, many such acts may and do occur among various individuals, whether speaking or not, and for a variety of reasons that may have no connection whatsoever to speech.

The reader may recall that the notion of supposedly varied "symptoms" of stuttering also surfaced, but only for a brief time, about the middle of the nineteenth century. In view of the frequency with which the claim of varied symptoms of stuttering has been made in modern times (for instance, Bloodstein 1981, 1995; Froeschels 1921, 1961; Johnson 1944a, 1944b; St. Onge 1963; Solomon 1932; Van Riper 1937, 1971), the idea clearly has held much more appeal in the twentieth century, most likely because it fits into psychological accounts of the disorder. Significantly, the idea has held great appeal for those who give considerable space in their accounts to notions involving learning. The idea that stuttering consists of a variety of "symptoms," which reportedly differ among those affected, fits very well into explanations of stuttering as individualized acquisition of disparate "behaviors."

All of the sources just cited speak quite authoritatively of the "great variety" of these so-called symptoms, implying that this is a fact of the disorder. The claim is evidently widely accepted, especially among the vast majority of those who subscribe to a belief in stuttering as "something psychological." However, beyond the matter of questioning the validity of these features as symptoms, there is a logistic issue as well. The — typically casual — notation regarding the extent of the purported variety easily gets out of hand, as epitomized in the statement by Froeschels (1961) that, in reference to "many thousands" of cases, he claimed that "no two cases ever had identical symptoms." This claim is exemplary of the loose casualness and extravagance of many statements made throughout the field by various "authorities;" statements that are accepted at face value and then repeated ever and anon as though they represent reality. In this particular instance even the claim of having personally examined "many thousands" of stutterers is itself highly questionable; but the implication of having made, and being able to remember, comparisons of every one of these cases to every other one should overwhelm anyone's credibility.[13]

In marked contradiction to the claims of the great variety of purported symptoms of stuttering, it now seems adequately documented that the only true symptoms are the speech features, the ubiquitous clonic and tonic markers by which stuttering has always been identified and which, in reality, characterize the disorder (see Wingate 1988: p. 9ff.).[14] Nonetheless, the claim of "variety of symptoms" persists, evidently because it is satisfying to various conceptual predilections.

AN OUTSTANDING CLINICIAN

Charles Van Riper stands out among those deserving of special mention in a history of stuttering, and with a commentary that is essentially positive. His contribution in the twentieth century is the most lengthy of all the notable figures in the field. His professional activity and achievement extended over the entire fifty-year period reviewed in this and the preceding two chapters.

Van Riper has been widely respected[15] for his clinical work with various defects of speech, but principally for his contributions in stuttering. A stutterer himself, much of what he did and had to say about the disorder clearly was influenced by his own experiences, both his personal recollections as a stutterer and from his clinical activity. However, this background did not overdetermine the orientation he expressed. Generally, his contributions were characterized by a certain eclecticism and a degree of flexibility that led to notable modifications in his position as time passed. He always gave considerable attention to psychological aspects of stuttering, especially the matter of stutterers' attitudes and reactions, including acceptance of word fears and the like. At the same time the stuttering itself remained his focal concern. In his long-term approach to the management of stuttering, the enduring core of his method was to work directly with speech production.

For a considerable length of time in his earlier writings Van Riper accepted the position that stuttering probably has multiple origins, varying from individual to individual. In fact, for some time he was inclined to favor the view that stuttering arises from pressures within the home.[16] However, he was always more interested in treatment of the problem than in speculation about its source, and over time his conviction about origin changed substantially. He came to believe, as did Bluemel, that stuttering is basically an inherent defect[17] which, in some instances, becomes compounded with the individual's own, largely unsuccessful, efforts to manage it. Although he consistently identified stuttering as a defect of speech, he always placed considerable emphasis as well on what he saw as the individual's reactions to the defect, and he considered these to be a major part of the overall problem, especially for cases in which the stuttering persisted. This dimension of his approach was based primarily in his own personal retrospection and clinical activity, rather than on objective research. A major fault that permeates the literature of stuttering in the modern era, it played a role in Van Riper's works as well. Nonetheless, he showed an ability to modify his conception of the nature of stuttering, a flexibility unusual among professionals in the field, especially those who are themselves stutterers. This flexibility was exemplified by the substantial change in his position regarding the supposed "development" of stuttering.

For some years he had accepted the "primary-secondary" scheme proposed by Bluemel. In fact, at one point Van Riper proposed an intermediate "stage," which he named "transitional" stuttering. Subsequently he even added a fourth stage. However, after following this scheme for some years, he repudiated the whole notion. His final statement on the matter of stages and the development of stuttering — for all such schemes, including his own — was that "it was all sheer folly" (Van Riper 1971: p. 101).

Van Riper was open and straightforward in his approach to treatment. He did not consider normally fluent speech to be the goal of therapy. Rather, he sincerely maintained that his treatment objective was to help stutterers achieve "fluent stuttering," and he regularly called attention to his own manner of speaking as prima facie evidence of what he tried to teach. Beyond the attention he always gave to certain psychological factors, the fundamentals of his treatment approach focused on teaching stutterers how to move through points of difficulty by drawing careful attention to the appropriate sequence of speech acts. The core of his method is represented in the well-known procedures of "cancellation" and "pull-out."[18] This method has been widely and successfully employed.

In many ways Van Riper stands as the twentieth-century counterpart of the outstanding English specialist of the nineteenth century, James Hunt (see Chapters 1 and 4), who, as reportedly described by Canon Kingsley, endeavored to teach stutterers "to speak consciously as other men speak unconsciously."[19]

FEEDBACK

By the late 1940s exploration of the earth's atmosphere and nearby space was well under way. The public followed these developments eagerly and, through the extensive media coverage of events, soon gained familiarity with some technological aspects of these achievements. The means by which the vehicles of exploration, rockets, were controlled was of special interest. A prominent aspect of this capability was the system of on-board self-correcting guidance control that kept the vehicles on course. The concepts of servo-systems and of "feedback"[20] as integral to the operation of such systems were understandable to anyone who was attentive to press and other media coverage of those fascinating events.

Delayed Auditory Feedback

Against this background context that featured complex, self-propelled machines having internal control systems dependent upon feedback, there occurred a unique coincidental event that was to have special repercussions for stuttering. In 1950 an acoustics engineer, Bernard Lee, reported having observed an interesting speech phenomenon during the course of testing some electronic equipment. He noted that if a person's speech, transmitted by microphone to the speaker's earphones, were delayed for a critical interval of about a fifth of a second, his speech was disrupted. Evidently the most intriguing aspect of the disruption effected by the delay was a tendency for the speaker to repeat certain syllables. Lee described this particular effect as "artificial stutter," and as illustration of the syllable repetition he had observed, he gave the example "aluminum-num" (Lee 1950).

The significance of this observation and report hinged on the word "artificial." Lee's description of his observation was defensible if the term "artificial" were taken to mean "not real" or "not actual," inasmuch as the syllable repetition he reported is of a word-final syllable. This anomaly is therefore not at all like actual stuttering, which almost invariably involves word-

initial syllables — certainly not word-final syllables. The distinction is absolutely critical. However, Lee's description was interpreted to mean that his report revealed "actual stuttering, artificially created." This interpretation led, for more than a decade, to a substantial literature and no little amount of research addressed to delayed auditory feedback (DAF) and its assumed analogue to stuttering vis-a-vis its supposed effect on normal speech.

The persisting theme propelling this activity was the belief that the servo-system concept offered the ultimate model for explaining stuttering. The basic assumption was that the cause of stuttering was to be found in some anomaly of the acoustic feedback "loop" in the (presumed) cerebral guidance system of speech production.

Eventually research findings yielded ample evidence that the disruption of normal speech effected by DAF does not resemble stuttering; in fact, is quite unlike stuttering. In certain important particulars, as noted above, this conclusion was evident from the beginning. However, the simple but critical difference in locus of the reported syllable repetition was completely ignored. The appealing notion of feedback, which was especially au courant at the time, had created a majority preoccupation. However, beyond the error of wrong position, there were a number of serious internal inconsistencies and contradictions within the attempts to explain stuttering as an acoustic feedback disorder (see Wingate 1976: pp. 227-239). Hardly the least of these contradictions is the fact that the speech of stutterers *improves* under DAF. In this respect it bears mention that the most common effect of DAF is to induce the speaker to slow his speech, in the manner of extending syllables. One might have expected that this finding, along with other observations regarding induced changes in speech, should have invited further exploration along these lines. However, sources having a focal interest in DAF have limited their attention to the auditory and feedback aspects of the phenomenon.[21]

Auditory Masking

During a period approximately concurrent with the excitement over delayed auditory feedback, considerable attention was also addressed to another auditory influence on stuttering: the effect of masking noise. Interest in the effect of masking noise was not precipitated by the DAF surge, but was revived by it. The active interest in auditory masking followed from earlier reports that persons who are deaf or very hard of hearing do not stutter. Among several ideas that had been advanced earlier to account for this observation, evidently the most appealing theme was the most obvious one, and also the most superficial: namely, that a person having a significant hearing loss doesn't hear himself talking. As one might guess, the core of this explanation centers in the belief, so widely held, that stutterers react to their speech defect, which makes it worse. Supposedly, a deaf individual could not be in this position, to wit: since the person cannot hear his speech he is not concerned about it; therefore, he just goes ahead and talks, and does so fluently. The reader might realize that such an explanation also involves the "feedback" notion, although on a different level than that proposed for DAF.

The use of auditory masking with stutterers was intended to mimic this supposed influence of organic hearing loss. The most effective masking source is "white noise," so called because it contains all frequencies of the audible spectrum. Experimentation addressed to the influence of masking noise on stuttering yielded two major findings.

First, it was found that masking noise is most effective when it is loud enough to be above the level of ordinary conversational speech. In fact, this loudness level is necessary in order to substantially reduce or eliminate the stuttering. This finding indicates that the beneficial influence of masking is only indirect, that is, through vocal changes it induces. In the professional literature concerned with auditory masking *per se* one finds occasional mention of the very compelling change in manner of speaking that results when masking is imposed on an individual with normal hearing; namely, that the person speaks much more loudly. This phenomenon, known as the Lombard effect, should be well known to anyone conversant with the subject matter of speech and hearing science. However, this very obvious change in manner of speaking that is induced by auditory masking was not readily considered as the essential vehicle for the observed reduction in stuttering. In common with the focus on delayed auditory feedback, sources caught up in a "feedback" explanation of auditory masking were evidently uninterested in exploring the dimensions of the change that clearly was wrought in the stutterers' manner of speaking.

The second major finding was that auditory masking produced results even when it was programmed electronically to be present only during the silent intervals in speech. This finding was of particular significance because it contravened both the "reaction" and "feedback" explanations of the beneficial influence of auditory masking.

Shadowing

In the early part of the period in which delayed auditory feedback attracted so much attention there appeared another feedback-inspired topic. Called "shadowing," it emerged as a coincidence from a study on dichotic listening, conducted as part of a body of research in speech recognition[22] pursued by an electrical engineer working in the field of telecommunications (see Cherry 1957). The objective of dichotic listening research is to shed light on various aspects of auditory processing in relation to laterality; implications of the findings are deduced from later assessment of participating subjects' performance. Our interest here is only in one dimension of the procedure itself, and its immediate result.

The essential procedure in dichotic listening research is to present different acoustic stimuli to each ear simultaneously, via earphones. In the Cherry study that yielded "shadowing," part of the procedure was to transmit connected speech (narrative material being read aloud) via one earphone and have the subjects repeat what they heard while listening to it. In this procedure then, what a subject repeats follows *immediately* what he or she hears being spoken; hence the name "shadowing."

In his extended writing on electrical transmission of speech (Cherry 1957) Cherry's approach was clearly couched in the concepts of information theory and quantal hypotheses. He viewed the production of speech itself as representing sets of habits, in which perceptual processes played a prominent role. He was thoroughly receptive to the feedback concept, which clearly fit well into his engineering background and his conceptual orientation. He was evidently impressed by B. S. Lee's (1950) report and, although he seems not to have made the erroneous interpretation of the word "artificial," he was nonetheless ready to assume that the feedback concept embodied in DAF represented an analogue for stuttering. In fact, he spoke of stuttering as "a perceptual problem" of the stutterer, in the auditory feedback sense of the term.

Cherry's work relating auditory function to stuttering was actually quite minimal (Cherry, Sayers, and Marland 1955, 1956; Cherry and Sayers 1956).[23] Moreover, it was addressed predominantly to the effects observed under auditory masking. The material dealing with shadowing, which was included in these reports, was presented only tangentially, being almost anecdotal in report form. Nonetheless, the topic of shadowing received the favored emphasis in his application of feedback ideas to stuttering. A central feature of this account was the claim that the change induced in the stutterer's speech while shadowing was the result of his having transferred perception of his own speech to that of the speaker being shadowed. The general impression conveyed in these reports was that the stutterer's speech when shadowing was a faithful copy of what he heard; also, the reports allowed the reader to entertain the image of the lead speaker (who read the narrative) speaking in an ordinary manner. Both of these impressions were very misleading; the speech of both participants (leader and shadower) was ill-described and neglected in the reports (see below).

Serious reservations about the value and significance of shadowing, certainly as presented, should arise if one looks carefully at what this work had to offer. Cherry stated (Cherry, Sayers, and Marland 1955) that the shadowing task "presents no difficulty to people of normal speech habits," which implies that any normal speaker can shadow what is spoken by any other normal speaker. However, this claim would surely be doubted by anyone who would undertake to replicate this activity by attempting to "shadow" someone speaking at ordinary conversational rate. The evident contradiction here is resolved by the revelation, noted in only one source (Cherry and Sayers 1956), that the narrative to be shadowed was spoken (evidently in all of Cherry's pertinent work) at approximately half the normal rate. Another clue to the nature of what the shadower heard was mentioned in Cherry, Sayers and Marland (1955), namely, that the narrative was "read by the operator steadily and continuously" (which suggests speaking in a slow, extended fashion — consistent with the relevation regarding rate noted above). Further, the subject was "taught to copy the intonation and rhythm" of what he was hearing.[24]

However, the resulting "shadowed" speech still was clearly not a very good copy of what was being heard. Cherry's notation of a typical performance stated that, in addition to sporadic errors and omissions, a subject's "spoken repetition tends to be in irregular detached phrases and . . . [is] . . . given in a singularly emotionless voice as though intoning" (Cherry 1957: p. 281).

It is remarkable that certain of these features, particularly the critical slow rate, not only were hardly mentioned in the reports regarding this phenomenon but were entirely ignored in review and interpretation of the results. Other features, such as the monotone vocal quality and the breaks and errors in the shadower's performance, were noted but their relevance to analysis and interpretation of the findings was completely disregarded.

The flurry of excitement about shadowing lasted for a relatively short while. Its theoretical value was difficult to justify and evidently pursuit of it led nowhere. Shadowing also had little discernible pertinence to the management of stuttering.

Something Salvaged

The failure of feedback notions to credibly account for the influence on stuttering of both DAF and auditory masking did not substantially deflect or limit an intent to capitalize on these obvious effects. The task of exploring the nature of these effects was clearly less attractive than endeavoring to harness their influence. Soon, specialized devices designed to duplicate these effects began to appear. These instruments will be considered later in this chapter.

RHYTHM AGAIN

As reviewed earlier (Chapter 4), the use of rhythm in treatment of stuttering derived from the sincere interest in and emphasis on good speech that characterized the elocutionary movement that burgeoned at the end of the eighteenth century. Discovery of rhythm's remarkable effect of ameliorating stuttering soon led to its active use for that purpose, and many respectable practitioners employed it as a significant part of their treatment method in the nineteenth century and into the early twentieth century. Around the turn of the twentieth century the establishments known as "the commercial schools" began to offer a special treatment program for stuttering. Evidently the use of rhythm played a substantial role in the methods used in these programs, which seem to have flourished at least into the 1920s.

Professional Repudiation

The emergence and rapid development in the mid-1920s of a formal organization intended to generate professionalism in working with disorders of speech[25] would bring about the demise of these private schools addressed to the treatment of stuttering. The professional association, closely linked to colleges and universities, carried an aura of authority and expertise that eclipsed the images of the private establishments. In addition, academically based programs typically charged nominal fees, if any. Moreover, the private institutes were severly criticized by some members of the young profession. The denigrating appellation "commercial schools" was, in fact, supplied by persons who had attained positions of influence in the growing professional association and who, for one reason or another, felt antagonism toward the private programs.[26] These critics contended that the schools were run by charlatans who, lacking appropriate training and knowledge, treated stuttering through the use of "tricks." The "trick" most denounced was the use of rhythm.

The fact that no one in the professional ranks understood the influence of rhythm clearly did not prevent them from denouncing its use. This ignorance of the effect of rhythm also did not dissuade many from offering a ready explanation for it.

Distraction. The clearly beneficial effect of rhythm has regularly been off-handedly dismissed as due to "distraction."   This explanation had surfaced occasionally in earlier times. Unfortunately, it has been repeated frequently in the extensive literature published since the establishment of the professional association.

It is especially pertinent to call attention here to two other speaking conditons that also are well known to effect   a remarkable amelioration of stuttering: singing and choral speaking. These conditions too have been claimed to produce their beneficial effect by distracting the stutterer from his stuttering. Moreover, the ameliorating influence of certain other conditions, including DAF and auditory masking, also has been explained as due to distraction.

Because the benefits of rhythm have been so regularly explained away by "distraction," but also because this explanation has been so widely applied, so frequently stated, and so routinely recited unthinkingly in respect to other effects as well, this is a good juncture at which to consider it briefly. And there is, at base, a more compelling reason to discuss it: namely, because it deserves a clarifying refutation.

It is important to recognize that "distraction" is undoubtedly the most ingenuous, superficial, and unreflective of the many indefensible explanations that have been offered in regard to stuttering. To accord it any credence whatsoever epitomizes an abysmal lack of basic attributes of a scientific attitude, such as inquiry, circumspection, and rationality. Moreover, its widespread acceptance and recitation by practitioners in the field reflects the catechismal orientation of so many, who nonetheless seem to believe that they try to understand stuttering.

The crucial, absolute fault of the distraction account is that the explanation it intends cannot possibly apply! The meaning of "distraction" is that a person's attention is effectively diverted from that to which he was previously attending; and the typical use of the term in respect to stuttering avers, or clearly implies, this intent. *However*, in none of the conditions that ameliorate stuttering can the individual be said to no longer have stuttering in mind. In fact, the stutterer himself is well aware that his stuttering has markedly diminished — which means that not only does he have stuttering in mind, but that it is most likely *foremost* in his mind. It would seem that this flagrant contradiction should long have been highly visible. Instead, it has obviously escaped recognition for a very long time, a fact that stands as additional testimony to the continued complacent superficiality of explanation in stuttering. Remarkably, the account is still readily accepted in some contemporary sources as "a viable hypothesis" (Conture 1990: pp. 276-277; see also Bloodstein 1993: p. 14 ff.).

Rhythm Returns

In spite of its *non grata* status, the use of rhythm in the management of stuttering reappeared in the early 1960s.[27] Its rebirth was effected through sources that lay outside the field of speech pathology, essentially in psychology and psychiatry, although a notable role was played by a recovering stutterer who had had long personal experience with the use of a metronome.

Had it not been for modern technological capability in electronics, an interest in the use of rhythm for treatment of stuttering might not have resurfaced. In 1963 a psychological journal published an article by two British practitioners, Meyer and Mair, that described the prototype of a miniaturized metronome and its use with stutterers.[28] Within a few years more sophisticated models of the device appeared; the most successful, the Pacemaster, was developed in Philadelphia. Its use was described in several publications of the psychiatry department of the University of Pennsylvania (Brady 1968, 1969, 1971). The unit itself is considered in the section on Modern Devices.

The reemergence of rhythm did not attract much notice. Over the next few years scattered investigations of it were conducted, and a few articles reported provisional use of it clinically. However, in the main it was met with disinterest. Among speech pathologists the general reaction to the therapeutic use of rhythm evidently remains essentially negative. More lamentable, the prevailing attitude toward rhythm's remarkable effect on stuttering is clearly one of indifference.

RECOVERY UNVEILED

For several years during the 1960s a spate of reports dealing with remission of or recovery from stuttering appeared in the professional literature. Not surprisingly the findings in these reports were a revelation to many persons in the field, essentially because the fact of recovery from stuttering had lain submerged for so long. Actually, it is rather more correct to say that evidence of remission had been long suppressed.

Clear evidence of spontaneous remission of stuttering had been presented in very early publications of the professional association in this country.[29] However, reference to these clear documentations of recovery was consistently omitted in subsequent journal and textbook sources. Undoubtedly such findings were ignored because they compellingly contradict the widely disseminated contention that stuttering typically — according to many sources, "invariably" — gets worse. This contention is embedded in the notion of stuttering as a vicious cycle of reaction-struggle-reaction-struggle.[30] For many years the only information on recovery presented to members of the profession had come in the form of occasional symposia at national conventions in which certain stutterers within the profession, who were considered to be "recovered" (although with some reservation), told their personal stories of why they believed their speech had improved. These accounts perforce omitted much pertinent information of the kind contained in the research on recovery.

The authoritative position within the profession in regard to stuttering recovery has not been limited to ignoring the evidence of its occurrence. In fact, even the *possibility* of spontaneous remission has been openly ridiculed by persons within the field through generalized criticism of counsel having been given parents of some stuttering children to the effect that their youngster would "grow out of it." Particularly in view of research findings, criticism of such counsel is highly presumptive and provincial. "Growing out of it" is just what is indicated by much of the evidence yielded by research dealing with recovery.

Various studies have reported differing rates of recovery among the populations studied, but the summary of a considerable amount of research reported by the mid 1970s[31] indicated that approximately half of the youngsters identified as stuttering in preschool years were no longer stuttering by the time they were about eight years of age. A major reason given for recovery, either directly or by implication, was maturational change. The research evidence on the extent of recovery by the time of mid-childhood would thus seem to require that any treatment dealing with children between the ages of two and nine should discount any claimed success rate by at least 50 percent. These findings also are especially pertinent to assertions regarding "prevention" of stuttering, a matter already considered in Chapter 8.

The research data also have revealed that recovery continues through the teen years and into adulthood as well, although the rate of recovery is evidently lower among postpubertal individuals. It was also found that recovery was not limited to those said to have been mild stutterers. In the older age range the reasons given for recovery almost invariably centered around a personal commitment to working at speech improvement. Success was often attributed to quite mundane but straightforward techniques, some of which would be decried by the typical speech therapist. In dramatic contrast, relatively few recovered stutterers who had had speech therapy gave such treatment much credit.

One more finding from the recovery literature deserves special mention because its significance relative to the role of fear. Among those stutterers who recalled having feared stuttering, many reported that the stuttering subsided prior to the time they became less fearful of its occurrence. Equally significant, in contrast, none reported that recovery was due to losing fear of stuttering.

LANGUAGE VARIABLES

As noted in Chapter 7, evidence for what came to be called "language factors" in stuttering appeared around 1940 in a series of reports by S. F. Brown,[32] based on his thesis and dissertation, both done at Iowa under the direction of Wendell Johnson. Evidently these findings did not arouse much interest at the time. Certainly they did not stimulate continued research along this line, except for one independent replication which, by the way, corroborated Brown's findings.

The first study in that first series, undertaken to discover which sounds were most difficult for stutterers, yielded equivocal results. However, extensions of this inquiry revealed that stutter events do not happen randomly in the speech sequence. It was discovered that the places (loci) where stutters occur are closely associated with various readily identifiable aspects of oral language expression. In the final article of that series Brown (1945), in summarizing his findings, identified four variables that he believed were "adequate to account for the loci of stuttering," and he concluded that there was "no indication of any additional factor." The variables he identified were as follows:

1. Type of phone: most consonants were associated with stuttering much more often than were vowels. As noted in preceding chapters, the consonant-vowel distinction had been noted several times before, in the nineteenth century. Brown's data qualified the literal consonant-vowel distinction with evidence that five consonants (/ h /, / ð /, / w /, / hw / and / t /) were stuttered no more often than vowels.
2. Grammatical class: nouns, verbs, adjectives, and adverbs were involved in a stutter much more often than were articles, prepositions, conjunctions, and pronouns.
3. Sentence position: stutters occurred more often with the first three words of a sentence than with later words.
4. Word length: stutters were more frequent with words of five letters or longer.

For some reason Brown failed to mention two other variables, both of which had been more outstanding in his findings than the four he listed: word-initial position, and stress-bearing syllable. One could have expected that word-initial position would stand out as significant; it has been noted so routinely in the history of stuttering that it stands as a universal feature of the disorder. Stress-bearing syllable, on the other hand, was a finding newly revealed in this early series.

The resurgence of interest in language variables, beginning in the early 1960s, took Brown's reports as the point of departure, and the extended inquiry in this vein has continued into the present time. Much of this research has centered around the four factors that Brown emphasized in his 1945 recapitulation, and the results obtained have continued to corroborate Brown's findings. Research during this period also contributed one additional dimension, namely, that stutter events also are inversely related to the frequency with which words can be expected to occur in actual use. That is, stutters are much more likely to be associated with less frequently used words.

As noted in Chapter 7, the authors[33] of the initial reports, eager to account for the findings in terms of stutterers' reactions, developed the explanation that each of these "language factors" had some form of "prominence" for stutterers. The notion of prominence, proposed as a rubric to encompass all of the "factors," actually centered in the idea of "meaningfulness," which, in turn, contained the assumption that it is the stutterer's concern about conveying meaning that is the ultimate, determining source of the difficulty he evidences (the stuttering).

In the subsequent research on language factors, which emerged twenty years later in the revival of interest in this topic, the idea of meaningfulness was for a time expressed through the concept of "information load," borrowed from psychologically based research on normal speech. The appeal of "information load" was that it seemed to offer a way to measure meaningfulness. However, within a few years the initial appeal of this framework faded, largely because of serious faults in the concept itself.

It is of special interest that more than ten years before publication of the "language factors" reports by Brown, Orton (1927, 1929) had expressed his inference that stuttering involves language function. Orton noted that certain well-established observations about stuttering suggested that the disorder is "related to the plane of the speech effort." This description implies that stuttering is some function of the level of complexity of an utterance. However, Orton's pithy observation, if even recognized, was not considered seriously until very recently.

For the most part the later research on language factors (post-1960) also carried forward Brown's assumptions that the factors he had identified were essentially independent variables and that the four he emphasized also were "adequate to account for the loci of stuttering." In fact, at this time a fair amount of the research was an expression of interest in determining a hierarchy of importance of these several factors. At the same time, some attention came to be addressed to such linguistic variables as syntax and prosody.

Inquiry into the former dimension was not particularly fruitful. However, research addressed to prosody yielded promising leads which, in addition, were seen to align well with notable observations made many times in the past about some connection between stuttering and voicing; for instance, the many nineteenth-century assessments that referred to "spasms of the glottis," and the notations by Hunt, Klencke, and Bluemel pointing out the significance of the *vowel*[34] rather than the initiating consonant. The focus on prosody and voicing also seemed clearly to articulate well with observations and research pertinent to what have come to be called the "ameliorative conditions" for stuttering.[35]

Eventually the several "language factors" were shown to be not separate and independent variables, but highly interrelated facets of a configuration centering on words as spoken in propositional context (Wingate 1988, Chapter 5). Of particular significance was the discovery that the essence of this configuration could be expressed through the two facets that Brown had omitted in his final summary: word-initial (actually, syllable-initial) position, and stressed syllable.

It was pointed out (Wingate 1988) that these two cardinal facets of the stutter event are isomorphic with the principal features of the syllable-structure hypothesis, an analysis of word structure generated from recent linguistic inquiry. As such, these particular language factors were proposed as the foci for a psycholinguistic conception of stuttering into which a range of other linguistically pertinent information about stuttering could be integrated.[36] It seems clear that findings emanating from psycholinguistics will continue to make substantial contributions to understanding stuttering.

Evidently, the analysis of language factors that placed emphasis on the central importance of voicing soon led to the construction of two special electronic devices designed to bring into focus the vocal dimension of the speech signal. These units are described in the section on modern devices.

Particularly in view of the attention that has come to be focused on voicing, it is of paramount importance to recognize that the integrative analysis of language factors (see above) led to identifying prosody, not simply voicing, as the major dimension of the speech signal deserving attention. Practitioners concerned with stuttering have for a long time addressed attention, and explanation, to laryngeal function (voicing, phonation) as central to stuttering, and this focus is still maintained in certain sources. However, it is not voicing per se that is faulty in stuttering. The problem arises when voicing must play its featured role in the service of language expression.

BACK TO THE FUTURE

Interest in neurological involvement in stuttering began to reappear in the late 1960s. Like the renascent interest in linguistic processes, attention to neurological dimensions has grown gradually, although intermittently, since that time.

This rejuvenated area of investigation has developed along two roughly separate lines of observation and inquiry. One approach is addressed to the occurrence of "acquired" stuttering, stuttering that became manifest following some demonstrable insult or known damage to the central nervous system. Instances of acquired stuttering have been reported to occur in association with various forms of aphasia, dysarthria, and apraxia and, as well, in other forms of damage to the brain resulting from penetrating wounds, closed-head injury, and infections.

It is of particular interest that the reports of these investigations have consistently included recognition that "stuttering" refers to sound or syllable repetitions and blockings in initial position. This recognition was evident not only in literal statement of these characteristics, but in the distinctions drawn between stuttering and other forms of disturbance in fluency that also are frequently seen in these conditions, such as articulation errors and efforts to correct them, or movement errors of other kinds. Distinctions also have been drawn between stuttering and other kinds of dysfluency that are typical of palilalia and those frequently found in Parkinsonism.

The other avenue of investigation of central nervous system function has employed various methods of assessing cerebral function in stutterers themselves, and vis-à-vis normal speakers. Prominent among such methods are dichotic listening and other assessments pertinent to cerebral lateralization, cortical blood flow, electroencephalography, and electrophysical techniques.

An overriding feature in all of this study of cerebral function relative to stuttering is the ever-present reference to differences in structure and function of the two cerebral hemispheres, particularly in respect to their participations in language. This abiding focus does not represent a literal revival of the cerebral dominance hypothesis, although the general idea of dominance of some sort or degree finds expression in various ways. Current efforts reflect, instead, the expanded knowledge of the brain and its operations that has been achieved over the intervening years. At the same time, it is somehow vindicating to the contributions of Orton and Travis that their work and concepts are by no means dismissed, nor even merely at the periphery of this renascent interest in the neurology of stuttering.

In relatively recent times, research interest in speech processes (as related to stuttering) also has reappeared. Most of this work carries reference to neurological substrates of speech production. Some of this research is oriented to or couched in a linguistic context, but this dimension still receives relatively little attention. A separate and more popular line of inquiry has been addressed to motor and physiological dimensions of oral expression per se. Much in this line is considerably removed from linguistic considerations; in fact, some of this type of research continues to carry within it an explanatory reference to psychological factors.

REAL GENETICS

In the late 1970s happenstance brought a revival of attention to the question of heredity in stuttering. The revival was represented almost exclusively in the work of Kenneth Kidd (1984), an outstanding geneticist whose work in other areas of human genetics led him to inquire into the heredity of stuttering. Over a period of several years his findings in regard to stuttering have corroborated the results from heredity studies done some forty years previously, along with intermittent clinical evidence, that stuttering does indeed "run in families." His analyses showed that two different genetic models provide a good fit to the data of stuttering. Although both models admit of some possible non-genetic influences, such contributions are essentially physiological in nature.

This topic of hereditary factors in stuttering contains a remarkable example of the persistence with which provincial beliefs within this field are retained. Kidd reported[37] that he had been approached several times by persons who seriously questioned whether he was aware of the article by M. Gray (1940, Chap-ter 7), their queries containing the supposition that knowing the contents of that publication would lead him to modify his analysis. The Gray article, presumed to constitute evidence for Johnson's claim of the "social heredity" of stuttering (see Chapter 7), was already known to Kidd, who had rejected it as "absurd."

NO PILL YET

As noted in Chapter 4, Potter (1882) reported that treatment with medicines available up to that time, and thought appropriate, were evidently of little use in the management of stuttering. Within the present century, especially since the 1940s, there have been sporadic attempts at medical treatment of stuttering in which a variety of drugs have been tried; these have included stimulants, sedatives, tranquilizers, vitamin supplements, and neuroleptics. Most often the medications tried have reflected the current, or individual, assumptions about the nature of the disorder. Beginning with the early efforts, and reflecting the psychodynamic views of stuttering active in that era, the medications attempted were those being used with some success in a variety of psychiatric disorders. Also, in view of the long-term beliefs that anxiety and tension are central features of stuttering, various sedatives have been tried over many years. With a reviving awareness that stuttering is more likely of neurologic than psychologic origin, drugs used in the control of certain neurologic conditions have received more attention.[38] At the same time, the possible value of certain medications has emerged by happenstance, as when a stutterer's fluency has been noted to improve consequent to taking some drug prescribed for another (physical) condition for which he was being treated.

Overall, the findings from use of a variety of drugs for stuttering have continued to be disappointing, although Brady's (1991) recent review suggests that certain new drugs currently being explored may have promise.[39] However, there is little reason to be optimistic about medication for stuttering until the development of some drug that is uniquely specific in its effect — a unique specificity that itself remains quite obscure. The attempts with drugs, couched in conceptions that stuttering is due to some generalized condition, overlook the substantial evidence that the disorder is somehow intimately and specifically involved with linguistic processing.

It is also pertinent here to mention hypnosis, a nonpharmacological treatment having possible influences similar to certain medications, especially tranquilizers. Periodically, hypnosis is suggested as a treatment for stuttering, for either or both objectives of inducing relaxation or "implanting" the suggestion of speaking fluently. Generally speaking, hypnosis has yielded the same kinds of results obtained with some drugs: an apparently beneficial effect for some cases, but typically mild and temporary. The outlook for hypnosis is similar to that for drugs, and for the same reason: both are what might be called "shotgun" methods that are also, in major respects, shots in the dark.

GATHERINGS OF "FACTS"

Intermittently in the twentieth-century literature on stuttering one finds publications addressed to recording the "facts" about the disorder. Most of these writings seem to have been well-intentioned, with the author endeavoring to set forth what, in his knowledge, appears to be established as dependable, broadly supported information significant to the disorder. However, a review of these sources quickly confirms the general axiom that facts are elusive. As one could expect, this axiom is particularly pertinent to stuttering. Many of the items in these lists have a very limited base and are colored by influences that range from mere happenstance to individual bias.

These lists, appearing spordically over seventy years in the twentieth century, contained varying numbers of items, sometimes with annotations explaining or justifying their inclusion in the list. The significance of the items in explaining the nature of stuttering was usually noted as well. If the items in such lists were truly acceptable as facts they could indeed contribute importantly to an understanding of stuttering. However, reservations about their value quickly arise when considering that the lists show little concordance, even among the eight simpler ones that appeared between 1913 and 1970.[40] For instance, the number of items per list ranges from five to thirteen; nineteen items appear only once; the best concordance (six out of eight) occurs only twice. The major flaw in compiling these lists was the lack of adequate criteria for including items. Of course, there was also no uniform criterial base subtending the several lists, a matter especially significant to a status as "fact."

The latest publications addressed to consideration of facts about stuttering appeared in print early in 1983. The three articles addressed to the matter[41] include much more material than that encompased in the earlier lists. They merit the attention of anyone having a serious, especially a professional, interest in stuttering even though some of this more recent literature repeats the clear limitations of the earlier lists. Also, one must keep in mind that the important matter of establishing clearly defensible criteria for "fact" status has not yet been addressed.[42]

It is notable that certain observations made by a number of nineteenth-century writers are prominent among the items mentioned regularly in these twentieth-century publications, particularly the following: the sex ratio; familial tendency; no stutter when singing.

MODERN DEVICES

In general there seems to be, within the profession, a rather limited and superficial awareness of appliances for stuttering. Particularly since the founding of the professional association, reference to devices, in the literature and through other sources, has typically been brief and negative. Standardly, devices have been soundly disparaged and dismissed as distractions, tricks, or nostrums.

Until fairly recent times the devices proposed as a means of mitigating stuttering have all been of the oral type. The best known of such devices, in terms of their mention in professional sources, were ones developed in the first half of the nineteenth century. The hostile attitude toward these oral appliances evidently reflects in some measure an insular bias regarding such instruments, but it seems also to have been due in considerable measure to having linked them associatively with the brief era of oral surgery for stuttering near the middle of that century. However, it is not appropriate to consider the early nineteenth century as "the era of devices." Oral devices to manage stuttering continued to surface throughout the nineteenth century, and a surprising number have appeared and received patents well into the twentieth century, both in this country and in Europe.[43] One seldom finds mention of them, and such references typically convey a sardonic air.

Electronic Appliances

As noted earlier in this chapter, the development and ready accessibility of miniaturized electronic components in the third quarter of the twentieth century made possible an entirely new kind of appliance, one whose influence is directed through the auditory channel. Two of these devices are designed with the simple intent of altering audition (auditory feedback) and can be described as auditory-interference devices. Both of these devices represent an effort to apply directly what had been observed in the era of excitement over the apparent role of auditory feedback: the effect of delayed auditory feedback and of auditory masking. Two other devices make use of the auditory channel as a means of emphasizing the vocal dimension of ongoing speech. Both represent the effort to implement a principle, derived largely from the psycholinguistic analysis of language factors in stuttering,[44] which points up the salience of the prosodic dimension of speech. A fifth device uses the auditory channel to deliver a rhythmic pulse. This instrument represents the many sources reporting the beneficial influence of rhythm.

Auditory-Interference Devices. At least one portable delayed auditory feedback apparatus was developed and promoted, but there is no clear record of its fate. Its actual use seems to have been both less widespread and shorter-lived than that of devices of the nineteenth century.[45] It is easy to appreciate that, in use as intended, this particular type of feedback device could be expected to soon lose any initial appeal it might have. It had a number of disadvantages. Not only would it be cumbersome because of the amount of hardware required but, more impressively, it would also be impractical and annoying when most needed — in conversation, where the need to wear earphones would pose continual problems. One can also anticipate continual frustration over problems in onset-offset control. Practical efforts to use a DAF apparatus evidently have receded into occasional employment for demonstration purposes in a clinical setting.

A portable auditory masking device, the Edinburgh Masker, attracted an uncertain amount of attention in the late 1970s and early 1980s. However, the instrument was never widely popular, and early in 1995 its manufacture was finally abandoned as an economic liability. Evidently a considerable portion of the limited acceptance attained by the device was due to the active promotional efforts of one stutterer who had found success in its use.[46] Its limitations were very much the same as those posed by the DAF apparatus.

Development of a very similar appliance called the Speech Rectifier, was reported in the *American Journal of Physical Medicine* in 1970.[47] Developed by a psychiatrist and a medical electronics firm, it was said to be the focus of a treatment program at a Speech Rectification Center in Los Angeles. However, use of this instrument evidently was not long-lasting.

The Voice Enhancers. Two appliances that focus on voicing have appeared on the market more recently (circa 1990). The simpler of the two, called the Fluency Master, consists of a tiny microphone with a short, thin tube attached to it. The microphone is pasted to the skin right behind the ear, directly over the mastoid bone, and the tube is led into a molded earpiece like that for a hearing aid. With this arrangement the wearer hears his speech via bone conduction, which substantially enhances the resonant (voiced) dimension of his speech.

One very obvious advantage of this device, in contrast to the two auditory-interference types, is that the sound is not foreign and does not induce the

Lombard effect. It is also much less cumbersome than the foregoing appliances. However, the benefits afforded by this device are not unique to it; as
noted by one stutterer (Weiss 1992), the same effect can be obtained by cup-
ping one hand tightly against the ear while placing the thumb on the mastoid
bone. Most likely the effect could also be achieved by simply occluding one
ear canal!

Prospective users of the device are expected to undergo training in its use. It
is of great interest that the training consists of rehearsing controlled utterances
that gradually increase in length, beginning with single-syllable words and
gradually increasing to brief sentences. Also most notable is the fact that these
exercises are produced at a very slow rate in which the vowel sounds are prolonged.

The second device of this type, called the Vocal Feedback Device (VFD),
clearly has the same objective as the Fluency Master; namely, to give users a
heightened awareness of their voicing. The principal feedback mode of the
Vocal Feedback Device is vibrotactile. The portable version of the basic device,[48] intended to be worn, has three elements: (1) a power pack, somewhat
larger than a cigarette pack, which can be attached to the user's belt; (2) a
transducer, approximately the size of two quarter-dollar U.S. coins, which is
positioned (by tape or band) either on the neck at the level of the larnyx[49] or on
the sternum; and (3) a microphone that is clipped to the shirt.

The Vocal Feedback Device has the same basic advantages as the Fluency
Master in terms of nature of influence and mode of implementation. Although
it also offers, with additional equipment, use of two more feedback channels,
even the basic unit is rather cumbersome, and the additional equipment adds
substantially to the paraphernalia.

With the Vocal Feedback Device, as with the Fluency Master, prospective
users go through a training program in which they are taught to speak very
slowly and deliberately. The VFD is, in fact, presented as an aid to learning a
method of speaking that focuses on rate control and continuous phonation as
pathways to fluency.

The objective of both of these two devices is very reminiscent of what all
three of Bates' devices of 1851 were designed to effect: namely, "an uninterrupted current of sonorous breath" (see Chapter 4).

The Beat Goes On. The device in focus here, called the Pacemaster, is a
miniaturized electronic metronome. It is small enough to fit in a standard be-
hind-the-ear hearing-aid case and is powered by a standard hearing-aid battery.
The rate of the beat is easily regulated with a partially exposed wheel
mounted in the case. The sound is transmitted to the auditory canal via a small
tube and earplug. The early version of the instrument had a volume control as
well, but was found to be unnecessary.

Users of the instrument are advised to begin with a slow beat, approximately
half of conversational speech rate, although individually adjusted. The rate is

then gradually increased as the user becomes comfortably successful with the new rate.

The unit is easy to use, simple to maintain, and no more obtrusive than a hearing aid. Although the sound is continuously present, the soft beat does not interfere with hearing acuity.

As noted earlier in this chapter, the Pacemaster came about through the collaboration of psychiatrists who were exploring the treatment of stuttering and a recovering stutterer who had had lengthy and rewarding experience in improving his speech through the use of a standard desk metronome. First reported in 1968, this instrument predates the other electronic devices. At this time many thousands of these little devices have been distributed all over the world to stutterers who continue to report success and satisfaction with their use.[50]

HELP YOURSELF

Another particularly significant development of the late 1970s was the emergence and substantial growth of stutterer self-help groups. This phenomenon has been coincidental with a number of social and cultural influences of the times, in particular the fervor of the 1960s with its intense concern for minority and individual rights, a heightened awareness of the disadvantaged, and the belated consideration for accommodating the handicapped. Within this context the stutterers' self-help movement expanded rapidly.

The more active of such groups have developed into formally organized associations, have a home office and chapters in many cities, publish a periodical, and hold conventions. In the United States the most vigorous association is the National Stuttering Project, based in Anaheim, California, which publishes a bimonthly periodical, *Letting Go.* The Canadian association is Speak Easy of Canada, based in St. John, Newfoundland. The major, and very active, self-help group in Great Britain is the Association for Stammerers, based in London. It publishes a quarterly, *Speaking Out,* that is distributed in other European countries as well. The British group is evidently the most active in the European League of Stuttering Associations (ELSA), a league of many national self-help associations in Europe. Similar national associations exist in many other countries around the world. Since 1986 representatives of these groups have come together four times in a World Congress of People Who Stutter. At the most recent congress, in 1995, an international federation of these associations was established. This International Stuttering Association, with headquarters in Germany, publishes a semiannual newsletter, *One Voice,* and is supporting development of an international Internet database on stuttering.

A reading of the literature of these associations reveals that they clearly have great value for their membership. At a personal level individual stutterers are afforded a special sense of community, are able to share experiences, feel less isolated, and learn from each other. In addition, the associations provide avenues for educating the public, enhancing employment access, and influencing relevant legislation.

Especially through some of the printed matter from these associations there is also a potential benefit for students of the disorder. In these sources one can find a certain amount of relief from the common textbook stereotypy about stutterers. Most contributors to the newsletters are stutterers who have had little exposure to the professional literature in the field. These predominantly lay stutterers report a considerable variety of individual experiences and express a range of personal views and attitudes that is refreshing. Some of these personal statements contain material of a nature that is not to be found in the sort of "case material" so regularly recounted in publications that originate within the profession. Nonetheless, one also will find in the pages of *Letting Go*, and in other publications from self-help groups, a considerable amount of the standard lore, common to expositions on stuttering, that is found in so many sources in the professional literature and also in other lay sources. In addition, certain clear "theoretical" biases appear, borne largely by individuals having some level of professional connection to the field of stuttering who have involved themselves in the self-help associations. One must therefore read these publications too with considerable circumspection.

It bears mention that current self-help groups had less formal precursors, which existed in more complacent times. One such group was the Kingsley Club,[51] active in Philadelphia between 1940 and 1950. It was organized by a William Smith, who was, significantly, successful as an attorney in spite of his stuttering. Members of the club, who numbered about 100 at its zenith, learned of it through a newspaper ad placed by Smith. All of the members, mostly adults, had had previous treatment (from speech therapy to psychiatry) that had not helped. Their monthly meetings centered around each individual speaking before the group, with liberal use of a desk metronome, a procedure reported to be generally beneficial among the club's members. The club gradually dissolved after the death of its founder, but at least several members were known to have continued use of the metronome method independently; one of them was instrumental in developing the Pacemaster.

ADDENDA AND REFLECTIONS

A similar section at the end of Chapter 4 presented, for the nineteenth century, a review of certain notable observations made about stuttering during that era, and also a summary of the major dimensions in approaches to treatment of that time.

There is little justification for repeating the nineteenth- and twentieth-century correspondences in observations about stuttering that were noted at the end of Chapter 4. It should be recognized, however, that certain items have been repeated with impressive frequency. There is also little reason for attempting to isolate reliable items of information new to the twentieth century. As pointed out in the section on "facts," many of the newer items, which might deserve a certain amount of consideration, would still not qualify as being particularly remarkable. On the other hand, there is justification for saying that, in the long run, there has not been much progress, even though a lot has happened.

Twentieth-Century Explanation

The nature of stuttering is hardly any better understood now than it was a century ago. In the nineteenth century and earlier, stuttering was addressed predominantly as a disorder of speech. Twentieth-century attention to stuttering has not built upon what went before; in fact, most of the relevant earlier information has been either ignored or repudiated. This state of affairs reflects principally the twentieth-century immersion of stuttering in the social sciences — especially psychology. Emerging at the beginning of the century, the disciplines encompassed under this general rubric have held forth the promise of revelation, which offered a wide range of enthralling possibilities for explanation and interpretation of the disorder. Explanatory attempts, loosely called "theories," have been a major preoccupation. The unfortunate result has been that what is currently "known" about stuttering consists of a melange of certain oft-repeated and widely affirmed observations; a certain amount of other data for which the documentation ranges from credible to contestable; a vast hodgepodge of conjecture, not recognized as such, that is couched in an incredible store of provincial but committed belief; and an unflagging penchant to continue looking elsewhere than directly at the disorder itself. And, as noted elsewhere in these pages, the typical twentieth-century "expert" on stuttering is, in varying measure, familiar with certain content from psychology but, in contrast, gives little evidence of knowing much about oral language processes.

Twentieth-Century Treatment

In respect to treatment, the situation is somewhat different but no better. In spite of the various explanatory notions proffered, essentially no new methods of treatment have emerged in the twentieth century. Other than the psychotherapies emanating from dynamic psychological accounts, treatment approaches do not emerge from any other "theory" of stuttering. A dramatic case in point is that, in spite of all the effort and attention devoted to explaining stuttering in terms of learning theory, there are no procedures based exclusively on such accounts.

Instead, treatment methods, procedures, and techniques exist quite independently of any particular "theory." Connections that may be claimed to exist between the two are contrived ex post facto, a maneuver in which extant treatment procedures are linked up verbally with some favored explanatory position. A representative example of such manipulation is revealed in Bloodstein's (1958) acknowledgment of fitting extant therapy methods to his explanatory contentions. In like vein, the supposed "operant programs" offered by, for instance, Ryan and Van Kirk (1971), Mowrer (1975, 1980) and Costello Ingham (1993) employ a procedure first reported early in the nineteenth century.[52] In both centuries the procedure reflects a simplistic grasp of oral language function; a limitation most regretable in the late twentieth century in view of the extensive advances in linguistics. Incidently, the purported operant programs do not really conform to actual operant method.

It is in respect to treatment that stuttering in the twentieth century contains a clearly direct lineage and continuity with preceding times. For most of the century stuttering has been immersed in some psychological orientation, in which a theoretical position is presumed to provide the rationale for treatment. However, in spite of this preoccupation with presumed psychological factors, the treatment efforts undertaken have almost universally dealt with *speech*. Furthermore, despite occasional assertions claiming a "new" method of treatment, one can readily find, usually quite close to the surface, that the crucial aspects of the procedure are either direct borrowings from the past that have long been recognized as worthwhile, or are some variant of a previously employed useful procedure. Most often the central feature(s) will be from among those included in the "speech specific" practices listed in the "Addenda and Reflections" in Chapter 4. It is particularly pertinent to emphasize that all such procedures involve measures for developing control over speech process.

FINIS

The last three chapters have covered the range of ideas about stuttering that have preoccupied attention to the disorder for more than half of the twentieth century. Although one can expect that most of these persuasions will continue to be pressed for some time to come, change is under way. There are indications that inquiry into this curious disorder is gradually, although very slowly, surfacing from its lengthy immersion in loose collections of assumptions, conjectures and beliefs which, unfortunately, are largely compoundings of twentieth century notions. Developments in the last decade of the century give evidence of an increasing interest in studying the disorder in regard to its obvious and undeniable character, namely, as a unique anomaly of oral language expression.

NOTES

1. Which might also be called "vernacular" psychology — the kind of everyday explanations of actions, behavior, and conduct that are based in casual personal or vicarious experience and couched in a variety of common terms that reflect some emotional effect or state (both positive and negative: e.g., fearful, excited, anxious, happy, embarrassed, relieved, etc.).

2. In almost every conversation I have had with a lay person in which the topic of stuttering comes up, the person has volunteered such an inference — sometimes as a question, but most often as an acknowledged fact.

3. One might add that in unsophisticated, lay accounts the "principles" are derived from common folklore type knowledge and experience.

4. Use of the pronoun "his" in discussions of stuttering can claim justification from one of the significant statistics of the disorder, namely that many more males than females stutter, by an overall ratio of four or five to one.

5. Freud's notions were received much more readily and enthusiastically in this country than in Europe. In fact, this situation continued to obtain throughout the twentieth century. See, for instance, Sargent (1964).

6. Notably Brill (1932) and Blanton (1931), Reed (1928) and Scripture (1912). Moreover, these discouraging reports echoed Freud's own reservations regarding psychoanalytic treatment of stuttering.

7. These three quotations exemplify the concept that psychodynamic symptoms have a cause, significance, and economy. See note 10, below.

8. Somewhat later Brutten and Shoemaker (1967) attempted to conform stuttering to this model. This effort too had many limitations (see Wingate 1976: p. 15ff.).

9. Of particular interest is the fact that Schuell neglected to incorporate into this explanation the seemingly contradictory evidence included in her review that more males than females "outgrow" stuttering.

10. These three dimensions are held to characterize the symptoms of psychodynamic disturbance: the *cause* inheres in the subconscious conflict; the *significance* somehow symbolizes that conflict; the *economy* represents symptom role in preventing overt expression of the underlying conflict.

11. Contentions (or implication) of such matters as "fear," "faulty learning," or "belief system" are not dealt with, or properly conceived, as underlyng disorder.

12. Ironically, it is the truly psychodynamic accounts that focus on the speech features.

13. In a 1955 statement (Froeschels 1956) the figure was "about sixteen thousand" stutterers. The claim of no two cases being alike indicates a paired-comparison process. To compare as few as 50 individuals, 2 at a time and *for one variable only*, would require 1,225 separate comparisons. For 100 cases the number of required comparisons would jump to 4,950. This value itself is rather beyond what even a remarkable memory could be expected to manage. Further, the number of required comparisons expands in like proportion as the number of cases increases. It is easy to extrapolate that for even 1,000 cases the number of required comparisons would be astronomical and quite beyond the capacity of any human memory.

14. The reader is also reminded of Potter's (1882: p. 76) critical observation about "varieties" of stuttering. See Chapter 4.

15. By some sources, almost revered. Sociable and friendly, he had a homespun, vernacular style of expression that was very appealing. This story-telling manner was well reflected in his authorship, after retirement, of tales recalled from his childhood, published under the nom de plume Cully Gage (see Gage 1977).

16. See, for instance, Van Riper 1958.

17. In the "recovered stutterers" symposium at the 1957 ASHA convention he remarked, with his characteristic good sense of humor, that he believed that even on his death-bed he would have trouble saying, "Farewell, dear world!" Nonetheless, he continued to show a predilection for emphasizing the role of emotion and featuring the presumed importance of reaction. For instance, in his last book (Van Riper, 1971) the

topic of fear recurs repeatedly; in fact, fear is central to one whole chapter (Chapter 7). Also, earlier in the same source (p. 15) he offered a definition of stuttering as "a word improperly patterned in time," but had to also include "and the speaker's reaction thereto."

18. This method is described succinctly in several editions of Van Riper's widely used book, *Speech Correction*.

19. The methods of other notable historical figures also come to mind in this context, such as Cotton Mather, who came to emphasize "deliberation" (see Bormann 1969), and Edward Warren's insistence that "slowness and deliberation are requisites" (see Warren 1837 [1977]).

20. The term "feedback" rapidly entered the lay vocabulary as an omnibus word that soon came to supplant more specific terms such as: "reply, reflections, opinion, consideration, review, thoughts, deliberations," etc.

21. This orientation has persisted in certain quarters; see, for example, Harrington (1987). Another interesting although tangential finding from some of the DAF research was the evidence of certain nonspecific anomalies of auditory processing among stutterer subjects. The significance of these findings remains unclear.

22. It seemed superfluous to mention in the text narrative that the subjects participating in this body of research had normal speech and hearing.

23. It is of some interest that Cherry used "stuttering" and "stammering" interchangeably. See pertinent discussion, Chapter 1.

24. If one tries "shadowing" it soon becomes evident that, in order to give the shadower a reasonable chance to perform with any level of success at all, the leader must make the adjustments of (1) slowing his speech considerably, and (2) speaking clearly and carefully.

25. The American Academy of Speech Correction, eventually to become the American Speech and Hearing Association. See Chapter 5.

26. Evidently those who were most outspoken in their criticism had attended one of these programs and did not like the method employed. This appraisal is attested in the only extant record of such personal reaction, which is reported by Clark (1964) in her summary of Bluemel's experience. There is reason to believe that W. Johnson, Van Riper, and Sheehan, all of whom were critical of the "commercial schools," had for some time attended one of them. In contrast, as noted in Chapter 5, other individuals in the profession also had attended such programs and spoke well of them.

27. One earlier article, describing what its author considered "a new method" that he called "syllable tapping," appeared in 1940. Written by a Dutchman (Van Dantzig 1940), it aroused no interest in this country even though it was published in the official organ of the American Speech and Hearing Association.

28. It is of particular interest that Meyer and Mair referred to their use of rhythm as a "new" method, as had Van Dantzig (1940).

29. A report from each of two different investigators: Bryne (1931) and Bryngelson (1938), in which the two populations totaled 1,800 stutterers.

30. The literal dimensions of this contradiction are clearly revealed in Chapter 7.

31. See Wingate 1976, Chapter 5.

32. An extended summary and review of Brown's reports are the subject of Chapter 3 in Wingate 1988.

33. Authors here refers essentially to Johnson and Brown. Johnson directed Brown's master's thesis and his doctoral dissertation, and he would almost certainly have led in

the interpretation of the findings. Incidentally, Brown also stuttered. (Authors of the few other studies evidently were not stutterers.)

34. The syllable nucleus, although not then identified as such.

35. See Glossary. These conditions are discussed in Wingate 1969 and 1970.

36. This integration is the substance of *The Structure of Stuttering* (Wingate 1988). In particular, the content in reference here is the subject of the four chapters that make up Part II of *Structure*.

37. Personal communication, April 27, 1984.

38. It is worth noting that interest in such medications has emerged in foreign sources. As noted in Chapter 5, work with speech disorders remained more within a medical framework on the continent.

39. Of three drugs reported more recently (Rothenberg et al. 1994; Althaus et al. 1995; Gordon et al. 1995), only one seemed to hold possible promise.

40. Bluemel (1913), Travis (1933b), Bender (1943), West (1943, 1958), Reid (1946), Karlin (1959), Sheehan (1970).

41. Andrews et al. (1983), Kent (1983), and Wingate (1983).

42. For instance, the lead article (Andrews et al.) included reference to a number of research reports that would not meet rigorous criteria. On such grounds one must accept that there is not much in the extensive research literature on stuttering that would seriously merit consideration as "fact."

43. See Katz 1977.

44. The major source referenced here is Wingate 1988. (Other sources that present evidence reflecting the importance of the prosodic dimension are in Wingate 1966c; 1967; 1969; 1970; 1976: Chapter 8; 1979).

45. Especially, for instance, those devised by Robert Bates (see Chapter 4).

46. Reported in *Letting Go*, 15, No. 6 (1995): 1. It is of interest that a similar device, reported in the same era (Donovan 1971), permitted the alternatives of steady or intermittent masking, or metronomic pacing.

47. Reference is listed under "News Notes" in the References.

48. The basic device uses vibrotactile feedback. Auditory feedback can be incorporated by adding earphones, and visual feedback added through use of a visual display monitor, a unit similar in size to the power pack. The apparatus is also offered in a large desk model, the "clinical VFD package."

49. One of the three devices developed by Robert Bates, noted in Chapter 4, created vibrotactile feedback via static pressure at the laryngeal site. As with the discovery by Weiss (1992) that manual enhancement of vocal feedback was as useful as the Fluency Master, one might also expect that simply placing one's thumb and forefinger at the laryngeal site would provide as good awareness of voicing as either of the appliances described here.

50. Personal conversations, Cy Libby, Associated Auditory Instruments, Upper Darby, Pa.

51. In honor of Canon Kingsley. See Chapter 4.

52. See Chapter 4 "Addendum."

PART V

DENOUEMENT

CHAPTER 10

Synopsis and Sequelae

The history of stuttering presented in the foregoing chapters has revealed a wide range of information about the disorder that can provide a realistic appreciation of its substance, and should serve to clarify efforts to understand its nature. The historical review also has identified certain circumstances that have afforded immediate benefit, as well as treatment principles and techniques that, used with success heretofore, are applicable in the present and for at least the foreseeable future.

The Synopsis of this final chapter is intended to bring into particular focus the major findings of this critical historical review. The section titled "Sequelae" is intended to emphasize, first, how those findings call for modifications in the way stuttering is conceptualized, and second, principles of and approaches to management of the disorder that are defensible in terms of what history reveals.

SYNOPSIS

Basics

First, it is clear that stuttering is an ancient disorder; it has been part of human history as least as long as human history has been recorded. That one can readily trace a history of the disorder is itself clear evidence of its existence as a recognizable and describable entity. As I noted in a previous publication,

throughout this long period one finds "ample reason to believe that everybody
has known what everyone else has been talking about" (Wingate 1988: pp. 8-9).

This much of what the history of stuttering tells us should be enough to end
the fuss and quibbling about identification of stuttering. The diversionary quar-
rel about the "reliability" of stuttering identification is a mid-twentieth-century
construction based on the demand posed by Wendell Johnson, and pressed by
his followers, that a clear *categorical* distinction be made between stutter
events and normal nonfluencies. It is a demand that requires concurrence in
respect to *all specific instances* of stutter. Even so, the reader is well reminded that the reliability values for such concurrence are regularly around .90,
values that should themselves quell the argument.[1]   As noted before in this
book, the current issue regarding identification can be readily resolved if there
is genuine intent to resolve it.

In addition to confirming that stuttering is a discriminable entity, the perennially recurring identification of the disorder tells us something else of great
importance — something that routinely is either ignored, dismissed, or trivial-
ized: namely, that stuttering is a *speech* disorder! Moreover, it is a *unique*
speech disorder — which is precisely why it has been so perennially and consistently identified over the long span of centuries! Furthermore, its uniqueness is
contained in the characteristics by which it has been so consistently identified:
principally, iterative fragments of speech (the "oscillations"), but also the evidently involuntary stoppages (the "fixations") in a speech sequence. These two
features have long been considered to reflect, as a common denominator, an
evident *inability* to proceed. By the early nineteenth century these characteristics had been assigned the succinct designations "clonic" and "tonic." Although vigorous efforts have been made since the 1930s to nullify, obscure, or
confound the reality of these characteristics, they remain the essential features
by which stuttering is identified.

It is relevant to mention here some of the more notable casual observations
about stuttering that have been made repeatedly over the years, especially in the
past two centuries, and which thereby can be considered substantial knowledge
on which we can rely in the attempt to understand stuttering and to treat it
realistically. In addition to what contribution these observations, as well as a
number of others, may eventually make to understanding and working with the
disorder, they constitute additional confirmation of its reliable identification,
inasmuch as these observations have been repeatedly associated with identified
stuttering.

Over the lengthy period mentioned above one finds, for instance, recurring
notation that the disorder is not manifest during singing; is minimized by
speaking to rhythm; is intermittent; runs in families; occurs more in males
than females; is most prevalent in childhood; diminishes spontaneously with
age; and improves through self-help efforts. In a slightly different vein, one
must add here that no treatment based solely upon, or derived from, any
claimed cause has produced cure — or, for that matter, even impressive and

sustained improvement.   Nevertheless, benefit has most frequently resulted from treatment that has centered in attention to speech process.

It is beyond the scope of this work to include many other matters, some of which require an amount of descriptive elaboration. However, there are some matters more specific to the twentieth century alone, essentially because they have been broached in this era. Most of these matters have been dealt with at length in preceding chapters, and some receive additional attention in subsequent sections of this chapter, but it seems appropriate to include mention of them in this summary review.

The quibbles about identifying and defining stuttering are adequately covered earlier in this section. To these we can add, as a general rubric, that there is no good reason to believe that stuttering is in any substantial sense a psychological problem. Under this heading we should include that there is no evidence that it is based in negative emotion; no evidence that stuttering is learned; no evidence that the word "stuttering" has ever done any harm; no evidence that stuttering arises out of normal nonfluency; no evidence that pressure regarding speech performance leads to stuttering; no evidence that early stuttering typically becomes more severe (in fact, there is clear evidence to the contrary); no evidence that parental actions have a negative effect (again, in fact, clear evidence to the contrary); and absolutely no evidence whatsoever that stuttering can be prevented.

The Concentration on Cause

The wish to identify a cause of stuttering is ageless, as are the contentions that the cause is understood. Statements about the cause of stuttering have appeared as frequently as reports of its identification. Unfortunately, while the identification of stuttering has remained reassuringly constant over the ages, the only evident constant in regard to its cause is the readiness with which someone has been more than willing to assert an explanation of cause.

The imputations of cause have varied considerably, and have fluctuated. It is especially pertinent to note that, whereas the identification of stuttering is based in perceivable reality, the attributions of cause have no objective base. Their sources include inference, induction, conjecture, fantasy, biases, and personal ruminations.

As might be expected, the various explanations for stuttering generally have reflected intellectual influences of the times in which they were offered. For instance, for centuries stuttering was explained in terms of the conjectured body humours; as the disciplines of anatomy and physiology developed, attention concentrated on body structures and their function; then, as psychology emerged from philosophy and became an independent discipline, explanations for stuttering were "discovered" in several veins of this new field.

It is this latest source of conjectures about cause that most concerns us. The emergence and rapid expansion of psychology constitute a benchmark in the history of stuttering. In all the centuries prior to the twentieth, attributions of the cause of stuttering came almost entirely from within medicine.[2]   Thus, conjectures on the cause of stuttering were put forth by a relatively small number of individuals who, through their privileged extraordinary education, possessed arcane knowledge seemingly pertinent to the subject.   However, these circumstances changed dramatically once individual psychology emerged and proliferated.[3]   As noted earlier in this book, many of the basic ideas in individual psychology are largely restatements of everyday experiences.   Also, certain more specialized concepts, which might rise from an esoteric origin within the discipline, are readily grasped, and subsequently expressed, by at least the reasonably educated layman.   This matter was ably addressed in an essay titled "Pop-Psych" that appeared in the October 7, 1966 issue of *Time* magazine. That essay continues to remain pertinent.[4]

The change in explanations of stuttering that accompanied the development of psychology is exemplified in the proliferation of "theories" of stuttering in the twentieth century;   almost all center around some psychological notion. Significantly, the major dimensions of these points of view are embodied in their reliance on case history content and testimonials from patients — hardly the substance of serious scientific investigation.   The considerable influence of these two sources of information on beliefs about stuttering is well illustrated by the importance that became widely attributed to fear.   Although fear had been mentioned in many accounts of stuttering over the centuries, it was never the featured variable.   Fear came to be accorded its prominent role in the explanatory accounts that have been mounted in the twentieth century, accounts that routinely have concentrated entirely on the presumed role of *negative* emotion.[5]

A closely related, actually integral, aspect of this twentieth-century phenomenon is the fact that a great deal of what has come to be accepted and believed about the disorder has been supplied by twentieth-century stutterers. For purposes of illustrative contrast, one must keep in mind that some of those persons writing about stuttering in the nineteenth century and earlier also were stutterers.[6]   However, what those stutterer-authorities had to say about the disorder had little influence beyond serving as a reference that might be cited by later writers.   This situation changed quite dramatically in the twentieth century, principally as a result of the formation of a professional organization addressed to disorders of speech and hearing.   Following the establishment of this professional association[7] in the mid-1920s, with its very rapidly expanding membership of novitiates, stutterer-authorities quickly rose to prominence. What these stutterers in this new era had to say about stuttering — a body of content that stemmed substantially from their own experiences and reflections — was readily and widely accepted.   It was then repeated and elaborated within the context of individual psychology, with which almost anyone could quickly become conversant.   Thereby, the foundation of what is now "known" about stuttering is based largely in what is predominantly a body of testimony — a collection of ideas derived from, or colored by, personal experiences.   The influence of this body of personal testimony has remained potent, largely through regular reaffirmation by a renewing cadre of stutterer-authorities and their entourages.

A Fertile Medium

Certain conditions endemic to the early formative period in the development of the professional association (Paden 1970: pp. 18-19, 50-53) have special relevance to the subject matter of stuttering, for they undoubtedly were conducive to the rise and influence of the stutterer-authorities. Paden pointed out that the founders of the association felt compelled to establish a professional organization because of two conditions that seriously concerned them: the low level of knowledge and training of large numbers of practitioners;[8] and the unscientific level of some of the articles and books then being published.

Unfortunately, these conditions continued to exist, within the association itself, for a number of years after its founding. Notably, even fourteen years after the association was established, concern about the inferior quality of convention papers was expressed in the report of the association's council. Further, reservations about the level and quality of professional activity continued for some time, as expressed in concern over the fact that, until 1950, convention papers and journal articles that were addressed solely to clinical content outnumbered papers and articles reporting research.

These conditions are particularly relevant to the subject of stuttering because, as the reader may recall (see Chapter 6), stuttering was the major preoccupation of the early membership of the association, and this interest held a clear predominance in both convention programs and journal articles for many years. These circumstances were highly conducive to the rise of stutterer-authorities. To the growing membership of the association — comprised largely of an enthusiastic and receptive audience, professionally aspiring but unsophisticated, ill-prepared and scientifically naive — the stutterer-authority was a massively persuasive figure. It was within this ambience, for instance, that Bluemel (1932) presented his "primary-secondary" notion. This entirely testimonial reflection, sincerely proposed as a basic insight, was blandly absorbed by a credulous audience, and thenceforth repeated and extended into a belief that still haunts the field. In spite of its vagueness, self-contradiction, and inconsistency with relevant facts, it continues to confound progress both in understanding the disorder and in dealing with it constructively.

It was not only the preponderant clinical reports and publications that were less than illustrious in substance. As reviewed earlier, the stuttering research itself that was reported during that era (in particular) also merits the opprobrium of inferior quality. Yet this research was not only readily accepted, it was the font of the expansive belief in stuttering as "learned behavior," along with the superstition about not speaking the word "stuttering." As the reader should recall, both of these notions were generated by Wendell Johnson, the most influential of the stutterer-authorities.[9]

The Preoccupation with Sounds

It is remarkable that for centuries, while the essential characteristics of stuttering, the classic "markers" (clonic and tonic), were regularly noted, and while so many statements about cause were offered, only in rare instances was careful attention directed specifically to what lies intermediate between identifying the disorder and stating a presumed cause of it. This intermediate subject, the process that obviously is disturbed — the speech sequence, should be, after all, the principal focus of interest.

Significantly, over the centuries the single most frequent observation about production aspects of stutterers' speech is the notation of greater difficulty with consonants than with vowels. This description, still widely accepted as a truism today, is an outstanding example of an instance in which trees obscure the forest. Observers have been fully impressed by what appears obvious, at a very literal level, and therefore are satisfied to deal simply with what they have observed. In this particular instance, the observer's focus on sounds, and then satisfaction with this preoccupation, have undoubtedly received consolidating support through the testimony volunteered by some stutterers — especially stutterer-authorities — regarding the belief in "difficult sounds."

For example, in the case of a stutter involving the word "keep," /k-k-k-kip/, the phoneme /k/ is understandably forced upon an observer's attention. It is also evidently the focus of attention for the stutterer himself, who may even report that he "has trouble with k's." In fact, some stutterers may go on to claim that "k" is (always) a "difficult sound" for them, or even that it is one among several "difficult sounds." Again certain stutterers, most likely those who have heard it from a speech therapist or other authority, may also say that "k" is a "feared" sound, or among their "feared" sounds.

In their absorbed, concrete preoccupation with the sound that is repeated (or prolonged), both observer and stutterer gain no appreciation of the fact that the difficulty actually must *not* be with that sound, since the sound is clearly being made; in fact, it is being made repeatedly, or too vigorously. If, however, one were to look circumspectly at the whole occurrence, it should become evident that the actual difficulty is in moving on to what should follow.

The foregoing analysis of the stutter event, which calls attention to what *follows* the obvious expression of anomaly, has been advanced a number of times in the history of the disorder. However, it has just as regularly been ignored or dismissed. As one might easily appreciate, Aristotle was the first person to describe stuttering in reference to what should follow the apparent problem: to wit, in his remarks relative to "joining syllables" and "uttering the next sound" (see Chapter 2). Aristotle's description remained unrecognized, or unappreciated, until very recently.

The essential idea involved in the analysis of a stutter event that emphasizes speech sequence reappeared at the beginning of the nineteenth century, and then more frequently near the end of the century. In 1803 Erasmus Darwin suggested that the difficulty lay in joining a consonant to the following vowel.

This description was repeated after mid-century by James Hunt, and again later in the century by several prominent figures in the field: Klencke, Kussmaul, and Alexander Graham Bell. Hunt was actually the first to refer to this "hallmark of stuttering"[10] as a failure of *transition*. Several decades later, both Bluemel (1913) and Froeschels (1913-1914) noted the "failure to connect consonant and vowel." More recently Van Riper (1954) remarked that the actual difficulty in stuttering lies in "the failure to connect sounds;" however, he did not note the crucial feature, that this failure to connect involves transition from consonant to vowel.

The recognition that a stutter event is correctly described as a failure of transition between phonemes thus had been noted, intermittently, for well over a century, and by persons of stature in the field. However, this occasional recognition did not bring the idea of transition into focus as a matter of any particular significance, or one deserving inquiry. Briefly put, it did not suggest any essential revision in the long-term orientation to stuttering as a problem with sounds themselves. Certain authors, Bluemel for instance, did point out that the concept of transition failure indicates that, contrary to standard conception, the problem lies with the vowel instead of the consonant. However, this deduction, with its very considerable significance for linguistic analysis, was pursued no further, other than in Bluemel's notion of "recoil of the vowel." This idea had uncertain promise for meaningful development, since it remained a focus on sounds. Nonetheless, it was dismissed by his contemporaries and its potential significance ignored. The long-term, widely accepted concern with speech sounds in stuttering — specifically, with those sounds participating in a "marker" of a stutter event — remained in place.

The focus on sounds reflects the idea that phonemes are distinct units, separate entities that have an independent reality and existence. It is from within the context of such a reification of sounds that they can become construed as "difficult" or "feared." This level of orientation to sounds can take conception of the stutter event no further than an implication of some motor (i.e., peripheral) disturbance in speech production. The field of stuttering has been at this impasse for a very long time. The continued preference for viewing stuttering as some problem of dealing with sounds (as such) reflects the persisting influence of the substantial lore-based belief in "difficult sounds" and the like, all of which originates in personal testimony, wherein appealing notions that impute psychological factors have remained persuasive.[11]

The idea that stuttering might involve more than a problem of making sounds was suggested initially in 1927 by Samuel Orton, who pointed out that a number of frequently reported observations about stuttering suggested involvement of the propositionality level of speech rather than emotional factors. However, Orton's suggestion was ignored, not only then but even when, a few years later, the findings of several studies began to implicate language dimensions in stuttering (see Chapter 8). His remarks regarding propositional level were not recalled (or at least not mentioned) for a long time (see Wingate 1988). Actually, and significantly, the novel findings that clearly indicated some involvement of language factors were interpreted as though they reflected a stutterer's reaction and fears, the well-entrenched favored notions.

It is of particular note that the line of investigation that yielded evidence of language factors resulted unexpectedly from what began as an intent to catalogue "difficult sounds" (Johnson and Brown 1935. See "Language Variables," Chapter 9). The findings of that initial study (on sounds) were disappointing in respect to the original objective; in fact, there was only very uncertain evidence for an actual "phonetic factor." On the other hand, the results of that study eventually played a key role in analyses subtending a psycholinguistic conception of the nature of stuttering (Wingate 1988).

The following section places this discussion of speech sounds, transition, and related matters in a larger context.

SEQUELAE

The content in this section is based upon and devolves from the historical foundations reviewed in the preceding pages, along with certain matters not previously discussed but which are especially relevant. The subsection titled "Orientation" is intended to set down certain evident truths about stuttering, revealed in this historical review, that call for a reorientation to how stuttering is viewed. The final subsection, "Management," identifies similar material that is especially pertinent to treatment of the disorder itself, as well as related matters involving the individual.

Orientation

The most important point to keep in mind, clearly attested in this history of stuttering, is that the cause of the disorder remains unknown. A corollary of this basic point is that any statement proposing to explain stuttering must be viewed with high level of suspicion and analyzed with the utmost care. In simpler terms, perhaps: no "theory" of stuttering merits acceptance, let alone devotion. A second corollary is that anyone professing to know the source of the disorder, or speaking as though he or she does, should also be considered highly suspect.

The second important point to keep in mind is that stuttering is a disorder of *speech*. As we have seen, it is by virtue of a certain anomaly in speaking that stuttering has been identified for centuries, and is so identified today. The corollary of this point is that it is in reference to this distinctive anomaly in one's speech, *and this anomaly alone*, that a person is said to be stuttering.

A third point, related inversely to the content of the points just stated, involves a prominent problem. This special problem is that, in spite of its practically universal acceptance, there is really no *good* reason to consider stuttering to be, in any substantial sense, a psychological problem.[12] The reader should refer to the "Basics" subsection earlier in this chapter for a brief summary of

specific items pertinent to this point. At the moment it seems important to emphasize that one should be especially cautious about claims regarding the presumed agency of fear, that ever-ready servant of speculation and logical lapse.
One should also be wary of claims invoking "anxiety," the over-valued, although prized, modern-day term frequently substituted, inappropriately, for
fear.[13] Undeniably, fear plays some — but a varying — role in occurrences
of stuttering but it is not the *cause* of stuttering. The continued preoccupation
with fear is a misdirecting obstacle.

These points underscore the assertion that it is long past time to begin the
study of stuttering for what it clearly is — a disorder of speech. More specifically, it is a disorder in the progression of speech. In this context it seems clear
that "speech" should be taken to mean *oral language expression*, not its more
circumscribed meaning of "motor performance." A corollary of this point is
that those who write about and those who work with stuttering must develop
some acumen regarding the substance of connected speech and of the processes
evidently involved in its production. Analysis of the literature on stuttering,
even contemporary writings, reveals that the vast majority of persons immersed
in the field have, at best, limited awareness of, or interest in such matters. As
discussed briefly in the first chapter, serious students of stuttering had best
become knowledgeable in this crucial area of study.

It is appropriate to note here that the perennial preoccupation with cause and
cure seems to reflect an unspoken assumption that, at base, stuttering is actually
a relatively superficial problem. One can appreciate that such a view is enhanced, if not engendered, by certain frequently made observations about stuttering, such as: its intermittency; that, on the average, it seems to occur in
only a small proportion of a stutterer's speech; that in many cases it seems
sensitive to external events, or is so reported; and so on. Within this assumption there appears to be the belief that a stutterer's linguistic system is intact;
that below this surface disturbance lies normal oral language capability, and
that it will be released once certain obstructions (such as fears, erroneous beliefs, bad habits, etc.) are neutralized. The findings in this historical review
itself suggest strongly that this is not a tenable position; that the disorder reflects some anomaly in the intricate processes of oral language expression.
There are many dimensions of evidence in support of this deduction; the interested reader is referred to Wingate (1988).

More on Speech Sounds, Transition, etc. The subsection headed "The Preoccupation with Sounds" included preliminary consideration of speech sounds
and transitions in respect to their involvement in stutter events. The next few
paragraphs will extend that assessment to include other aspects of speech process involved in a stutter event, especially vis-a-vis their occurrence in the
normal speech sequence.

Continuing from what was presented earlier, there is another important matter to consider with respect to the place and role of sounds (phonemes) in a
stutter event. Recall that Erasmus Darwin, in his astute observation regarding

joining consonant to vowel, specified *initial* consonant, which means *word-initial* consonant. The matter of word-initial position is not often mentioned in the literature of stuttering; certainly it is hardly ever emphasized.[14] Perhaps the omission is an oversight, which might represent that this matter is simply taken for granted. But it is a matter that must not be left unconsidered for any reason! It is a matter that deserves principle consideration. Word-initial position is as much a part of stutter identification as are the apt descriptive terms "clonic" and "tonic." Word-initial (actually, syllable-initial; see below) is where clonic and tonic happen! Word-initial is not only obvious to the observer of stutter events; it is constantly, although most often inadvertently, affirmed by stutterers themselves. That is, although stutterers do not regularly speak analytically of stutter locus, word-initial position is clear in whatever reference they give. Specifically, if speaking of "difficult sounds," stutterers mean only those sounds as they occur at the beginning of a word. Conversely, if speaking of "difficult words," those words are identified in terms of their initial sound. It is this fact of initial position per se, much more than whatever phoneme may occur there, that is especially significant to understanding the stutter event.

It is important to recognize that, fundamentally, "word-initial" means "syllable-initial," a broader rubric that also, significantly, happens to encompass all instances of stutter occurrence. Syllable-initial is the more comprehensive, and correct, description of the locus of stutter events.

Both initial position and (phonetic) transition are supra-phonetic dimensions. Although they involve phonemes, they transcend them. It follows that they transcend the level of conception and analysis embodied in the focus on speech "sounds." They are more than phonemes, in that both involve connection to something else — in a sequence. That "something else" is, most immediately, the nucleus of the syllable.

Several crucial features of the speech "stream" must be borne in mind in the effort to understand stuttering at levels beyond observation of the immediate stutter event. It is critically important to recognize (1) that the syllable is the basic structure of speech; (2) that the essential feature of the syllable is its nucleus, which is invariably a vowel form;[15] (3) that most syllables have initiating and terminating consonantal phonemes (although these boundaries meld in connected speech); and (4) that the continuity of normal speech represents procession via syllable nuclei.

In normal utterance the syllable-initiating phonemes (consonants) are inextricably bound to their syllablic nuclei, which are vowel forms. In a stutter event, in contrast, the integrity of the syllable is destroyed: the initiating phoneme, a consonant, remains separated from the syllable nucleus.

In normal utterance, both initial position and transition reflect movement, movement into the syllable nucleus—and then on into succeeding nuclei. Movement, borne through the substance of syllable nuclei, is the essence of the external properties of speech, manifested as flow. It is movement, the essence of flow — of *fluency* — that is disturbed in stuttering.

It has been well documented that the syllable fractures that constitute stutter events always involve a particular locus—syllable-initial position with intended transition. Analysis and integration of the many linguistic aspects of stuttering vis-a-vis normal speech (Wingate 1988) reveal a third dimension of a stutter event that this locus involves: namely, linguistic stress. Importantly, linguistic stress is expressed through the syllable nucleus, the vowel form. Thus, adding to what was described in the preceding paragraph, it follows that the syllable fracture in stuttering constitutes an interruption of movement into a stress prominence.

The "stream" of ordinary, normal speech is fundamentally an undulating tone borne via the successions of syllable nuclei. The variations in this undulating tone are principally variations in stress, which, reflecting typically subtle shifts in loudness, duration, and pitch, are expressed through sequential syllable nuclei. In normal speech these variations are expressed concurrently, and in concert with, the phonetic sequences, and are integral with them to the meaning of the message being expressed.

The stress patterning that constitutes the undulating tone of the speech "stream" is referred to as the *prosody*, or *melody* of oral language expression. The "stuff" of this undulating tone, this carrier of the speech signal, is voicing.[16] The next section will highlight a repeated finding in this history of stuttering; namely, that some level of emphasis on voicing emerges consistently in conditions reported to have a beneficial effect on stuttering—and in the core techniques of, supposedly varied, treatment methods.

Management

Treatment. Over the centuries those treatment efforts that have yielded benefit to stutterers have, in one way or another, had a direct effect on the individual's speech.

Pertinent review should begin by recalling efforts that may be listed under "speech improvement," largely because the earliest well-documented report of treatment effort was clearly of this sort. I am referring here to the record of Demosthenes, and Satyrus (see Chapter 2). A long hiatus followed, with Chervin being the next significant figure to espouse such a method, and who reported that success with stuttering in his time was proportional to how well treatment approached "the simple and natural means" of working directly on speech performance, as reported for Demosthenes. Chervin's position was echoed in other sources of his era, as well as later: in the outstanding achievements of James Hunt, who taught stutterers "to speak consciously as other men speak unconsciously"; in the contributions of elocution in general; and in the successes of, for example, Warren, Klencke, Kussmaul, and the Gunthers.

Although the latter figures carried the speech improvement form of treatment into the twentieth century, this straightforward method became obscured in the early decades by the distracting influences unleashed by the growth of psychology, in which the "messiahs" (West 1959) appeared and were active. Interestingly, a partial essence of a "speech improvement" approach appeared later, almost covertly, in a method presented as a means of teaching stutterers to stutter fluently — the method developed by Van Riper.

Van Riper always placed much emphasis upon dealing with a stutterer's feelings and attitudes, but the real core of his approach addressed very directly the matter of producing sequences in speech. A careful reading of his widely used and highly successful method reveals that in the heart of the method — the techniques of "cancellation" and "pull-out" — there is a clear concentration on slow, deliberate speaking as the means of emphasizing the appropriate pattern in a sequence of phonemes. In the course of the stutterer's learning supposedly "other and better ways of stuttering" (Van Riper 1973: p 327), he is essentially being assisted, through means actually considered as subsidiary, to become more aware of his speech production.

The essential substance of Van Riper's method can be conveyed through a brief description of "cancellation," the basic procedure. The stutterer "cancels" having stuttered a word by saying it again several times, but in a special way. The recitation involves several progressive steps of rehearsal (which need not be restated here) in each of which the word is to be said in a "strong, deliberate, slow-motion kind of utterance in which the sequencing of motoric components is somewhat slowed and obviously highly controlled. . . . The cancelled word does not sound the same as it would were it spoken normally. It is slower, stronger, spoken more carefully and consciously" (p. 326).[17]

The limitation of the Van Riper method is that it is addressed principally to words, and specifically to words that were stuttered. However, it does teach something about basic aspects of sequencing in speech. One should note that it incorporated certain techniques widely employed in earlier treatment methods that were addressed to a broader spectrum of speech production, as reviewed in Chapter 4, techniques that continue to reappear, unacknowledged, in many supposedly different treatment methods.

Certain purportedly modern approaches to treatment also are actually centered in basic and simple speech improvement process, even though other activities are presented as the crux of the approach. A good illustration is found in a publication (Guitar 1980) that was presented as an integration of contemporary therapies. Actually the "integration" turned out to be a comparison between therapies belonging in the "stuttering modification" category and those that fit the "fluency shaping" type. As the author noted, the orientation of the first type focuses on reducing the stutterer's emotional reactions, which are presumed to be the source of his stuttering; the orientation of the latter is preoccupied with the notions of conditioning and reinforcement, which are presumed to be the means by which stuttering is to be unlearned.[18] However, the difference between these two types of approach is only superficial. In the course of pursuing their supposed separate and different goals, both approaches — through acts treated as means incidental to the intended implementation of those goals — "help the stutterer become more fluent by teaching him to talk, at least temporarily, in a modified, controlled, or purposeful fashion" (p. 15). Further, the activities employed incidentally by both approaches yield similar-sounding speech patterns "in which words are spoken with a prolonged, gradual onset" (p. 16).

Upon reasonably attentive inspection of the supposedly varied therapies that may be catalogued today (see, for instance, Peins 1984; Peters and Guitar 1991; Culatta and Goldberg 1995), one will find that the supposed "variation" is to be found largely in various constructions and activities that constitute conceptual superstructures, which reflect certain beliefs about stuttering. The superstructures contain many features that careful observation and critical analysis will show to be superfluous or tangential. The central base of the therapies, in contrast, consists of certain long-established, regularly employed techniques that deal directly with speech. Their common method is revealed in terms that reappear in the descriptions of these supposedly varied therapies, such as slow, prolonged, easy-onset, controlled, deliberate, careful. References like this were employed regularly in descriptions of stuttering treatment in earlier times, especially in the nineteenth century, wherein the problem was addressed solely as a disorder of speech.

Voicing—Always There. It is time now to reintroduce the matter of voicing. The terms in focus at the end of the preceding paragraph refer to actions that are accomplished through voicing. The extent to which voicing is the essence of these activities seems to have gone unrecognized. Evidently persons treating stuttering in the nineteenth century, and earlier, did not routinely recognize that these activities all resolve to a common base in voicing, although a connection to voice was realized much more frequently then than among proponents of recent "therapies." One should recall that the intermittent references to "spasms of the glottis" clearly indicated awareness of interruption in voicing.

We can move on to recall other circumstances in which the central role of voicing has been either evident, recognized, or deducible from incisive analysis of circumstances. One should keep in mind that emphases on voicing typically have an accompanying reduction in rate.

Among the many and varied oral devices created to alleviate stuttering, the prominent role of voicing was pointedly affirmed in those devices intended to "maintain a current of sonorous breath." Other oral devices, intended to either support or restrict oral structures, had the practical result of emphasizing voicing through minimizing articulation. Similarly, the reduced oral movements central to the Leigh-Yates-American method and comparable techniques had the net effect of emphasizing voicing. The same can be said of the effect of lingual surgery.

The reader should recall that certain circumstances have been widely demonstrated to have a dramatically beneficial effect on stuttering, namely, singing, speaking to rhythm, and choral speaking. The prominence of voice in singing should be self-evident;[19] voicing also is clearly predominant in speaking to rhythm, and in choral speaking.

Certain modern-day experimental influences — auditory masking and de-layed auditory feedback — which some sources evidently still view as some form of corrective auditory feedback, also induce a prominence of voicing, which provides a more likely source of their value for stuttering than some hypothesized direct, or indirect, auditory linkage. In respect to feedback ef-forts, we should recall that the latest "feedback" type devices for stuttering are designed to enhance voicing.

One can readily find voicing to be the central dimension in many well-used therapy techniques. For instance, it should be quite obvious in the use of "prolongation" and in "slowing down," but should also be readily perceived in "easy onset," in which the "onset" is the on-glide to the syllable nucleus, wherein voicing is begun early (and with deliberation). Similarly, voicing is easily seen to be central to certain special techniques such as those introduced by Froeschels: initially, "breath chewing"[20] and later, "ventriloquism tech-nique." It is of some interest that, in his presentation of ventriloquism tech-nique (Froeschels 1950), he mentioned, but only in passing, that "modulation of the voice is of great significance."

Recognizing the centrality of voicing in those treatment techniques that have for so long produced amelioration of stuttering should provide the fulcrum for efficacious treatment of stuttering independent from the provincialisms of contrived "theories." Not only does the rationale derive substance from a lengthy pragmatic precedent, it is also consistent with a credible, objectively documented analysis of how stuttering is clearly a disorder of speech. These two substantial bases of support provide a framework for treatment within which various appropriate techniques can be incorporated, assuming that their purpose within the rationale is made clear. Additionally, the range of proce-dures accessible within this framework allows educated therapists a consider-able degree of flexibility and creativity. These dimensions, the mark of a true clinician, are stultified and rendered feeble by the prescribed routines and se-quences of stuttering therapy "programs." They also are compromised by ap-proaches characterized by preoccupation with psychological superficialities.

A new era in the treatment of stuttering will require that those who would implement the defensible approach to treatment that emerges through lessons from the history of the disorder must become better educated about the process they are intending to repair — speech. Within the past half century much valuable and pertinent knowledge has accrued in the fields of speech science and psycholinguistics, and a speech therapist well prepared to work with stut-tering should be familiar with it.

A new era of stuttering treatment must also bring with it the ability and will-ingness to slough off the platitudes and nostrums that have spread so vigorously and entangled the field in this past half century, and still remain so broadly accepted. Such revision can also be expected to limit, even turn back, the mushrooming of "methods," most of which have a superstructure of indefensible rationale, overblown terminology, unsupportable contentions, and unnecessary activities.

Concerning certain of the psychologically based preoccupations that still beset treatment efforts, two points should be made briefly. First, neither the therapist, nor the therapist's mentor, nor the patient should be indulged in regard to a preoccupation with reaction, fear, or attitudes. These matters cannot, of course, be blithely dismissed, but one must constantly pursue the effort to relegate them to the limited role they can be shown to play. Second, in any *human* learning circumstance, the learner brings to the situation three variables: (1) the motivation to learn; (2) the ability to do what is to be learned; and (3) a cognitive capacity through which he can understand what is going on. What the learner needs from the outside is a source of instruction.[21] What one learns is dependent upon the instruction given, understanding the instruction, and successfully following it. Recognized achievement of learning is its own "reward." The achievement is not dependent upon the external "delivery" of some presumed "reinforcement." It is presumptuous to believe that such gestures are anything more than redundant; appealing and satisfying to some practioners, but nonetheless redundant.

Counseling. It is most appropriate to begin this section by giving special attention to the meaning of the word "counsel" and its derived forms "counselor" and "counseling."

Any good modern dictionary will define these words in terms of *advice.* In particular, "counseling" means "to give advice to; advise."[22] Unfortunately, in certain areas that borrow so much of their substance from psychology, the meaning of the term became aggrandized to imply a kind of psychotherapeutic midwifery; not necessarily "real" psychotherapy, but something quite beyond giving advice. As a clear example of the unjustifiable intrusion occasioned by this expansion, one can find, in a number of sources, the recommendation that parents be counseled regarding (the unwarranted assumption of) "their part" in a child's stuttering.

The movement to expand counseling into something more than giving advice may well have originated from (or at least have been encouraged by) the book, *Counseling and Psychotherapy,* by Carl Rogers.[23] Published in 1942, it appeared when belief in stuttering as a psychological problem was vigorously growing.

Therapists of stuttering who are instructed or encouraged to deal with the feelings, attitudes, and emotions of stutterers and persons close to the stutterer are being led into activity for which they are, on the whole, improperly prepared. A line from An Essay on Criticism by Alexander Pope is pertinent here: "A little learning is a dangerous thing." The full spirit of this adage has been well captured in William Allen White's amendment: "A little learning is not a dangerous thing to one who does not mistake it for a great deal." Unfortunately, this caution does not seem to be routinely incorporated in many sources addressing the management of stuttering.

The counseling afforded by speech therapists should consist predominantly of advice; advice broadly based on what the therapist should know about speech, and about stuttering as a disorder of speech, and on knowledge specific to stuttering that has been objectively determined and corroborated over its lengthy history. The advice must be forthright regarding especially the matters of no known cause and no guarantee of cure. These admissions should lead quickly to confession of the general inadequacy and untenability of the many "theories" of stuttering. It follows that any statement representing any such point of view should be adequately identified as such, accompanied with pertinent caveat.

There are a number of well-documented and supportable items of knowledge about stuttering, revealed in this history, that should be included in the advice imparted to stutterers or their families. A special set of such items is listed under "Basics" in this chapter. Developing a complete list of such items might turn out to be a worthwhile undertaking. Culatta and Goldberg (1995: p. 156-157) suggest that disclosure laws may soon raise legal issues in regard to stuttering treatment. They give as an example an instance in which failure to have disclosed the known hereditary factor might, in time to come, result in a lawsuit. One should add that even now someone may well find sufficient basis for litigation in the serious misrepresentations that are readily found in various "theory"-based approaches to management, and the counseling proffered.

NOTES

1. The issue is discussed earlier (see Chapter 8). The reader is reminded that this demand contradicts Johnson's earlier criticism of categorization. It also seems pertinent to recall here that the same authors who find bona fide values of .90 not good enough to indicate reliability are nonetheless willing to claim even questionably derived values no greater than .60 as being tantamount to a value of 1.00 for the notion of "consistency."

2. As noted, first the humours doctrine, then anatomy-physiology.

3. That is, the psychology of the person, to contrast with particular specialties within the broad framework of psychology, such as sensation and perception; physiological psychology; comparative psychology; etc.

4. Consider, for instance, the extent of "counseling" afforded by bartenders, omitting for the moment such obvious sources as the clergy, best friends, etc. The fact that such counseling may miss the mark is beside the point. In a similar vein, the concepts of conditioning and reinforcement have been readily assimilated by many lay persons. Actually, the essential principles were well appreciated and employed by animal trainers long before the academic nomenclature was applied to them.

5. As noted previously, earlier accounts mentioned some link between emotional arousal and stutter occurrence, but those accounts included positive as well as negative emotion. Exclusive emphasis on negative emotion is a hallmark of twentieth-century psychological accounts.

6. A special case in point is Edgar Werner, founder and editor of *The Voice* (see Chapter 4). Potter (1882) identified fourteen stutterers among the authorities he cited; there were a number of others.

7. The American Academy of Speech Correction, which would soon become the American Speech and Hearing Association.

8. Who would soon become association members.

9. The influence of the stutter-authorities, notably Johnson, Van Riper, and Sheehan, is also perpetuated through publications of an influential lay source, the Stuttering Foundation of America. Known as the Speech Foundation of America until a few years ago, it was originated and wholly supported by a wealthy stutterer, Malcolm Fraser, who heavily favored views consistent with those expressed by the men noted here.

10. The words of Alexander Graham Bell.

11. The persisting attention to sounds is exemplified in Peters and Hulstjin (1987), a compilation of papers presented at an international conference. (See Wingate 1989) Papers of a second conference (Peters, Hulstjin, and Starkweather, 1991) showed some apparent advance. A third conference, titled "Speech Motor Production and Fluency Disorders" was held in June 1996.

12. Any more than reason to propose the same for epilepsy or Tourette's syndrome, for both of which precipitative and reactive psychological elements have been demonstrated.

13. This casual equivalence in usage marks a specific instance of the superficiality of borrowings from psychology. These two terms have different meanings in psychological literature.

14. In the eight sources, reported in Chapter 9, that present a list of facts about stuttering, none mentions the matter of stutter occurrence in word-initial position. Interestingly, one (Bluemel, 1913) listed that stuttering does *not* occur on word-*final* sounds, a corollary that also receives little attention..

15. "Vowel form" is intended as a generic term, to include vowels, dipthongs and the occasional triptophong—resonant phonemes that can serve as the nuclei of stressed syllables.

16. Because of its very unique nature, there should perhaps be an esoteric term for this activity. "Vocalization," used previously (Wingate, 1969; 1970; 1988), although more appropriate in certain contexts, seems to invite confusion with "phonation." "Voicing" is preferrable here, especially to emphasize its identity with vowel forms as well as the historical connections.

17. In view of the cardinal features of "cancellation," it is of some interest that Van Riper remarked on several occasions that telling a stutterer to slow down "doesn't work" (personal conversation). Importantly, there are different ways to slow one's speech.

18. The reader should recognize these two types as representing the two popular forms of psychological accounts of stuttering. Guitar's (correct) identification of these types was as follows: the former "refers to an approach to stuttering based on the theory that most of the stutterer's problems in speaking are the result of avoiding or struggling with . . . repetitions and/or prolongations"; the latter "is based on operant conditioning and programming principles, e.g., successive approximations of antecedent stimulus events, use of reinforcement of appropriate responses, and so on."

19. It is also amply demonstrated in research (see Wingate 1976: pp. 193-196). Further, the evident superior effect of singing and rhythm can be attributed to the fact that the "patterns" focus on syllable nuclei (see Wingate 1976: pp. 209-212).

20. The rationale for this technique was indeed strange, especially coming from a physician. Froeschels (1956) averred that "the *identity* [sic] of voiced chewing and speaking can be understood if we consider the fact that one can chew food and talk at the same time without any mutual interruption" (p. 45; italics added).

21. In actuality, this source may be written only, or written and personal communication, or only personal. In the learning circumstance with which we are concerned here, it seems most appropriate to provide at least the personal instruction. However, I have met "very much improved" stutterers who claimed to have achieved their success from a written source only.

22. *Webster's New World Dictionary of the American Language, Second College Edition.*

23. C. R. Rogers, *Counseling and Psychotherapy* (Boston: Houghton Mifflin, 1942).

Glossary

ACCESSORY FEATURES. Extraneous movements that sometimes accompany the cardinal features of stuttering (the elemental repetitions and prolongations). Accessory features are of two levels: (1) speech related movements, and (2) ancillary movements (other movements not directly involved in speaking).

AGE OF ENLIGHTENMENT. A European intellectual movement of the 17th and 18th Centuries that celebrated and emphasized the use of reason.

AMELIORATIVE CONDITIONS. Those conditions under which stutterers evidence very little or no stuttering. The most effective of such conditions are singing, speaking to rhythm, speaking in chorus, auditory masking while speaking, and speaking under delayed auditory feedback.

ANNO DOMINI. Here, meaning literally the beginning of the Christian era.

AUTOMATIC SPEECH. Word, phrase, or sentence utterances that are not appropriate to circumstances and have no evident meaningful reference. Typically occurring in the speech efforts of aphasics, an observation that prompted this classification. See PROPOSITIONAL SPEECH.

CHOREA. Any of a group of disorders of the nervous system characterized by brief, rapid, irregular jerking movements caused by involuntary muscular contractions of the limbs, face, trunk, and head. Also called St. Vitus's Dance.

CLONIC.   Medical term meaning "characterized by alternate contraction and relaxation of muscles." Perceived as oscillation, iteration; hence, application of the term to the elemental repetitions, one of the two characteristic features of stuttering. See also TONIC.

DEXTRAL.   A technical reference to right-sided.   The term comes directly from the Latin *dextra*, meaning "right" in the directional sense.   The word "right" has other, evaluative or judgmental, significances. All forms of "dextra" have positive meanings, for example: "dexterous" and similar derivative forms that mean to be skillful, adroit, clever, capable.   Note also the masculine given name "Dexter," meaning "the right, the good"; also, being placed "at the right" is the honored position; etc.   For contrast, see SINISTRAL.

DIDACTIC.   Of teaching, instruction.

DIS.   A prefix carrying the connotation of separation or negation.   Used to construct words having a very general reference.

DYS.   A prefix carrying the connotation of bad, abnormal.

ELOCUTION.   The art of public speaking or declaiming.

EOANTHROPUS.   "Dawn" man; here, simply, earliest man.   Whether one thinks in terms of homo erectus or homo habilis (the latter evidently older by some million-plus years) is not of particular concern in the present context. (Homo erectus is estimated to have lived some 200,000 yrs ago.)

EPHPHATHA.   A pertinent reference from the Bible.   In an early book of the New Testament (Mark, estimated to have been written before A.D. 56) it is written that Jesus was brought

one that was deaf, and had an impediment in his speech; and they beseech him to put his hand upon him. And he took him aside from the multitude, and put his fingers into his ears, and he spit, and touched his tongue; And looking up to heaven, he sighed, and saith unto him, Ephphatha, that is, Be opened. And straightway his ears were opened, and the string of his tongue was loosed, and he spake plain. (Mark 7: 32-37)

ETYMOLOGY.   The origin and development of a word.

EUGENICS.   [Greek "good" + "genes"].   Improvement of the race through controlled mating.

EUPHEMISM.   [Greek "good" + "speech"].   Using a "nicer," less offensive or more acceptable form of expressing something: e.g., "passed away" in place of "died."

GENERAL SEMANTICS.   A system of beliefs propounded by Alfred Korzybski in which the central tenet seems to have been that words control our
thought. The following three selections are Korzybski's own statements, reproduced here verbatim largely to show the recondite eccentricity of his thinking
and writing.

Definition of General Semantics.   General Semantics formulates a new *experimental*
branch of natural science, underlying an empirical theory of human evaluations and
orientations; involving a definite neurological mechanism, present in all humans.   It
discovers direct neurological methods for the *stimulation* of the activities of the human
cerebral cortex and the direct introduction of beneficial neurological 'inhibition,' which
restore nervous balance to the over-stimulated human nervous systems. It discovers also
that most human difficulties are due to *intensional* orientations and languages and the
solution of many of them can be brought about by *extensional* orientations and languages, which is accomplished simply and automatically by a few elementary linguistic
extensional devices. The meaning of a term in extension consists of the objects to
which the term may be applied; its meaning in intension consists of the qualities which
are possessed by the objects bearing the name' (Jevons). In the case of General Semantics we deal with intensional and extensional *orientations* and *attitudes,* which represent a broader problem than the one defined by Jevons.

Intensional orientations are based on verbal definitions, associations, etc., largely
disregarding observations as if they would involve a 'principle' of 'talk first and never
mind life facts.' *Extensional orientations* are based on ordering observations, investiga-
tons, etc., *first*, and the verbalization next in importance. Thus the extensional attitudes
are based on the *natural order of evaluation*, making a natural theory of values possible,
and leads to a workable theory of adjustment or 'sanity.' Intensional orientations, then,
represent the reversal of the natural order of evaluation, and must introduce factors of
misevaluation or maladjustment in human lives. ("Outline of General Semantics," presented by Korzybski at the First American Congress for General Semantics, March 1,
1935,   first two paragraphs.)

General semantics is not any 'philosophy,' or 'psychology,' or 'logic,' in the ordinary
sense. It is a new extensional discipline which explains and trains us how to use our
nervous systems most efficiently. It is not a medical science, but like bacteriology, it is
indispensable for medicine in general, and for psychiatry, mental hygiene, and education
in particular. In brief, it is the formulation of a new non-aristotelian system of orientation which affects every branch of science and life. The separate issues involved are not
entirely new; their methodological formulation *as a system* which is workable, teach-
able and so elementary that it can be applied by children, is entirely new. (Introduction
to the second edition cf *Science and Sanity* 1941, pp. xi-xii.)

General Semantics turned out to be an empirical natural science of non-elementalistic
evaluation, which takes into account the living individual, not divorcing him from his
reactions altogether, nor from his neuro-linguistic and neuro-semantic environments, but
allocating him in a *plenum* of some values, no matter what. (Preface to the third edition
of *Science and Sanity,* 1948, p. viii.)

GIBBOUS.   Here, designating the moon or a planet in the phase in which more than half but not all of the disk is illuminated.

GLOSS.   This term has several meanings relative to the use of words. The sense intended here is "to cover up or make appear right by specious argument or by minimizing."

ITERATIVE.   Done repeatedly.

LEARNING; THE PARADIGMS.   In psychological laboratories addressed to the study of how organisms learn, the basic process is   referred to as "conditioning," of which there are two major types: classical conditioning, and instrumental conditioning.
    In classical conditioning, so called because it replicates the original procedure reported by Pavlov, there is an unconditioned stimulus (UcS) which is necessary and adequate to elicit a response (R). If another (originally immaterial) stimulus is associated sufficiently often with the adequate stimulus, the former will, in due time (then called the conditioned stimulus [CS], become able to the elicit the response (which is now a conditioned response [CR], "conditioned" to that specific CS). The hallmark of classical conditioning is that the occurrence of the response does not influence the circumstances of the process.   (This learning theory paradigm shows up in only one account of stuttering, and then as only part of the explanation.)
    Instrumental Conditioning bears this name because what the organism does (the R) is *instrumental* in the occurrence of the reinforcement (of that R). There are several types of instrumental conditioning:
    1. instrumental reward: some act of the organism results in immediate positive reinforcement whenever that act is performed. The reference example is the delivery of a food pellet when a bar is pressed. There are two forms of this type:
        a. respondent: this form incorporates a stimulus which, though initially inadequate, comes to elicit the act (R) through its repeated association with the reward (whereby the stimulus becomes conditioned, a CS)
        b. operant: this form omits mention of any stimulus that elicits the act. The act is simply considered from the time it occurs — is "emitted." It too is said to be acquired via the effect of a reward that is contingent upon its occurrence.
    2. instrumental escape: some act of the organism (R) terminates or substantially reduces a noxious circumstance (UcS). The reference example is that pressing a bar turns off the electrification of the floor on which the animal is situated.
    3. instrumental avoidance: some act of the organism (R), performed in response to a signal (S), enables it to avoid a noxious condition (UcS). The reference example is that by pressing a bar when a buzzer sounds, the animal avoids delivery of an electric shock.

LINGUISTIC UNIVERSALS.   Features and aspects of language form and function that are found to be similar across most languages.

MOLIÈRE   (*ne* Jean Baptiste Poquelin, 1622-1673).   Considered by many critics to be the world's greatest writer of comedies.   His plays ridiculed the weakness, foolish actions, and false values of the people of his times.

MYRMIDON.   An unquestioning follower or subordinate.

ONOMATOPOEIA.   The sound of a word imitates or resembles its referent, e.g., rush, whirr, shriek, bomb, chickadee.

PARADIGM.   Model, explanatory base, structure.

PARADOX.   Something self-contradictory in fact.

PHLEBOTOMY.   Blood-letting; an old medical practice based on the humours doctrine of illness. The objective was to bring the humours into balance.

PHONETIC SYMBOLISM.   Some aspect of the phonetic structure of a word suggests the word's referent.

PHRENOLOGY.   A system claiming that character and mental faculties are revealed in the configuration of the skull.

PRESCIENCE.   Foreknowledge, sense of something impending.

PROPOSITIONAL SPEECH.   Spontaneous speech, newly generated and appropriate to the circumstances, that conveys a meaningful message obviously intended by the speaker. John Hughlings Jackson (1835-1911), an outstanding British neurologist, offered this characterization of typical normal verbal utterances as contrasted to abnormal "automatic speech" (see earlier) typically produced by aphasics. Propositional speech is also to be distinguished from "phatic" statements, such as the readily elicited, highly routinized brief utterances occurring as salutations.

PSYCHOANALYSIS.   This term is properly used to refer to the psychological position created by Sigmund Freud, both his "theory" of psychosexual development and the treatment method he espoused.   Psychoanalysis began as a method of treating neurosis, especially hysteria (Breuer and Freud 1895). Its central treatment techniques of free association and catharsis (talking out), first employed by Joseph Breuer, a Viennese colleague of Freud, replaced hypnosis as the favored treatment. The method was first presented in Breuer's celebrated report "The Case of Miss Anna O." Actually, the case was subsequently recognized to have been misdiagnosed: the young woman was most likely suffering from tubercular meningitis, which was treated successfully at a Swiss sanatorium—she lived another fifty years.

RENAISSANCE.   Literally, "rebirth": the great revival of art, literature, and learning in Europe in the fourteenth, fifteenth and sixteenth centuries, marking the intellectual transition out of the medieval world into the modern.

SEMANTOGENIC.   [from Greek: semanto (word-meaning) + genic (source, cause)]. Therefore, "caused by the meaning of a word; caused by a word."

SEPSIS.   Poisoning caused by the absorption into the blood of pathogenic microorganisms, as from putrefying material.

SINE QUA NON.   [Latin "without" + "which" + "not"] Absolute prerequisite; essential.

SINISTRAL.   A technical reference to "left-sided." The term comes directly from the Latin sinistra which had the meaning of both "left" and "sinister" ("portending evil"). The connection between "left" and "evil portent" relates, historically, to the relative rarity of left-handedness. Being oddities, individuals "marked" in this way were considered to be "possessed," usually by the devil. The left is traditionally the side of evil; for instance, in magical rites, moving deliberately to the left is an appeal to evil influences. Note also "left-handed compliment"; "gauche"; etc. For contrast, see DEXTRAL.

SPEECH FEATURES.   The essential observable characteristics in speech that characterize stuttering. See CLONIC and TONIC.

SPONTANEOUS GENERATION.   (also: abiogenesis) An ancient belief, accepted in early science as well, that living organisms can arise out of nonliving matter (supposedly exemplified in the appearance of maggots in decaying organic matter).

STUTTERING, DEFINITION OF.   The following is a defensible current definition of stuttering. Objective and descriptive, it appears in *Churchill's Medical Dictionary* (1989). Unfortunately, definitions of this sort have not appeared in the literature on stuttering for many years (but cf. West, Robert, below).

stuttering: A speech disorder affecting the fluency of production, often characterized by repetitions of certain sounds, syllables, words, or phrases, and by the prolongation of sounds and blocking of the articulation of words. Severer forms may be associated with facial grimacing, limb and postural gestures, involuntary grunts, or impaired control of airflow. The severity of symptoms may vary with the speaker's situation and audience. Stuttering usually begins in childhood and is commoner in males than in females. It is unusual to find evidence of neurological dysfunction in the confirmed adolescent or adult stutterer. Management varies from attempts to control respiratory activity, or in the measured production of syllables and words, to psychotherapy aimed at readjusting the self-image of the individual and his place in the community. Often several therapeutic methods are used in combination. Also *stammering, psellism, lingual titubation, battarism* (seldom used), *batturismus* (seldom used), *dysphemia* (seldom used), *dysarthria literalis* (seldom used), *dysarthria syllabaris spasmodica* (seldom used), *balbuties* (Obs.).

SWIFT, JONATHAN (1667-1745). One of the greatest English satirists.

TONIC. Medical term meaning "state of sustained muscular contraction." Perceived as arrest of movement; hence, application of the term to prolongation of sound or posture, one of the two characteristic features of stuttering.

WEST, ROBERT. Author of a classic statement in definition of stuttering:

Stuttering is characterized by sudden and frequent spasms, tonic and clonic, (usually limited to the neuro-muscular mechanism of speech, but sometimes spreading to other somatic nervous and muscular systems) during which the flow of speech is interrupted, and in the intervals between which the speech, though fluent, may exhibit vocal tenseness and even, in some cases, articulatory clumsiness. There are many varying pictures of stuttering spasms: blocking in the explosive phase of the sounds b, p, d, t, g, and k; repetitions of these sounds; the holding of fricative sounds such as s, θ, and f; the laryngeal blocking on voiced continuants; the inspiratory gasps that interrupt the expiratory movements of speech. Sometimes the chief locus of the spasms disturbing speech seems to be the musculature of the face and lips, sometimes that of the tongue, again that of the larynx, or yet again that of the respiratory machinery. Acoustically the stuttering may appear to be even a mere hesitation in the onward flow of speech. (West, 1933; West et al. 1937)

(Note that the entire definition is addressed to *speech process.* The term "spasms," considered prejudicial, could be readily supplanted by a more innocuous word without altering the value of the statement.)

ZEITGEIST. The intellectual-cultural orientation and attitudes characteristic of a particular period of time.

References

Adams, M. R., L. M. Webster, and D. I. Maxwell (1967). Comments on: "Stuttering adaptation and learning." *Journal of Speech and Hearing Disorders* 32, 192-195.

Adams, S. (1932). A study of the growth of language between two and four years. *Journal of Juvenile Research* 16, 269-277.

Allen, W. S. (1953). *Phonetics in Ancient India*. London: Oxford University Press.

Althaus, M., H. J. Vink, R. B. Minderaa, S. M. Gorhuis-Brouwer, and M. D. Oosterhoff (1995). Lack of effect of clonidine on stuttering in children. *American Journal of Psychiatry* 152, 1087-1089.

Anderson, L. O. (1923). Stuttering and allied disorders: An experimental investigation of underlying factors. *Comparative Psychology Monographs* 1, 1-78.

Andreski, S. (1972). *Social Sciences as Sorcery*. New York: St. Martin's Press.

Andrews, G., S. Hoddinott, A. Craig, P. Howie, A.-M. Feyer, and M. Neilson, (1983). Stuttering: A review of research findings and theories circa 1982. *Journal of Speech and Hearing Disorders* 48, 226-246.

Annett, M. (1978). Genetic and non-genetic influence on handedness. *Behavioral Genetics* 9, 227-249.

Armstrong, D. F., W. C. Stokoe, and S. E. Wilcox (1995). *Gesture and the Nature of Language*. Cambridge: Cambridge University Press.

Arnott, N. E. (1828) *Elements of Physics*. Edinburgh.

Bacon, Francis (1651). *Sylva Sylvarum: or, A Natural History in Ten Centuries*. London: W. Rawley.

Baker, S. J. (1948). Speech disturbances: A case for a wider view of paraphasias. *Psychiatry* 11, 359-366.

Balken, E. R., and J. H. Masserman (1940). The language of phantasy. *Journal of Psychology* 10, 75-86.

Ballard, P. B. (1912). Sinistrality and speech. *Journal of Experimental Pedagogy* 1, 298-310.

Beech, H. R. and F. Fransella (1968). *Research and Experiment in Stuttering*. London: Pergamon.

Bender, J. F. (1943). The prophylaxis of stuttering. *Nervous Child* 2 181-198.

Blanton, S. (1931). Stuttering. *Mental Hygiene* 15, 271-282.

Blood, G. W. (1985). Laterality difference in child stutterers: heterogeneity, severity levels, and statistical treatments. *Journal of Speech and Hearing Disorders* 50, 66-72.

Bloodstein, O. (1944). Studies in the Psychology of Stuttering: XIX. The relationship between oral reading rate and severity of stuttering. *Journal of Speech Disorders* 9, 161-173.

Bloodstein, O. (1958). Stuttering as an anticipatory struggle reaction. In Eisenson, J. (ed.), *Stuttering: A Symposium*. New York: Harper and Row.

Bloodstein, O. (1981) *A Handbook on Stuttering*. Chicago: National Easter Seal Society.

Bloodstein, O. (1984). Stuttering as an anticipatory struggle disorder. Chapter 9 in R. F. Curlee and W. H. Perkins (eds.), *Nature and Treatment of Stuttering*. San Diego: College-Hill.

Bloodstein, O. (1990). On pluttering, skivering and floggering: A commentary. *Journal of Speech and Hearing Disorders* 55, 392-393.

Bloodstein, O. (1993). *Stuttering: The Search for a Cause and Cure*. Boston: Allyn and Bacon.

Bloodstein, O. (1995). *A Handbook on Stuttering*. (5th ed.) San Diego: Singular.

Bluemel, C. S. (1913). *Stammering and Cognate Defects of Speech*. New York: Stechert.

Bluemel, C. S. (1932). Primary and secondary stammering. *Proceedings of the American Society for the Study of Speech Disorders*, 91-102. Also in *Quarterly Journal of Speech* 18 (1932), 187-200.

Bluemel, C. S. (1957). Presentation in Symposium of "Recovered" Stutterers, annual convention of the American Speech and Hearing Association, Cincinnati, Ohio.

Boorstin, D. J. (1983). *The Discoverers*. New York: Random House.

Bormann, E. G. (1969) Ephphatha, or some advice to stammerers. *Journal of Speech and Hearing Research* 12, 453-461.

Brady, J. P. (1968). A behavioral approach to the treatment of stuttering. *American Journal of Psychiatry* 125, 843-848.

Brady, J. P. (1969). Studies of the metronome effect on stuttering. *Behavior Research and Therapy* 7, 197-204.

Brady, J. P. (1971) Metronome conditioned speech retraining for stuttering. *Behavioral Therapy* 2, 129-150.

Brady, J. P. (1991) The pharmacology of stuttering: A critical review. *American Journal of Psychiatry* 148, 1309-1316.

Breuer, J., and Freud, S. (1955) *Studies on Hysteria*. London: Hogarth. [Originally published 1895]

Bridgman, P. W. (1927). *The Logic of Modern Physics*. New York: The Macmillan Co.

Brill, A. A. (1932). Speech disturbances in neurosis and mental diseases. *Quarterly Journal of Speech Education* 9, 129-135.

Brookshire, R. H. (1967). Comments on: "Stuttering adaptation and learning." *Journal of Speech and Hearing Disorders* 32, 195-198.

Brown, S. F. (1945). The loci of stutterings in the speech sequence. *Journal of Speech Disorders* 10, 181-192.

Brutten, E. J., and J. E. Dancer (1980). Stuttering adaptation under distributed and massed conditions. *Journal of Fluency Disorders* 5, 1-10.

Bryne, M. E. (1931). A follow-up study of one thousand cases of stutterers from the Minneapolis Public Schools. *Proceedings of the American Society for the Study of Disorders of Speech*.

Bryngelson, B. (1938). Prognosis in stuttering. *Journal of Speech Disorders* 3, 121-123.

Budge, E. A. W. (1978). *An Egyptian Hieroglyphic Dictionary, Vol. 2*. New York: Dover.

Burdin, G. (1940). The surgical treatment of stuttering, 1840-1842. *Journal of Speech Disorders* 5, 43-64.

Burke, K. (1945). *A Grammar of Motives*. New York: Prentice-Hall.

Carroll, J. B. (1953). *The Study of Language*. Cambridge, Mass.: Harvard University Press.

Carroll, J. B. (1956). *Language, Thought and Reality: Selected Writings of Benjamin Lee Whorf*. New York: John Wiley and Sons.

Castiglioni, A. (1941). *A History of Medicine*. Translated and edited by E. B. Krumbhaar. New York: Alfred A. Knopf.

Catford, J. C. (1977). *Fundamental Problems in Phonetics*. Bloomington: Indiana University Press.

Catton, B. (1963). *The Battle of Gettysburg*. New York: American Heritage.

Chase, S. (1938). *The Tyranny of Words*. New York: Harcourt, Brace.

Chase, S. (1956). *Guides to Straight Thinking*. New York: Harper.

Chase, S. (1969). *Danger—Men Talking: A Background Book on Semantics and Communication*. New York: Parents Magazine Press.

Cherry, E. C. (1953). On the recognition of speech with one, and with two ears. *Journal of the Acoustical Society of America* 25, 975-979.

Cherry, E. C. (1957). *On Human Communication*. Cambridge, Mass.: MIT Press.

Cherry, E. C., and B. M. Sayers (1956). Experiments upon the total inhibition of stammering by external control and some clinical results. *Journal of Psychosomatic Research* 1, 233-246.

Cherry, E. C., B. M. Sayers, and P. Marland (1955). Experiments on the complete suppression of stammering. *Nature* 176, 874-875.

Cherry, E. C., B. M. Sayers, and P. Marland (1956). Some experiments on the total suppression of stammering. *British Psychological and Sociological Bulletin* 30, 43-44.

Chervin, A. (1867). *Du Begaiement Considere comme Vice de Pronunciation*. Paris.

Churchill's Medical Dictionary. (1989). Philadelphia: W. B. Saunders.

Claiborne, J. H. (1917). Stuttering relieved by reversal of manual dexterity. *New York Medical Journal* 105, 577-581, 619-621.

Clark, R. M. (1964). Our enterprising predecessors and Charles Sydney Bluemel. *Asha* 6, 108-114.

Clark, R. M., and F. P. Murray (1955). Alterations in self-concept. Chapter 7 in D. Barbara (ed.), *New Directions in Stuttering*. Springfield, Ill.: Charles C Thomas.

Conture, E. G. (1990). *Stuttering*. 2nd ed. Englewood Cliffs, NJ.: Prentice-Hall.

Cooper, E. B., and C. S. Cooper (1991). A fluency disorders prevention program for preschoolers and children in the primary grades. *American Journal of Speech-Language Pathology* 1, 28-31.

Costello Ingham, J. M. (1993). Behavioral treatment of stuttering children. In R. F. Curlee (ed.), *Stuttering and Related Disorders of Fluency*. New York: Thieme-Stratton.

Craig, A. R., and M. Kearns (1995). Results of a traditional acupuncture intervention for stuttering. *Journal of Speech and Hearing Research* 38, 572-578.

Culatta, R., and S. A. Goldberg (1995). *Stuttering Therapy: An Integrated Approach to Theory and Practice*. Boston: Allyn and Bacon.

Cull, R. (1835). *Stammering and Its Cure*. London: Cadell and Murray.

Daly, J. A., and J. C. McCrosky (eds) (1984). *Avoiding Communication Shyness, Reticence and Communication Apprehension*. Beverly Hills, Calif.: Sage Publications

Davis, D. M. (1939). The relation of repetitions in the speech of young children to certain measures of language maturity and situational factors. Part I. *Journal of Speech Disorders* 4, 303-318.

Davis, D. M. (1940). The relation of repetitions in the speech of young children to certain measures of language maturity and situational factors. Part II and Part III. *Journal of Speech Disorders* 5, 235-246.

Dollard, J., and N. E. Miller (1950). *Personality and Psychotherapy*. New York: McGraw-Hill.

Donovan, G. E. (1971). A new device for the treatment of stuttering. *British Journal of Disorders of Communication* 6, 86-88.

Eiseley, L. (1958). *Darwin's Century*. New York: Doubleday.

Eldridge, M. (1968). *A History of the Treatment of Speech Disorders*. Edinburgh: E. and S. Livingstone.

Evans, R. B., and W. A. Koelsch (1985). Psychoanalysis arrives in America: The 1909 Psychology Conference at Clark University. *American Psychologist* 40, 942-948.

Fisher, M. S. (1932). Language patterns of preschool children. *Journal of Experimental Education* 1, 70-85.

Fisher, M. S. (1934). Language patterns of preschool children. *Child Development Monographs*, No. 15.

Fletcher, J. M. (1914). An experimental study of stuttering. *American Journal of Psychology* 25, 201-255.

Fletcher, J. M. (1928). *The Problem of Stuttering*. New York: Longmans, Green.

Freeman, D. (1983). *Margaret Mead and Samoa: The Making and Unmaking of an Anthropological Myth*. Cambridge, Mass.: Harvard University Press.

Freud, S. (1936). *The Problem of Anxiety*. New York: Norton.

Froeschels, E. (1913-14). Zur Pathologie des Stotterns. *Archiv fur Experimentelle und Kleine Phonetik* 1, 372-380.

Froeschels, E. (1921). A study of the symptomatology of stuttering. *Monatschrift fur Ohrenheilkunde* 55, 1109-1112.

Froeschels, E. (1943). Survey of the early literature on stuttering, chiefly European. *Nervous Child* 2, 86-95.

Froeschels, E. (1950). Ventriloquism: A technique for stutterers. *Journal of Speech and Hearing Disorders* 15, 336-337.

Froeschels, E. (1956). Pages 41-47 in E. Hahn (ed.), *Stuttering: Significant Theories and Therapies*. Stanford, Calif.: Stanford University Press.

Froeschels, E. (1961). New viewpoints on stuttering. *Folia Phoniatrica* 13, 187-201.

Froeschels, E., O. Dillrick, and I. Wilhelm (1932). *Psychological Elements in Speech.* Boston: Expression Co.

Gage, C. (1977). *The Northwoods Reader.* Au Train, Mich.: Avery Color Studios.

Gans, E. (1981). *The Origin of Language: A Formal Theory of Representation.* Berkeley: University of California Press.

Gibbon, E. (1911). *A History of the Decline and Fall of the Roman Empire, Vol. 3.* New York: Bigelow, Brown Co.

Goguen, J. A. (1968-69). The logic of inexact concepts. *Synthese* 19, 325-373.

Goldman-Eisler, F. (1952). Individual differences between interviewers and their effects on interviewee's conversational behavior. *Journal of Mental Science* 98, 660-671.

Goldman-Eisler, F. (1954). A study of individual differences and interaction in the behavior of some aspects of language in interviews. *Journal of Mental Science* 100, 177-197.

Goldman-Eisler, F. (1955). Speech-breathing activity--a measure of tension and affect during interviews. *British Journal of Psychology, General Section* 46, 53-63.

Goldman-Eisler, F. (1957). Speech production and language statistics. *Nature* 180, 1497.

Goldstein, M. A. (1940). Speech without a tongue. *Journal of Speech Disorders* 5, 65-69.

Good, J. M. (1827). *The Study of Medicine.* New York: Collins and Hannay.

Gordon, C. T., G. M. Cotelingam, S. Stager, C. L. Ludlow, S. D. Hamburger, and J. L. Rapoport (1995). A double-blind comparison of clomipramine and desipramine in the treatment of developmental stuttering. *Journal of Clinical Psychiatry* 56, 238-242.

Gorman, M. (1962). *General Semantics and Contemporary Thomism.* Lincoln: University of Nebraska Press.

Graves, Robert. (1934). *I, Claudius; from the Autobiography of Tiberius Claudius.* New York: H. Smith and R. Haas.

Graves, Robert. (1935). *Claudius the God and His Wife Messalina.* New York: H. Smith and R. Haas.

Gray, M. (1940). The "X" family: A clinical and laboratory study of a "stuttering" family. *Journal of Speech Disorders* 5, 343-348.

Gray, P. (1993). The assault on Freud. *Time,* November 29, pp. 47-51.

Greenberg, J. H. (ed.) (1963) *Universals of Language.* Cambridge, Mass.: MIT Press.

Greenberg, J. H. (1965). The word as a linguistic unit. In C. E. Osgood, and T. A. Sebeok (eds.), *Psycholinguistics: A Survey of Theory and Research.* Bloomington: Indiana University Press.

Guitar, B. (1980). *Stuttering: An Integration of Contemporary Therapies.* Memphis, Tenn.: Speech Foundation of America.

Guthrie, W. (1951). The development of rhetorical theory in America 1635-1850 — V: The elocution movement — England. *Speech Monographs* 18, 17-30.

Haagensen, C. D., and W. E. B. Lloyd (1943). *A Hundred Years of Medicine.* New York: Sheridan House.

Hahn, E. F. (1943). *Stuttering: Significant Theories and Therapies.* Stanford, Calif.: Stanford University Press.

Hahn, E. S. (1956). *Stuttering: Significant Theories and Therapies.* 2nd ed. Stanford, Calif.: Stanford University Press.

Halle, M. (1900). Ueber storungen der athmung bei stottem. *Monatschrift fur Spracheilkunde* 10, 225-236.

Hamilton, W. (1854). On Robert Bates's Instruments for the Cure of Stammering. (Report of the Committee on Science and the Arts of the Franklin Institute of the State of Pennsylvania) *Journal of the Franklin Institute*, April.

Hamre, C. E. (1992). Stuttering prevention I: Primacy of identification. *Journal of Fluency Disorders* 17, 3-23.

Harrington, J. (1987). Stuttering, delayed auditory feedback, and linguistic rhythm. *Journal of Speech and Hearing Research* 31, 36-47.

Harris, B. (1979). Whatever happened to little Albert? *American Psychologist* 34, 151-160.

Harrison, H. P. (1958). *Culture under Canvas: the Story of Tent Chautauqua*. New York: Hastings House.

Hayakawa, S. I. (1941). *Language in Action*. New York: Harcourt, Brace.

Hedley, W. S. (1900). *Therapeutic Electricity*. Philadelphia: P. Blakiston's Son and Co.

Hejna, R. F. (1955). A study of the loci of stuttering in spontaneous speech. Doctoral dissertation, Northwestern University, Evanston, Ill.

Hill, H. (1944a). Stuttering: I. A critical review and evaluation of biochemical investigations. *Journal of Speech Disorders* 9, 245-261.

Hill, H. (1944b). Stuttering: II. A review and integration of physiological data. *Journal of Speech Disorders* 9, 289-324.

Hinton, L., J. Nichols, and J. J. Ohala (1994). *Sound Symbolism*. Cambridge: Cambridge University Press.

Hogewind, F. (1947). Speech therapy in the Netherlands. *Speech* 11, 2, 20-21.

Hollingworth, H. I. (1930). *Abnormal Psychology*. New York: Ronald.

Householder, F. W. (1946). On the problem of sound and meaning: An English phonestheme. *Word* 2, 83-84.

Hull, C. L. (1943). *Principles of Behavior*. New York: Appleton-Century-Crofts.

Hunt, J. (1861). *Stammering and Stuttering*. Hastings, England: Ore House. (Republished 1967 by Hafner Publishing, New York.)

Jacoby, G. W. (1901). *Electrotherapy, Vol. 2*. Philadelphia: P. Blakiston's Son and Co.

Johnson, W. (1930). *Because I Stutter*. New York: Appleton.

Johnson, W. (1932). The influence of stuttering on the personality. *University of Iowa Studies in Child Welfare*, Vol. 5, No. 5.

Johnson, W. (1933). An interpretation of stuttering. *Quarterly Journal of Speech* 19, 70-76.

Johnson, W. (1934). Stuttering in the preschool child. *University of Iowa Studies in Child Welfare*, No. 37.

Johnson, W. (1938). The role of evaluation in stuttering behavior. *Journal of Speech Disorders* 3, 85-89.

Johnson, W. (1941). The problem of stuttering from the point of view of general semantics. Paper presented at the Second International Congress of General Semantics, University of Denver, Denver, Colorado.

Johnson, W. (1944a). The Indians have no word for it: Stuttering in adults. *Quarterly Journal of Speech* 30, 456-465.

Johnson, W. (1944b) The Indians have no word for it: Stuttering in children. *Quarterly Journal of Speech* 30, 330-337.

Johnson, W. (1946). *People in Quandaries: The Semantics of Personal Adjustment.* New York: Harper and Row.

Johnson, W. (1949). An open letter to the mother of a stuttering child. *Journal of Speech and Hearing Disorders* 14, 3-8.

Johnson, W. (1955). The descriptional principle and the principle of static analysis. Chapter 43 in W. Johnson, and R. R. Leutenegger (eds.), *Stuttering in Children and Adults.* Minneapolis: University of Minnesota Press.

Johnson, W. (1956). Stuttering. Chapter 5 in W. Johnson, S. F. Brown, J. F. Curtis, C. W. Edney, and J. Keaster (eds.), *Speech Handicapped School Children.* New York: Harper and Row.

Johnson, W. (1957). Panel of "recovered" stutterers. Annual convention of the American Speech and Hearing Association, Cincinnati, Ohio.

Johnson, W. (1961a). Measurements of oral reading and speaking rate and disfluency of adult male and female stutterers and nonstutterers. *Journal of Speech and Hearing Disorders*, Monograph Supplement 7, 1-20.

Johnson, W. (1961b). *Stuttering and What You Can Do About It.* Minneapolis: University of Minnesota Press.

Johnson, W. (1962). A comment on "Evaluation and stuttering." *Journal of Speech and Hearing Disorders* 27, 390.

Johnson, W. (1967). Stuttering. In W. Johnson, and D. Moeller (eds.) *Speech Handicapped School Children.* New York: Harper and Row.

Johnson W., and Associates (1959). *The Onset of Stuttering.* Minneapolis: University of Minnesota Press.

Johnson, W., and S. F. Brown (1935). Stuttering in relation to various speech sounds. *Quarterly Journal of Speech* 21, 481-496.

Johnson, W., S. F. Brown, J. F. Curtis, C. W. Edney, and J. Keaster (1948). *Speech Handicapped School Children.* (1st ed.) New York: Harper and Row.

Johnson, W., S. F. Brown, J. F. Curtis, C. W. Edney, and J. Keaster (1956). *Speech Handicapped School Children.* (2nd ed.) New York: Harper and Row.

Johnson, W., S. F. Brown, J. F. Curtis, C. W. Edney, and J. Keaster (1967). *Speech Handicapped School Children.* (3rd ed.) New York: Harper and Row.

Johnson, W., and M. Inness (1939). Studies in the psychology of stuttering : XIII. A statistical analysis of the adaptation and consistency effects in relation to stuttering. *Journal of Speech Disorders* 4, 79-86.

Johnson, W., and J. R. Knott (1936). The moment of stuttering. *Journal of Genetic Psychology* 48, 473-479.

Johnson, W., and J. R. Knott (1937). Studies in the Psychology of Stuttering: I. The distribution of moments of stuttering in successive readings of the same material. *Journal of Speech Disorders* 2, 17-19.

Johnson, W., and R. Leutenegger (1955). *Stuttering in Children and Adults.* Minneapolis: University of Minnesota Press.

Johnson, W., and L. S. Millsapps (1937). Studies in the psychology of stuttering: VI. The role of cues representative of past stuttering in a distribution of stuttering moments during oral reading. *Journal of Speech Disorders* 2, 101-104.

Jonas, G. (1977). *Stuttering: The Disorder of Many Theories.* New York: Farrar, Straus and Giroux.

Karlin, I. W. (1959). Stuttering: Basically an organic disorder. *Logos* 2, 61-63.

Katz, M. (1977). Survey of patented anti-stuttering devices. In R. W. Rieber (ed.). *The Problem of Stuttering.* New York: Elsevier.

Kelso, J. A. S., E. L. Saltzman, and B. Tuller (1986). The dynamical perspective on speech production: data and theory. *Journal of Phonetics* 14, 29-59.

Kent, R. D. (1983). Facts about stuttering: Neuropsychologic perspectives. *Journal of Speech and Hearing Disorders* 48, 249-254.

Kidd, K. K. (1977). A genetic perspective on stuttering. *Journal of Fluency Disorders* 2, 259-269.

Kidd, K. K. (1984). Stuttering as a genetic disorder. In R. Curlee, and W. Perkins (eds.), *Nature and Treatment of Stuttering: New Directions.* San Diego: College Hill.

Klencke, H. (1844) *Die Storungen des menschlichen Stimm und Sprachorgans.* Cassel.

Klencke, H. (1862). *Die Heilung des Stotterns.* Leipzig.

Klingbeil, G. M. (1939). The historical background of the modern speech clinic. *Journal of Speech Disorders* 4, 115-132.

Kluckhohn, C. (1954). Culture and behavior. Chapter 25 in G. Lindzey (ed.), *Handbook of Social Psychology, Vol. 2.* Reading, Mass.: Addison-Wesley.

Kolakowski, L. (1989). *The Presence of Myth.* Translated by Adam Czerniawski. Chicago: University of Chicago Press.

Korzybski, A. H. S. (1921). *Manhood of Humanity: The Science and Art of Human Engineering.* New York: E. P. Dutton.

Korzybski, A. H. S. (1933). *Science and Sanity: An Introduction to Non-Aristotelian Systems and General Semantics.* Lancaster, Pa.: Science Press Printing Co.

Kowalczyk, P. A., and E. Yairi (1995). Features of F2 transitions in fluent speech of children who stutter. Paper (SA 664) presented at the 1995 Convention of the American Speech Language Hearing Association, Orlando, Fla.

Kussmaul, A. (1877). Disturbances of speech. Ziemssen's *Encyclopedia of the Practice of Medicine* Vol. 14. New York.

Labov, W. (1973). The boundaries of words and their meanings. In C.-J. N. Bailey, and R. W. Shuy, *New Ways of Analyzing Variation in English.* Washington, D.C.: University of Georgetown Press.

Langford, C. H. (1942). Moore's notion of analysis. In P. A. Schliff (ed.), *The Philosophy of G. E. Moore.* New York: Tudor.

Lee, B. S. (1950). Some effects of sidetone delay. *Journal of the Acoustical Society of America* 22, 639-640.

Lee, B. S., W. E. McGough, and M. Peins (1973). A new method for stutter therapy. *Folia Phoniatrica* 25, 186-195.

Lemert, E. M. (1951). *Social Pathology.* New York: McGraw-Hill.

Lemert, E. M. (1972). *Human Deviance, Social Problems and Social Control.* Englewood Cliffs, N.J.: Prentice-Hall.

Lenneberg, E. H. (1967). *Biological Foundations of Language.* New York: John Wiley and Sons.

Lewis, G. A. (1907). *Home Cure for Stammerers.* Detroit: Winn and Hammond.

Lieberman, P. (1988). *On the Origins of Language: An Introduction to the Evolution of Human Speech.* Boston: University Press of America.

Lum, P. (1958). *Fabulous Beasts.* London: Thames and Hudson.

Mahl, G. F. (1956a). Disturbances and silences in the patient's speech in psychotherapy. *Journal of Abnormal and Social Psychology* 53, 1-15.

Mahl, G. F. (1956b). Disturbances in the patient's speech as a function of anxiety. Paper presented at the meeting of the Eastern Psychological Association, March 23-24, Atlantic City.

Mahl, G. F. (1956c). "Normal" disturbances in spontaneous speech. Paper presented at the meeting of the American Psychological Associaton, August 30-September 5, Chicago.

Marler, P. (1975). On the origin of speech from animal sounds. Pages 11-37 in J. F. Kavanagh, and J. E. Cutting (eds.), *The Role of Speech in Language*. Cambridge, Mass.: MIT Press.

Martin, L. (1986). Eskimo words for snow: A case study in the genesis and decay of an anthropological example. *American Anthropologist* 89, 2, 443-444.

McCarthy, D. A. (1930). The language development of the preschool child. University of Minnesota Institute of Child Welfare Monograph Series, No. 4. Minneapolis: University of Minnesota Press.

McCarthy, T. A. (1991). *Ideals and Illusions*. Cambridge, Mass.: MIT Press.

McCormac, H. (1828). *A Treatise on the Causes and Cure of Hesitation of Speech or Stammering*. London: Smith, Elder and Co.

McNeill, D. (1987). *Psycholinguistics: A New Approach*. New York: Harper and Row. Chapter 6.

Meigs, J. A. (1852). Clinical report on Robert Bates' cure for stammering. *Clinic of Jefferson Medical College*. Surgeon General's Office Library, February 21, 1852.

Mettler, C. C. (1947). *History of Medicine*. Philadelphia: P. Blakiston.

Meyer, V., and J. M. Mair (1963). A new technique to control stammering: A preliminary report. *Behavior Research and Therapy* 1, 251-254.

Miller, N. (1944). Experimental studies of conflict. Chapter 14 in J. McV. Hunt (ed.), *Personality and the Behavior Disorders*. New York: Ronald.

Moeller, D. (1972). *Living with Change: The Semantics of Coping*. New York: Harper and Row.

Moeller, D. (1976). *Speech Pathology and Audiology: Iowa Origins of a Discipline*. Iowa City: University of Iowa Press.

Morrison, T. (1974). *Chautauqua: A Center for Education, Religion and the Arts in America*. Chicago: University of Chicago Press.

Morton, J. B. (1950). *Camille Desmoulins; and Other Studies of the French Revolution*. London: Werner Laurie.

Mowrer, D. M. (1975). An instructional program to increase fluent speech of stutterers. *Journal of Fluency Disorders* 1, 25-35.

Mowrer, D. M. (1980). *A Program to Establish Fluent Speech*. Columbus, Ohio: Charles E. Merrill.

Mowrer, O. H. (1956). Two-factor learning theory reconsidered, with special reference to secondary reinforcement and the concept of habit. *Psychological Review* 63, 114-125.

Muir, F. L. (1964). Case studies of selected examples of reticence and fluency. M.A. Thesis, Washington State University.

Murphy, J. M. (1976). Psychiatric labeling in cross-cultural perspective. *Science* 191, 1019-1028.

Newman, S. S. (1941). Behavior patterns in linguistic structure: a case study. Pages 94-106 in L. Spier, A. I. Hallowell, and S. S. Newman (eds.), *Language, Culture and Personality: Essays in Memory of Edward Sapir*. Menasha, Wis: Sapir Memorial Publication Fund.

News Notes (1970). Treatment of stuttering. *American Journal of Physical Medicine* 49, 330.

Nicolosi, L., E. Harryman, and J. Kresheck (1978). *Terminology of Communication Disorders: Speech, Language, Hearing.* Baltimore: Williams and Wilkins.

O'Neill, Y. V. (1980). *Speech and Speech Disorders in Western Thought before 1600.* Westport, Conn.: Greenwood Press.

Onslow, M. (1995). A picture is worth more than any words. *Journal of Speech and Hearing Research* 38, 586-588.

Orton, S. T. (1927). Studies in stuttering. *Archives of Neurology and Psychiatry* 18, 671-672.

Orton, S. T. (1929). A physiological theory of reading disability and stuttering in children. *New England Journal of Medicine* 199, 1047-1052.

Orton, S. T., and L. E. Travis (1929). Studies in Stuttering: IV. Studies of action currents in stutterers. *Archives of Neurology and Psychiatry* 21, 61-68.

Paconcelli-Calzia, G. P. (1941). *Geschichtzahlen der Phonetik: 3000 Jahre Phonetik.* Hamburg: Hansischer Gildenvealog.

Paden, E. P. (1970). *A History of the American Speech and Hearing Association, 1925-1958.* Washington, D.C.: American Speech and Hearing Association.

Page, M., and R. Ingpen (1985). *The Encyclopedia of Things that Never Were: Creatures, People and Places.* Adelaide, Australia: Paper Tiger Press.

Paster, G. K. (1993). *The Body Embarrassed.* Ithaca, N.Y.: Cornell University Press.

Pastore, N. (1949). *The Nature-Nurture Controversy.* New York: King's Crown Press.

Paulson, R. E. (1983). *Language, Science and Action.* Westport, Conn.: Greenwood Press.

Peins, M. (ed.) (1984). *Contemporary Approaches in Stuttering Therapy.* Boston: Little Brown & Co.

Perello, J. (1976). *The History of the International Association of Logopedics and Phoniatrics.* Barcelona: Editorial Augusta, S.A.

Perkins, W., J. Rudas, L. Johnson, and J. Bell (1976). Stuttering: discoordination of phonation with articulation and respiration. *Journal of Speech and Hearing Research* 19, 509-522.

Perkins, W., J. Rudas, L. Johnson, and J. Bell (1986). Stuttering: discoordination of phonation with articulation and respiration. Chapter 4 in G. H. Shames, and H. Rubin (eds.), *Stuttering: Then and Now.* Columbus: Charles E. Merrill.

Perkins, W. H., R. D. Kent, and R. F. Curlee (1991) A theory of neurolinguistic function in stuttering. *Journal of Speech and Hearing Research* 34, 734-752.

Peters, H. F. M., and W. Hulstijn (eds.) (1987). *Speech Motor Dynamics in Stuttering.* New York: Springer-Verlag.

Peters, H. F. M., W. Hulstijn, and C. W. Starkweather (eds.) (1991). *Speech Motor Control and Stuttering.* New York: Elsevier.

Peters, T. J., and B. Guitar (1991). *Stuttering: An Integrated Approach to Its Nature and Treatment.* Baltimore: Williams and Wilkins.

Phillips, G. M. (1968). Pathology of the normal speaker. *Speech Monographs* 35, 39-49.

Phillips, G. M., L. Kelly, and R. B. Rubin (1991) *Communication Incompetencies.* Carbondale Ill.: University of Southern Illinois Press.

Potter, S. O. L. (1882). *Speech and Its Defects.* Philadelphia: P. Blakiston, Son and Co.

Prins, D. (1968). Pre-therapy adaptation of stuttering and its relation to speech measures of therapy progress. *Journal of Speech and Hearing Research* 11, 740-746.

Prins, D., and C. P. Hubbard (1988). Response contingent stimuli and stuttering: Issues and implications. *Journal of Speech and Hearing Research* 31, 696-709.

Pullam, G. K. (1991). *The Great Eskimo Vocabulary Hoax.* Chicago: University of Chicago Press. Chapter 19.

Quinting, G. (1971). *Hesitation Phenomena in Adult Aphasic and Normal Speech.* The Hague: Mouton.

Rapaport, H. (1989). *Heidegger and Derrida: Reflections on Time and Language.* Lincoln: University of Nebraska Press.

Read, A. W. (1938). Speech defects and mannerisms among slaves and servants in colonial America. *Quarterly Journal of Speech* 24, 397-401.

Records, M. A., R. C. Heimbuch, and K. K. Kidd (1977). Handedness and stuttering: A dead horse? *Journal of Fluency Disorders* 2, 271-282.

Reid, L. D. (1946). Some facts about stuttering. *Journal of Speech Disorders* 11, 3-12.

Remnick, D. (1995). Fool Britannia. *New Yorker,* January 16, 79-83.

Robbins, S. D. (1919). A plethysmographic study of shock and stammering. *American Journal of Physiology* 48, 285-323.

Rockey, D., and P. Johnstone (1979). Medieval Arabic views on speech disorders: Al Razi (c. 865-925). *Journal of Communication Disorders* 12, 229-243.

Rothenberger, A., H. S. Johannsen, H. Schultze, H. Amorosa, and D. Rommel (1994). Use of tiapride on stuttering in children and adolescents. *Perceptual and Motor Skills* 79, 1163-1170.

Rubin, H. J. (1960). Further observations on the neurochronaxic theory of voice production. *Archives of Otology and Laryngology* 72, 207-211.

Ryan, B., and R. Van Kirk (1971). *Programmed Conditioning for Fluency: Program book.* Monterey, Calif.: Monterey Learning Systems.

St. Onge, K. R. (1963). The stuttering syndrome. *Journal of Speech and Hearing Research* 6, 195-197.

Sanford, F. H. (1942). Speech and personality. *Psychological Bulletin* 39, 811-845.

Sapir, E. (1915). Abnormal types of speech in Nootka. *Anthropological Series, Canada Department of Mines, Geological Survey,* Memoir 62, No. 5.

Sargent, W. (1964). Psychiatric treatment here and in England. *Atlantic Monthly* 214 (July), 88-95.

Savithri, S. R. (1987). Speech pathology in ancient India: A review of the literature. *Journal of Communication Disorders* 20, 437-445.

Savithri, S. R. (1988). Speech and Hearing Science in ancient India: A review of Sanskrit literature. *Journal of Communication Disorders* 21, 271-317.

Schoolfield, L. (1938). The development of speech correction in the nineteenth century. *Quarterly Journal of Speech* 24, 101-116.

Schuell, H., (1946). Sex differences in relation to stuttering: Part I. *Journal of Speech Disorders* 11, 277-298.

Schuell, H. (1947). Sex differences in relation to stuttering: Part II. *Journal of Speech Disorders* 12, 23-38.

Scramuzza, V. M. (1940). *The Emperor Claudius.* Cambridge, Mass.: Harvard University Press.

Scripture, E. W. (1904). *The Elements of Experimental Phonetics.* New York: Scribner.

Scripture, E. W. (1912). *Stuttering, Lisping and Correction of the Speech of the Deaf.* New York: Macmillan.

Selmar, J. W. (1991). *Help! This Child Is Stuttering.* Austin, Tex.: Pro-Ed.

Sheehan, J. G. (1953). Theory and treatment of stuttering as an approach avoidance conflict. *Journal of Psychology* 36, 27-49.

Sheehan, J. G. (1958). Conflict theory of stuttering. Pages 123-166 in J. Eisenson (ed.), *Stuttering: A Symposium.* New York: Harper and Brothers.

Sheehan, J. G. (1970). The known and the unknown. Chapter 8 in J. G. Sheehan (ed.), *Stuttering: Research and Therapy.* New York: Harper and Row.

Sheridan, T. (1762). *A Course of Lectures on Elocution.* London: W. Strahan. Reissued 1968 by Benjamin Blom, New York.

Smith, M. E. (1926). An investigation of the development of the sentence and extent of vocabulary in young children. *University of Iowa Studies in Child Welfare,* Vol. 3, No. 5.

Snidecor, J. (1945). Why the Indian does not stutter. *Quarterly Journal of Speech* 33, 493-495.

Soderberg, G. A. (1962). What is "average" stuttering? *Journal of Speech and Hearing Disorders* 27, 85-86.

Solomon, M. (1932). Stuttering as an emotional disorder. *Proceedings of the American Speech Correction Association* 2, 118-121.

Sortini, A. J. (1955). Twenty years of stuttering research. *Journal of the International Council for Exceptional Children* 21, 181-183.

Speaking Out (1994). The quarterly magazine of the Association for Stammerers. Winter issue, p. 12.

Spence, K. W. (1960). *Behavior Theory and Learning.* Englewood Cliffs, N.J.: Prentice-Hall.

Spotting and stopping stuttering. (1983) Changing Times. October, pp. 64-67.

Stager, S. V., C. L. Ludlow, C.T. Gordon, M. Cotelingam, and J. L. Rapoport (1995). Fluency changes in persons who stutter following a double blind trial of Clomipramine and Desipramine. *Journal of Speech and Hearing Research* 38, 516-525.

Stam, J. H. (1976). *Inquiries into the Origin of Language.* New York: Harper and Row.

Starkweather, C. W., S. R. Gottwald, and M. M. Halfond (1990) *Stuttering Prevention.* Englewood Cliffs, N.J.: Prentice- Hall.

Steer, M. D., and W. Johnson (1936). An objective study of the relationship between psychological factors and the severity of stuttering. *Journal of Abnormal and Social Psychology* 31, 36-46.

Stein, L. (1942). *Speech and Voice.* London: Methuen.

Stevens, S. S. (1955). Psychology and the science of science. Chapter 3 in M. H. Marx (ed.), *Psychological Theory.* New York: Macmillan.

Stewart, J. L. (1960a). Studies of North American Indians of the Plains, Great Basin and Southwest. Paper read at the ASHA Convention, Los Angeles.

Stewart, J. L. (1960b). The problem of stuttering in certain North American Indian societies. *Journal of Speech and Hearing Disorders,* Monograph Supplement 6, April.

Stocking, G. W. (1968). *Race, Culture and Evolution.* New York: Free Press.

Stromsta, C. (1965). A spectrographic study of disfluencies labelled as stuttering by parents. *De Therapis Vocis et Loquelae* 1, 317-320.

Stromsta, C. (1986). *Elements of Stuttering.* Oshtemo, Mich.: Atsmorts Publishing.

Studdert-Kennedy, M. (1975). From continuous signal to discrete measage: Syllable to phoneme. In J. F. Kavanaugh, and J. E. Cutting (eds.), *The Role of Speech in Language*. Cambridge, Mass.: MIT Press.

Sussman, H. M., and P. F. MacNeilage (1975). Hemispheric specialization for speech production and perception in stutterers. *Neuropsychologia* 13, 19-26.

Swadesh, M. (1971). *The Origin and Diversification of Language*. Chicago: Aldine-Atherton.

Sweet, H. (1877). *Handbook of Phonetics*. Oxford: Clarendon Press. (Also, 1970. College Park, Md.: McGrath.)

Symmes, D., and M. Biben (1988). Conversational vocal exchanges in squirrel monkeys. Pages 123-132 in D. Todt, P. Goedeking, and P. Symmes (eds.), *Primate Vocal Communication*. New York: Springer-Verlag.

Ten Cate, M. J. (1902). Ueber der untersuchung der athmung bei sprachfehlern. *Monatschrift fur Spracheilkunde* 12, 247-259.

Thelwall, J. (1805). Stuttering. *London Medical and Physical Journal* 13, 450-455.

Thelwall, J. (1806). Stuttering. *London Medical and Physical Journal* 14, 256-259.

Thelwall, J. (1810). *A Letter to Henry Cline on Imperfect Developments of the Faculties, Mental and Moral, as well as Constitutional and Organic; and on the Treatment of Impediments, of Speech*. London: R. Taylor and Co.

Thelwall, J. (1812a). *Illustrations of English Rhythmus*. London: J. M. McCreary, Blackhorse Court.

Thelwall, J. (1812b) *Selections for the Illustration of a Course of Instructions on the Rhythmus and Utterance of the English Language*. London: J. M. McCreary, Blackhorse Court.

Thornton, E. M. (1983). *Freud and Cocaine—The Freudian Fallacy*. London: Blond and Briggs.

Travis, L. E. (1925). Muscular fixation of the stutterer's voice under emotion. *Science* 62, 207-208.

Travis, L. E. (1926). A phono-photographic study of the stutterer's voice and speech. *Psychological Monographs* 36, 109-141.

Travis, L. E. (1927a). Studies in Stuttering: I. Disintegration of the breathing movements during stuttering. *Archives of Neurology and Psychiatry* 18, 673-690.

Travis, L. E. (1927b). Studies in Stuttering: II. Photographic studies of the voice in stuttering. *Archives of Neurology and Psychiatry* 18, 998-1014.

Travis, L. E. (1928). A comparative study of the performances of stutterers and normal speakers in mirror tracing. *Psychological Monographs* 39, 45-50.

Travis, L. E. (1929). Recurrence of stuttering following shift from normal to mirror writing. *Archives of Neurology and Psychiatry* 21, 386-391.

Travis, L. E. (1933a). A neurological consideration of stuttering. *Spoken Word* 1, 3-11.

Travis, L. E. (1933b). Speech Pathology. Chapter 16 in C. Murchison (ed.), *A Handbook of Child Psychology*. Worcester, Mass.: Clark Univ. Press.

Travis, L. E. (1934). Dissociation of homologous muscle function in stuttering. *Archives of Neurology and Psychiatry* 31, 127-133.

Travis, L. E. (1937). Brain potentials and the temporal course of consciousness. *Journal of Experimental Psychology* 21, 302-309.

Travis, L. E. (1940). The need for stuttering. *Journal of Speech Disorders* 5, 193-202.

Travis, L. E. (1957). The unspeakable feelings of people, with special reference to stuttering. Chapter 29 in L. E. Travis (ed.), *Handbook of Speech Pathology*. New York: Appleton-Century-Crofts.

Travis, L. E. (1978a). Neurophysiological dominance. *Journal of Speech and Hearing Disorders* 43, 275-277.

Travis, L. E. (1978b). Cerebral dominance theory of stuttering, 1931-1978. *Journal of Speech and Hearing Disorders* 43, 278-281.

Travis, L. E., and L. B. Fagan (1928). Studies in Stuttering: III. A study of certain reflexes during stuttering. *Archives of Neurology and Psychiatry* 19, 1006-1013.

Travis, L. E., and R. Y. Herren (1929). Studies in Stuttering: V. A study of simultaneous antitropic movements of the hands of stutterers. *Archives of Neurology and Psychiatry* 22, 487-494.

Travis, L. E., and W. Johnson (1934). Stuttering and the concept of handedness. *Psychological Review* 41, 534-562.

Travis, L. E., and D. B. Lindsley (1933). An action current study of handedness in relation to stuttering. *Journal of Experimental Psychology* 16, 258-270.

Trilling, L. (1953). *The Liberal Imagination: Essays on Literature and Society*. Garden City, N.J.: Doubleday.

Van Dantzig, M. (1940). Syllable-tapping, a new method for the help of stammerers. *Journal of Speech Disorders* 5, 127-131.

van den Berg, Jw. (1957). Sur les theories myo-elastique et neuro-chronaxique de la phonation. *Review de Laryngologie de Bordeaux* 74, 495-512.

Van Riper, C. (1937). The effect of devices for minimizing stuttering on the creation of symptoms. *Journal of Abnormal and Social Psychology* 32, 185-192.

Van Riper, C. (1954). *Speech Correction: Principles and Methods*. Englewood Cliffs, N. J.: Prentice-Hall.

Van Riper, C. (1957). Symptomatic therapy for stuttering. Chapter 27 in L. E. Travis (ed.), *Handbook of Speech Pathology*. New York: Appleton-Century-Crofts.

Van Riper, C. (1958). Experiments in stuttering therapy. Pages 275-390 in J. Eisenson (ed.), *Stuttering: A Symposium*. New York: Harper and Brothers.

Van Riper, C. (1971). *The Nature of Stuttering*. Englewood Cliffs, N.J.: Prentice-Hall.

Van Riper, C. (1973). *The Therapy of Stuttering*. Englewood Cliffs, N.J.: Prentice-Hall.

Van Riper, C. (1992a). Some ancient history. *Journal of Fluency Disorders* 17, 25-28.

Van Riper, C. (1992b). Stuttering? *Journal of Fluency Disorders* 17, 81-84.

Van Riper, C., and K. Hull (1955). The quantative measurement of the effect of certain situations on stuttering. Chapter 8 in W. Johnson, and R. R. Leutenegger (eds.), *Stuttering in Children and Adults*. Minneapolis: University of Minnesota Press.

Walker, J. (1781). *Elements of Elocution*. London: Robinson.

Walker, J. (1787). *The Melody of Speaking*. London: Robinson.

Warren, E. (1837). Remarks on stammering. *American Journal of Medical Science* 21, 75-99. Reprinted 1977, in *Journal of Communication Disorder* 10, 159-179; and as pp. 159-179 in R. W. Rieber, *The Problem of Stuttering*, New York: Elsevier North-Holland.

Watson, J. B. (1913). Psychology as a behaviorist views it. *Psychological Review* 20, 158-177.

Watson, J. B. (1914). *Behavior: An Introduction to Comparative Psychology*. New York: Holt, Rinehart and Winston.

Watson, J. B. (1916). The place of the conditioned reflex in psychology. *Psychological Review* 23, 89-117.

Watson, J. B. (1919). *Psychology from the Standpoint of a Behaviorist.* Philadelphia: Lippincott.

Watson, J. B. (1924). *Behaviorism.* New York: W. W. Norton.

Watson, J. B., and R. Rayner (1920). Conditioned emotional reactions. *Journal of Experimental Psychology* 3, 1-14.

Webster, W. G. (1986). Neuropsychological models of stuttering: II. Interhemispheric interference. *Neuropsychologia* 24, 737-741.

Weiss, D. A. (1948). The International Society for Logopedics and Phoniatry. *Speech* 12, 2, 15.

Weiss, D. M. (1992). Fluency enhancing systems . . . for free! *Letting Go* 12, 2, 4-5.

Wells, G. A. (1987). *The Origin of Language.* LaSalle, Ill.: Open Court Publishing.

West, R. (1933). *Disorders of Speech and Voice.* Madison, Wis.: College Typing Co.

West, R. (1943). The pathology of stuttering. *Nervous Child* 2, 96-106.

West, R. (1958). An agnostic's speculations about stuttering. Pages169-222 in J. Eisenson (ed.), *Stuttering: A Symposium.* New York: Harper and Brothers.

West, R. (1959). Speech science in the first half of the twentieth century. Pages 24-28 in *Re-establishing the Speech Profession.* Speech Association of the Eastern States.

West, Robert W. (1968). Necrology. *Asha* 10, 8, 331-332.

West, R., M. Ansberry, and A. Carr (1957). *The Rehabilitation of Speech.* New York: Harper and Brothers.

West, R., L. Kennedy, and A. Carr (1937). *The Rehabilitation of Speech.* New York: Harper and Brothers.

Whipple, G. M. (1911). The left-handed child. *Journal of Educational Psychology* 2, 1-78.

Whorf, B. L. (1940). Science and linguistics. *Technological Review* (MIT) 42, 6, 229-31, 247-248. Reprinted in J. B. Carroll (ed.), *Language, Thought and Reality: Selected Writings of Benjamin Lee Whorf.* Cambridge, Mass.: MIT Press, 1956.

Williams, W. J. (1972). *General Semantics and the Social Sciences,* Chapter 4. New York: Philosophical Library.

Wingate, M. E. (1962a). Evaluation and Stuttering, Part I: Speech characteristics of young children. *Journal of Speech and Hearing Disorders* 27, 106-115.

Wingate, M. E. (1962b). Evaluation and Stuttering, II: Environmental stress and critical appraisal of speech. *Journal of Speech and Hearing Disorders* 27, 244-257.

Wingate, M. E. (1962c). Evaluation and Stuttering, III: Identification of stuttering and the use of a label. *Journal of Speech and Hearing Disorders* 27, 368-377.

Wingate, M. E. (1964a). A standard definition of stuttering. *Journal of Speech and Hearing Disorders* 29, 484-489.

Wingate, M. E. (1964b). Recovery from stuttering. *Journal of Speech and Hearing Disorders* 29, 312-321.

Wingate, M. E. (1966a). Stuttering adaptation and learning: I. The relevance of adaptation studies to stuttering as "learned behavior." *Journal of Speech and Hearing Disorders* 31, 148-156.

Wingate, M. E. (1966b). Stuttering adaptation and learning: II. The adequacy of learning principles in the interpretation of stuttering. *Journal of Speech and Hearing Disorders* 31, 211-218.

Wingate, M. E. (1966c). Prosody in stuttering adaptation. *Journal of Speech and Hearing Research* 9, 550-556.

Wingate, M. E. (1967). Slurvian skill of stutterers. *Journal of Speech and Hearing Research* 10, 844-848.

Wingate, M. E. (1969). Sound and pattern in "artificial" fluency. *Journal of Speech and Hearing Research* 12, 677-686.

Wingate, M. E. (1970). Effect on stuttering of changes in audition. *Journal of Speech and Hearing Research* 13, 861-873.

Wingate, M. E. (1976). *Stuttering: Theory and Treatment*. New York: Irvington-Wiley.

Wingate, M. E. (1979). The loci of stuttering: grammar or prosody? *Journal of Communication Disorders* 12, 283-290.

Wingate, M. E. (1983). Speaking unassisted: Comments on a paper by Andrews et al. *Journal of Speech Disorders* 48, 255-263.

Wingate, M. E. (1984a). Fluency, disfluency, dysfluency and stuttering. *Journal of Fluency Disorders* 9, 163-168.

Wingate, M. E. (1984b). The recurrence ratio. *Journal of Fluency Disorders* 9, 21-29.

Wingate, M. E. (1986a). Physiological and Genetic Factors. Chapter 3 in G. H. Shames and H. Rubin (eds.), *Stuttering: Then and Now*. Columbus: Charles E. Merrill.

Wingate, M. E. (1986b). Adaptation, consistency and beyond: I. Limitations and contradictions. *Journal of Fluency Disorders* 11, 1-36.

Wingate, M. E. (1986c). Adaptation, consistency and beyond: II. An integral account. *Journal of Fluency Disorders* 11, 37-53.

Wingate, M. E. (1988). *The Structure of Stuttering*. New York: Springer-Verlag.

Wingate, M. E. (1989). Review of H. F. M. Peters and W. Hulstjin (eds.), *Speech Motor Dynamics in Stuttering*. New York: Springer-Verlag, 1987.

Wingate, M. E. (1990). Fifty-eight years of stuttering research: Extending the Sortini analysis. Unpublished research.

Wyllie, J. (1894). *The Disorders of Speech*. Edinburgh: Oliver and Boyd.

Yairi, E. (1995). Early intervention in early childhood stuttering: Myths and facts. Paper (F-1110) presented at the annual convention of the American Speech Language and Hearing Association, Orlando, Fla.

Yearsley, J. (1844). Stammering. *The Lancet*, 244-248.

Further Reading

Appelt, A. (1911). *The Real Cause of Stammering and its Permanent Cure*. London: Methuen.

Bigelow, H. R. (1892). *Plain Talks on Electricity and Batteries, with Therapeutic Index*. Second Edition. Philadelphia: P. Blakiston, Son & Co.

Blanton, S. (1916). The University of Wisconsin Speech Clinic. *Journal of Educational Psychology* 7, 253-260.

Boorstin, D. J. (1993). *The Creators*. NewYork: Vintage Books.

Bryant, Pearl (1941). Speech re-education in the nineteenth century. Unpublished Ph.D. dissertation, Northwestern University.

Camac, C. N. B. (1931). *Imhotep to Harvey: Backgrounds of Medical History*. New York: P. B. Hoeber. Republished, 1973, by Milford House, Inc., Boston.

Cavendish, R. (Ed.) (1983). *Man, Myth and Magic*, Vols. 3 and 6. London: Marshall Cavendish Ltd.

Dolan, J. P., and W. N. Adams-Smith (1978). *Health and Society: A Documentary History of Medicine*. New York, The Seabury Press.

Goraj, J. T. (1963). A report on three European speech facilities. *Asha* 5, 860-864.

Gould, J. E. (1961). *The Chatauqua Movement*. Buffalo: State University of New York Press.

Haller, M. H. (1984). *Eugenics: Hereditarian Attitudes in American Thought*. New Brunswick: Rutgers University Press.

Harms, E. (ed.) (1943). Special Issue: Stuttering in Children. *The Nervous Child* 2, 79-205.

Kester, D. G. (1950). The development of speech correction in organizations and in schools in the United States during the first quarter of the 20th Century. Doctoral dissertation, Northwestern University.

Kitz, R. J., and L. D. Vandam (1986). A History and Scope of Anesthetic Practice. Pages 3-15 in Miller, R. D. (ed.), *Anesthesia, 2nd Edit., Vol I*.

MacLeod, E. (1945). A short history of speech therapy: III. Speech therapy in Britain and America. *Speech* 9, 1, 10-12.

McLeod, A. L. (1955). Speech therapy in Australia. *Speech* 19, 1, 27-28.

Schultz, D. P. (1969). *A History of Modern Psychology*. New York: Academic Press.

Stecher, S. (1964). Speech therapy techniques in Germany. *Asha* 6, 157-159.

Van Riper, C. (1970). Historical Approaches. Chapter 2 in Sheehan, J. G. (ed.), *Stuttering: Research and Therapy*. New York: Harper and Row.

Van Thal, J. H. (1945). A short history of speech therapy: I. Past history. *Speech* 9, 1, 7-12.

Van Thal, J. H. (1945). A short history of speech therapy: II. Speech therapy on the continent of Europe. *Speech* 1, 9-10.

Vincent, J. H. (1886). *The Chautauqua Movement*. Boston: Chautaqua Press. Republished, 1971, Freeport, N.Y.: Books for Libraries Press.

Wallace, K. R. (1943). *Francis Bacon on Communication and Rhetoric*. Chapel Hill, N.C.: University of North Carolina Press.

Wallace, K. R. (1954). *History of Speech Education in America*. New York: Appleton-Century-Crofts Inc.

Watson, R. I. (1963). *The Great Psychologists: Aristotle to Freud*. New York: Lippincott.

Name Index

Subject Index

accessory features, 55, 86, 171, 217
adaptation effect, 119-23, 134
Age of Enlightenment, 30, 217
ameliorative conditions, 179, 184, 217
American Academy of Speech
   Correction, 70, 215
American Speech & Hearing
  Association,
    beginnings of, 70
    membership increase, 81, 84, 105,
    215
anesthesia, 30, 54n. 2
anthropology, 57, 64ff, 109
anxiety, 158, 207
articulation, 37
    animal magnetism, 56
    anticipatory struggle hypothesis, 138-39,
    148
automatic speech, 31, 165, 217
avoidance, 114, 117, 138-41, 148, 158

Because I Stutter, 111-12, 133
behavior, 61, 120-23, 137, 141-45
   overuse of term, 143
behaviorism, 62, 65-66, 89, 94ff, 166
"block," the, 13
Bogue Institute, 72
"bounce," the, 132

cancellation, 174, 210
cause
   featured in definitions, 147-48, 155
   preoccupation with, 201, 207, 214
   unknown, 147, 156, 206, 207
cerebral dominance, 77ff, 185
Chautauqua movement, 34
child labor legislation, 34, 57
choral speaking, 211-12
chorea, 41-42, 48, 217
clonic, 2, 42, 85, 113, 132
    144, 172, 200, 204-8, 218. *See*
    also tonic.
commercial schools, 72, 178, 196
conditioning, 62, 95
conflict theory, 169-70
consistency effect, 119-22, 152, 160
consonants, 43, 74
continuity hypothesis, 139, 151
cultural anthropology, 35, 66
cultural determinism, 65, 89ff, 166

deaf, 169
deconstruction, 105-6
definition, 98, 135, 138, 146-49, 155, 161,
   201
development of stuttering, 85, 157, 173

About the Author

MARCEL E. WINGATE is Professor, Department of Speech & Hearing Sciences, Washington State University. As a clinical psychologist, he became interested in stuttering in an era when it was almost universally considered to be psychological in origin.

ISBN 0-89789-530-4

90000>

EAN

9 780897 895309

HARDCOVER BAR CODE

DATE DUE
